The Friendship of the Barbarians

XENOPHON AND THE PERSIAN EMPIRE

Steven W. Hirsch

Published for Tufts University by
University Press of New England
Hanover and London, 1985

University Press of New England

Brandeis University
Brown University
Clark University
University of Connecticut
Dartmouth College

University of New Hampshire
University of Rhode Island
Tufts University
University of Vermont

Copyright 1985 by Tufts University

All rights reserved. Except for brief quotation in critical articles or reviews, this book, or parts thereof, must not be reproduced in any form without permission in writing from the publisher. For further information contact University Press of New England, Hanover, NH 03755.

Printed in the United States of America

Library of Congress Cataloging in Publication Data
Hirsch, Steven W., 1950–
  The friendship of the barbarians.
  Bibliography: p.
  Includes index.
  1. Greece—History—Expedition of Cyrus, 401 B.C.
  2. Cyrus, the Younger, d. 401 B.C. 3. Xenophon.
  4. Xenophon. Anabasis. I. Title.
  DF231.32.H57 1985   935'.05'0924   85–40586
  ISBN 0–87451–322–7

The maps on pp. xii–xiv are reproduced from *Early Greece* by Oswyn Murray, with the permission of the publishers, Stanford University Press and Fontana Paperbacks. © 1980 by Oswyn Murray.

For my father, Wallace L. Hirsch

Contents

PREFACE / ix
MAPS / xii–xiv
Introduction / 1
1. Attitudes toward Persia in the Philosophical and Technical Works / 6
2. Trust and Deceit in the *Anabasis* / 14
3. *Agesilaus*: The Making of a Panhellenic Hero / 39
   APPENDIX A. The *Hellenica* and the Composition of the *Agesilaus* / 56
   APPENDIX B. Xenophon and Isocrates / 57
4. The *Cyropaedia* and History / 61
   APPENDIX. Plato and the *Cyropaedia* / 97
5. The King's Eye / 101
   APPENDIX A. Testimonia from Greek Sources / 131
   APPENDIX B. Intelligence Networks in the Ancient World / 134
6. Xenophon, Plato, and Persia / 140

NOTES / 149
BIBLIOGRAPHY / 197
INDEX / 209

Preface

By one of those ironies which are so frequent in the study of history, the relative paucity of written materials surviving from within the Achaemenid Persian Empire has made scholars largely dependent on Greek sources for their knowledge of its history and civilization. The Persians have been seen by posterity through the eyes of an alien people who, at the least, did not fully understand their ways and were often inclined to be hostile. As a result, it is particularly important to determine both the biases of our Greek sources and the validity of the information about Persia which they convey.

Xenophon, the Athenian soldier, farmer, and writer on historical, philosophical, and technical topics, is one of our chief sources of information about the Persian Empire in the first half of the fourth century B.C. This book addresses the issues both of Xenophon's attitudes toward the Persians and of his reliability as a historian. For this purpose, Xenophon's works can be divided into two categories: those with a significant historical component (insofar as their subject matter is primarily past events)—the *Anabasis*, *Agesilaus*, *Cyropaedia*, and *Hellenica*—and those which are predominantly philosophical or technical. The Introduction discusses Xenophon in his historical context, briefly summarizes some trends in modern scholarship, and poses the problem with which this book will be concerned. Chapter 1 surveys the most revealing passages on Persia and Persians in the philosophical and technical works. Chapters 2 through 4 examine Xenophon's treatment of Persia in the *Anabasis*, the *Agesilaus*, and the *Cyropaedia*. Chapter 5 presents a test case for Xenophon's knowledge about Persia—the problem of the Persian official called "the King's Eye." The final chapter compares x / Preface

Xenophon's attitudes toward Persia with those of his contemporary and peer, Plato. The results of this investigation mandate a reevaluation, and in many cases a rejection, of traditional dogmas about the attitudes of Xenophon in particular and of fourth-century Greeks in general. In many passages Xenophon evinces a reasonable and moderate, and sometimes a clearly favorable, attitude toward the Persians. The extent and reliability of Xenophon's knowledge about Persia, even in an enigmatic work such as the *Cyropaedia*, is much greater than most classicists have recognized, and he is clearly a valuable source of information about the history, peoples, and customs of ancient Iran. Finally, an appreciation of the extent to which Xenophon's literary purposes influenced his historical treatment of the Persians should contribute to a better understanding of those works in which Persia plays a conspicuous role. Xenophon was a major figure in fourth-century literature, and he participated in the creation or early development of several genres which became prominent in later Greek and Latin literature—memoir, novel, philosophic dialogue, prose encomium. This reevaluation of Xenophon as writer and thinker will, I hope, give impetus to recent stirrings of renewed interest in him and his works.

It is a pleasure to thank the many people who have assisted me in one way or another. My deepest respect and gratitude are reserved for my teachers at Stanford University: Antony E. Raubitschek, who planted the seeds of this project in his seminar on Xenophon and who has always been so generous with his time and his ideas; Michael H. Jameson, whose high standards have both guided and inspired me; Mark W. Edwards, for his sage advice; and John Nicols, for his gentle prodding. In recent years I have benefited from my association with colleagues in the Departments of Classics and History at Tufts University, and I owe a special debt of thanks to John W. Zarker and Peter L. D. Reid for their unflagging support and encouragement. A number of colleagues around the country have read drafts of some or all of the manuscript and have generously shared their knowledge with me. I am especially grateful to John K. Anderson, and also to David Stronach, Richard N. Frye, Michael N. Weiskopf, and J. Joel Farber.

I am obligated, as well, to a number of institutions: to Stanford University, for financial support throughout my graduate years; to Tufts University, for providing a stimulating environment in which to teach and pursue research; and to the Center for Middle Eastern Studies at Harvard University, for making library resources available.

I have been fortunate to have the services of a fine and patient typist in Maria Freitas, a thorough and skillful copy editor in Ann Hawthorne, and an astute indexer in Nicholas D. Humez. The kindness and cooperation of the staff of the University Press of New England have been most welcome.

My obligations to my family are exceeded only by my affection. Finally, none of this would have been possible without the love and companionship of my wife, Janet Rose.

TUFTS UNIVERSITY
MEDFORD, MASSACHUSETTS
OCTOBER 31, 1984

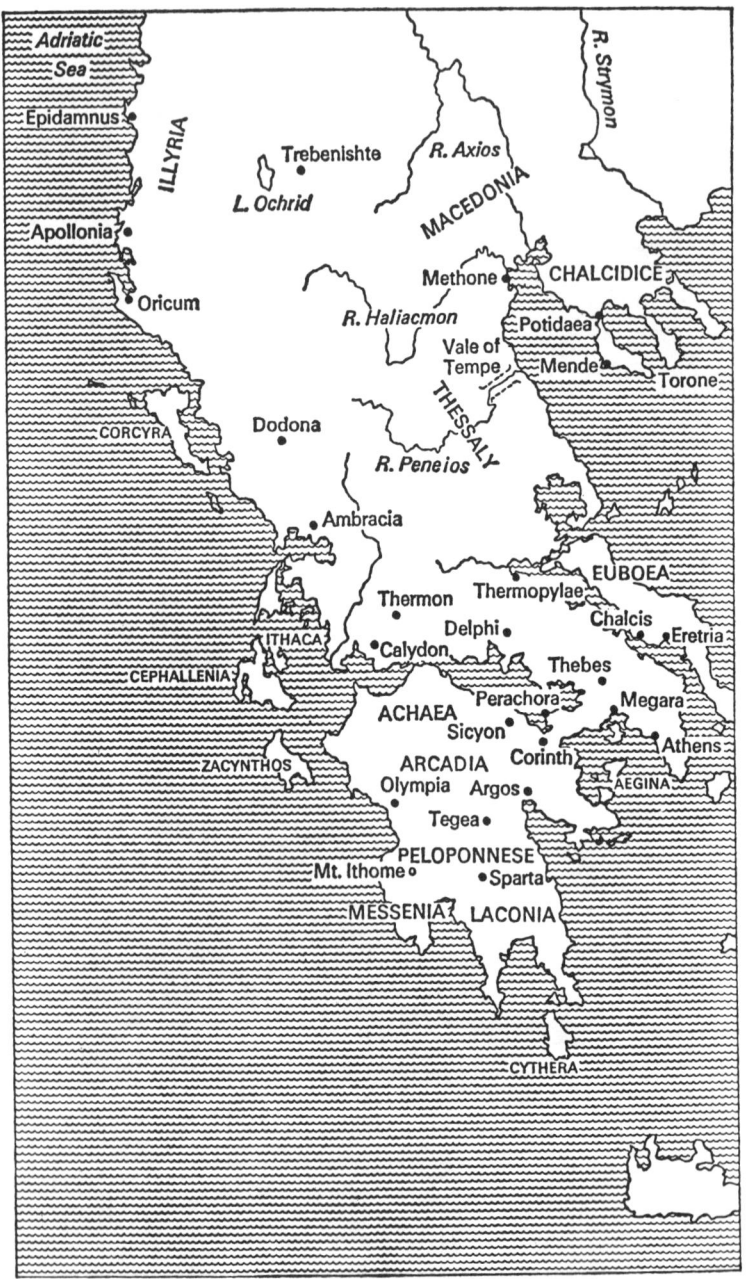

Greece and the Aegean

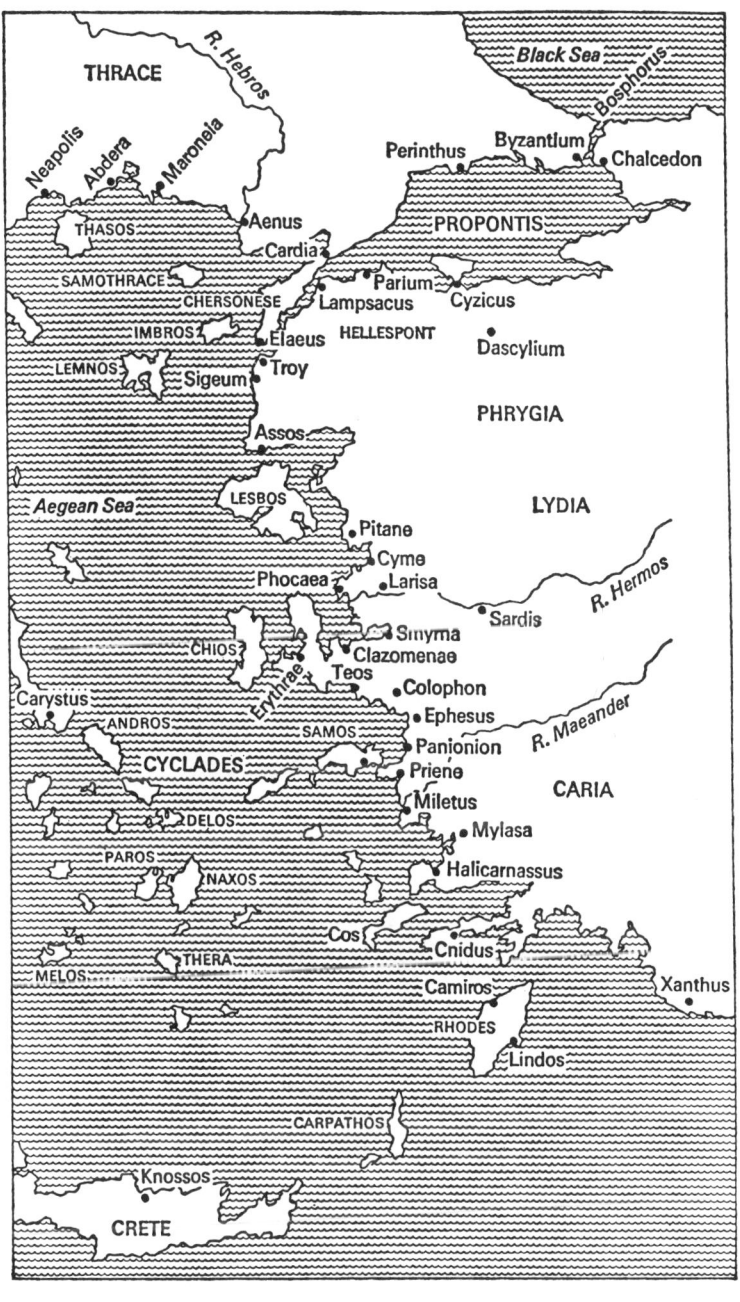

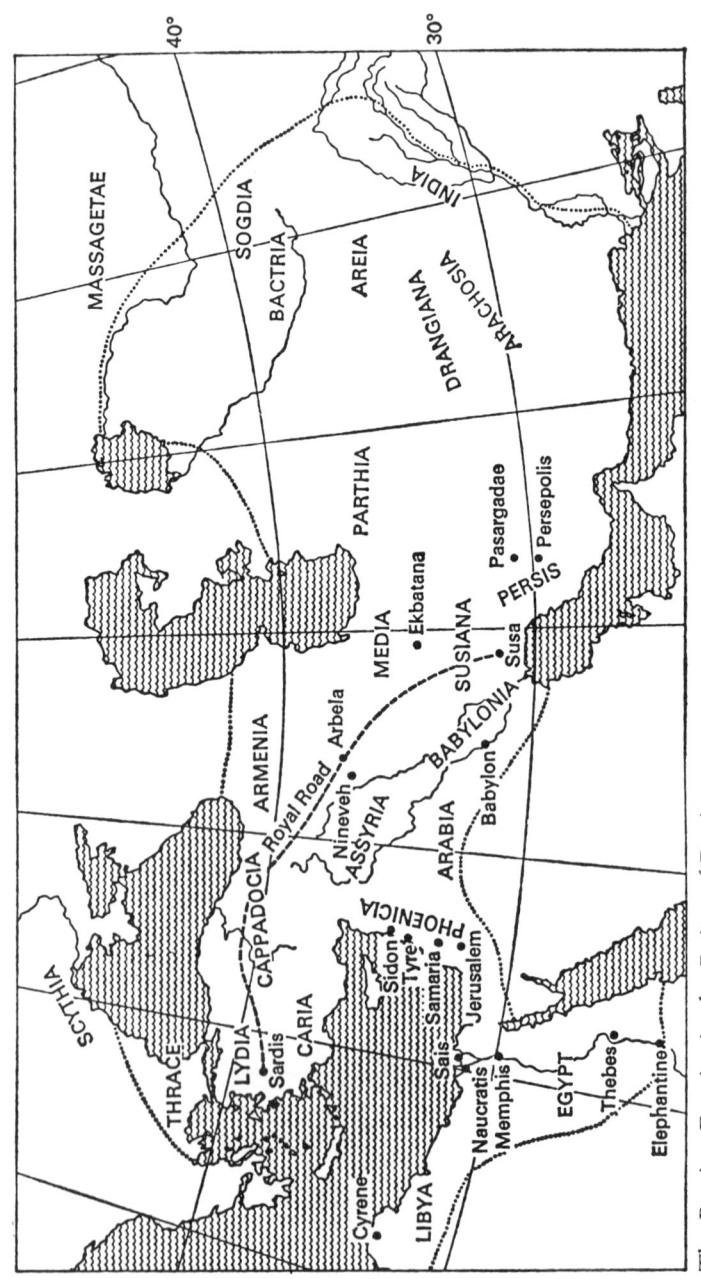

The Persian Empire in the Reign of Darius

The Friendship of the Barbarians

Introduction

καὶ οὔποτε ἐρεῖ οὐδεὶς ὡς Ἕλληνας ἀγαγὼν εἰς τοὺς βαρβάρους, προδοὺς τοὺς
τὴν τῶν βαρβάρων φιλίαν εἱλόμην. . . .
And never shall any man say that I, after leading Greeks into the land of
the barbarians, betrayed the Greeks and chose the friendship of the
barbarians. . . .
—the Greek mercenary commander Clearchus to his troops during the march to
Babylonia in 401 B.C. (*Anabasis* 1.3.5)

In the first decades of the fourth century B.C.[1] the Greeks of the mainland, clustered in their small, contentious city-states, once again had to look East and ponder the intentions of the mighty Persian Empire. By providing crucial assistance to Sparta in the last years of the Peloponnesian War, Persia had regained much of the prestige which she had lost in the wars of the early fifth century and again appeared to be in a position to threaten the independence of the Greeks. Despite their persistent internal rivalries, the Greeks' conception of themselves was defined largely in terms of what set them apart from "barbarians" (*barbaroi*, "foreigners"). But what exactly were their conceptions of and attitudes toward the Persian Empire and the Persian people? Clearly, the question of Greek attitudes toward Persia has significant historical implications; for attitudes—the estimation which one people forms about the motives, disposition, and character of another—can significantly affect the course of events in a confrontation between civilizations. As with so many other questions concerning the ancient world, however, enforced reliance on literary evidence makes it notoriously difficult to ascertain the prevailing general attitude, since it is always dangerous to assume that the well-born Greek intellectuals whose works survive necessarily represent the thoughts and ideals of the common people.

Xenophon offers a promising point of access to fourth-century

2 / Introduction

Greek attitudes toward Persia. He grew up in the last decades of the fifth century in Athens,[2] where there was a notably high degree of public awareness of the events of recent history. Athenian orators of the period tirelessly recalled the glorious achievements of their forefathers in repulsing the Persian invaders at Marathon in 490 and at Salamis ten years later. With the growth of Athenian naval power in subsequent decades, the Persians were driven out of the Aegean and the coastal regions of Asia Minor. But having reached maturity in the latter stages of the Peloponnesian War, Xenophon was also a witness to the fact that it was Persian gold which enabled Sparta to build fleets and ultimately triumph over Athens in 404.

This much was known to every Athenian at the turn of the fourth century. Xenophon is special in that he had firsthand experience of the Persian Empire, of both its rulers and its subject peoples. In 401 he joined a corps of Greek mercenaries hired by the Persian prince Cyrus and participated in the latter's ill-fated attempt on the throne of his brother, King Artaxerxes II. Cyrus and his army drove swiftly into the heart of the empire and prevailed over the king's forces in a hard-fought battle at Cunaxa near Babylon. However, Cyrus himself fell in the battle. Deprived of their patron, the Greek troops overcame great difficulties and fought their way home. Xenophon played a vital part as an elected commander on this perilous march, which he commemorated in the *Anabasis*. After their return to the Hellenic zone of culture, Xenophon and the remnant of the Greek mercenaries took service with the Spartans, and under the leadership of Dercyllidas and King Agesilaus they engaged in a series of campaigns against the Persian satraps in western Asia Minor.

Sensing a curiosity about Persia among contemporary Greeks,[3] Xenophon capitalized on his knowledge and experience by making Persia a prominent topic in several works. This and the fact that all his works have survived make him a valuable source of information about fourth-century Greek perceptions of Persia. As a self-styled expert on Persia he may be indicative of informed Greek opinion, and through his considerable literary output he may be presumed to have influenced the attitudes of the Greeks of his day and afterward.[4]

The results of this investigation must be set against what is otherwise known, or believed to be known, about Greek attitudes toward Persia in the fourth century.[5] Many moderns share the assumption that most Greeks of the later classical period regarded the Persians as cowardly, slavish, effeminate, lascivious, and untrustworthy. In this they have been unduly influenced by the panhellenic polemics of the Athenian orator Isocrates, who repeatedly urged a united Greek crusade against the Persian "barbarian."[6] Recalling the escape from Persia of Cyrus' Greek troops (and grossly exaggerating the ease with which they accomplished it), Isocrates attributed the success of this venture to the degeneracy of the Persians:

> And none of these things has happened by accident, but all of them have been due to natural causes; for it is not possible for people who are reared and governed as are the Persians, either to have a part in any other form of virtue or to set up on the field of battle trophies of victory over their foes. . . . Most of their population is a mob without discipline or experience of dangers, which has lost all stamina for war and has been trained more effectively for servitude than are the slaves in our country. (As for) those, on the other hand, who stand highest in repute among them . . . their whole existence consists of insolence toward some, and servility towards others—a manner of life than which nothing could be more demoralizing to human nature. Because they are rich, they pamper their bodies; but because they are subject to one man's power, they keep their souls in a state of abject and cringing fear. . . . They are faithless to their friends and cowardly to their foes; their lives are divided between servility on the one hand and arrogance on the other; they treat their allies with contempt and pay court to their enemies. . . . So ingrained in our nature is our hostility to them that even in the matter of our stories we linger most fondly over those which tell of the Trojan and Persian Wars, because through them we learn of our enemies' misfortunes.
>
> (*Panegyricus* 150–58)[7]

But there are reasons for doubting whether Isocrates' diatribes represent the feelings of most fourth-century Greeks,[8] and whether Isocrates fully believed what he said. Plato, in the *Republic* (5.470B–C), also urges the Greeks to stop warring among themselves and to turn their aggression against the barbarians.[9] Yet passages in other works indicate that he was aware of the basic speciousness of simplistically dividing the world into Greeks and barbarians (*Statesman* 262D, *Theaetetus* 174–75). Isocrates and Plato almost certainly had similar motives: to end the internecine warfare which plagued the Greek city-states in the fourth century by providing the Greeks with a common objective and channeling aggressive impulses into hatred for the barbarian. Isocrates' lack of success in arousing substantial popular support for his projects should serve as a warning that most Greeks did not share his views about the Persians.

There is at present no consensus among scholars as to Xenophon's attitude toward the Persians. Most commentators, in line with traditional assumptions about Greek attitudes in general, insist that he held the Persians in low esteem. Some would even echo the extreme formulation of Delebecque: "... sa vie durant Xénophon gardera ancrée au fond du coeur sa haine du caractère barbare."[10] On the other hand, a minority opinion holds that Xenophon admired the Persians and thereby prefigured the Hellenistic Age, with its meeting and melding of races and cultures. This disagreement exists not only because Xenophon says different things about the Persians at different times, but also because scholars attempting to grapple with these contradictions differ fundamentally in their approaches to his writings. In this context, it is convenient to borrow the terms *Analysts* and *Unitarians*, employed in other areas of classical philology. The Analysts believe that Xenophon's ideas and attitudes varied over time in response to changes in Greek political affairs and in Xenophon's personal situation. They use these perceived shifts in attitude to create a chronology of Xenophon's works, relating them to the events of his life and times. The Unitarians claim that Xenophon maintained a basic consistency in his attitudes. They propose that the best way to understand his thought is to examine his treatment of major themes throughout his works; in their view, the various works tend to complement and build upon one another. To be sure, these points of view are not necessarily mutually exclusive: Analysts accept a certain amount of consistency in Xenophon's thinking, and Unitarians concede that Xenophon's ideas underwent some development. Both approaches, however, are subject to grave difficulties. On the one hand, the apparent contradictions in Xenophon's attitudes toward the Persians are not easily reconciled. On the other hand, the Analysts' approach involves a damning circularity: the chronology of Xenophon's political development is first inferred from the works, and then the attitudes expressed in the works are neatly fitted into this chronological scheme.[11]

Because there are in fact few secure footholds for dating the majority of Xenophon's writings, I am reluctant to predicate my own interpretations on tenuous chronological constructs. Instead, I offer a pair of suggestions for grappling with the contradictions in

Xenophon's attitude toward the Persians. First, it may be a mistake to expect Xenophon to hold a simple and consistent attitude on such a highly charged topic as the Persian Empire, which both dazzled and terrified the Greeks of the classical period. How many of us today, in matters of equivalent significance for our own times, are not torn between rational analysis and emotional reaction? Second, the attitude expressed by Xenophon in a given passage may be more a function of his theme and purpose in that particular context than an indication of his final judgment on the matter. These considerations make it easier to deal with the uncomfortable fact that he uses the Persian king both as a model for the ideal administrator in the *Oeconomicus* and as a paradigm of vice and effeminate luxury in the *Agesilaus*. Seen in this light, the question of Xenophon's attitude toward the Persians is as much a literary as a historical problem.

Xenophon has also been at the center of a controversy of a different sort. It is probably fair to say that most classicists have doubts about the extent of Xenophon's real knowledge of the Persian Empire, especially with respect to the information in one of his most important works, and the one in which Persia plays the most prominent role, the *Cyropaedia*.[12] On the other hand, many Iranologists have long treated the *Cyropaedia* and Xenophon's other works as major sources of information for the history, institutions, and culture of the Persian Empire. The primary reason that classicists and Iranologists have formed very different conclusions about the historical value of sources such as the *Cyropaedia* is that until quite recently there was only limited contact between the disciplines: Iranologists often lacked the historiographic expertise to evaluate the aims, methods, and biases of Greek authors, while classical historians tended to be unaware of the discoveries of specialists in Iranian archaeology and philology. The increasing cooperation between the two disciplines both demands and makes possible a reconsideration of the historical value of Xenophon's testimony about Persia.

1

Attitudes toward Persia in the Philosophical and Technical Works

In Xenophon's essentially philosophical or technical works (that is, all except the *Anabasis*, *Agesilaus*, *Cyropaedia*, and *Hellenica*), Persia necessarily plays a limited part. While references to Persia in these works are not frequent, they are nonetheless worth examining since in these instances, where Xenophon is perhaps less likely to be under constraints of theme or subject matter and may choose to speak of Persia solely out of personal interest or knowledge, one may hope to discern something of his true feelings. In most cases the references provide little or no insight into his attitudes toward Persia.[1] However, in several cases, particularly in the *Oeconomicus*, a treatise on estate management, they are highly revealing. The two passages that permit the most significant inferences are *Oeconomicus* 14.6–7 and *Oeconomicus* 4.

Oeconomicus 14.6–7 reads:

ἐγὼ οὖν καὶ τούτων, ἔφη, προσφέρων ἔνια καὶ ἄλλα τῶν βασιλικῶν νόμων προφερόμενος πειρῶμαι δικαίους περὶ τὰ διαχειριζόμενα ἀπεργάζεσθαι τοὺς οἰκέτας. ἐκεῖνοι μὲν γὰρ οἱ νόμοι ζημίαι μόνον εἰσὶ τοῖς ἁμαρτάνουσιν, οἱ δὲ βασιλικοὶ νόμοι οὐ μόνον ζημιοῦσι τοὺς ἀδικοῦντας, ἀλλὰ καὶ ὠφελοῦσι τοὺς δικαίους· ὥστε ὁρῶντες πλουσιωτέρους γιγνομένους τοὺς δικαίους τῶν ἀδίκων πολλοὶ καὶ φιλοκερδεῖς ὄντες εὖ μάλα ἐπιμένουσι τῷ μὴ ἀδικεῖν.

By applying some of these clauses and other enactments found in the Persian king's code, I try to make my servants upright in the matters that pass through their hands. For while those laws only penalise the wrongdoer, the king's code not only punishes the guilty, but also benefits the upright. Thus, seeing that the honest grow richer than the dishonest, many, despite their love of lucre, are careful to remain free from dishonesty.[2]

In this passage Ischomachus, a Greek country squire who is, for all practical purposes, a mouthpiece for Xenophon in the treatise, is discoursing on ways to make servants honest. He reveals that, in addition to the precepts of the famous Athenian lawgivers, Draco and Solon, he draws upon the Persian king's laws. Whereas Athenian laws only punish wrongdoers, the king's laws both punish wrongdoers and reward those who act justly. Rewards for just behavior entice even the greedy into right action. The implication is clear that the king's laws are in this one respect superior to those of the great Athenian lawgivers. An analogy is drawn between Ischomachus, as master of his estate and servants, and the Persian king, as master of his empire and its inhabitants. The king is thereby portrayed as a fair master and an ideal administrator, a theme which recurs in *Oeconomicus* 4.

Other passages in Xenophon imply a similar conception of Persian practice. According to *Oeconomicus* 4.8 and *Anabasis* 1.9.19, Persian governors who take good care of their territory and its inhabitants are well rewarded, whereas those who have been negligent are removed from office and punished. Describing the education of noble Persian youths at the royal court, Xenophon states that the boys learn *sophrosyne*—moderation and self-control—by observing men being honored and dishonored by the king (*Anabasis* 1.9.3–4). The younger Cyrus encourages justice by rewarding those who practice it, thereby gaining eager, honest, and loyal followers (*Anabasis* 1.9.16–17). Likewise the elder Cyrus encourages *philotimia*—the eager and ambitious pursuit of excellence—by bestowing rewards and honors (*Cyropaedia* 8.1.39, 8.6.11).

Plato shares Xenophon's admiration for the king's laws. At several points he praises Darius as a great lawgiver, whose laws have preserved the Persian Empire down to Plato's day, and calls him the equal of such distinguished Greek legislators as Lycurgus and Solon.[3] Darius himself, in the monumental inscription on the rock face at Behistun, claims: "Within these countries, the man who was loyal, him I rewarded well; (him) who was evil, him I punished well; by the favor of Ahuramazda these countries showed respect toward my law."[4]

Thus it appears that Xenophon is correct in claiming that the

8 / Attitudes toward Persia

provision for both reward and punishment was a singular feature of Persian law, and it is clear that he regards the Persian system as superior to the Greek in this respect.

Chapter 4 of the *Oeconomicus* is a lengthy discussion of the Persian king's concerns and conduct in matters of war and agriculture. Critobulus has asked Socrates which branches of knowledge he should cultivate. Socrates replies that they should not be ashamed to imitate the Persian king, who pays close attention to war and agriculture.

As to matters of war, he exacts tribute and orders the governors to provide maintenance for the troops protecting their territory. He installs garrisons in the citadels and makes annual inspections of the troops (except garrison troops) at the "places of muster." He rewards officers and governors who have provided well for their troops and punishes those who have neglected these duties. In like manner he makes inspection of the country, rewarding governors who have cared well for the land and people and punishing those who have not. There are two classes of officers, one ruling over the inhabitants and laborers and collecting tribute from them, the other ruling the local troops and garrisons. The civil and military governors are in a position to report on one another if they do not do their jobs properly.

Wherever the king resides or visits, he ensures that the "paradises" (the carefully tended parks and gardens of Persian royalty and nobility) are full of all the good things which the earth has to offer, and he spends much of his time in them. When he gives rewards, he first rewards those who have distinguished themselves in war, and second those who have best administered the land. The younger Cyrus (Xenophon's former patron) claimed that he deserved the prize for both endeavors, priding himself as much on caring for the land as on his feats as a warrior. Socrates claims that Cyrus would have been an excellent ruler had he lived; throughout his campaign to seize the Persian throne, while many abandoned the cause of the king, no one deserted Cyrus. Finally, Socrates tells of the time when Cyrus showed the Spartan admiral Lysander the paradise at Sardis; as Lysander marveled at it, Cyrus confessed that he himself had laid it out and planted many of the trees, such exercise being regular for him.

Thus the main thrust of Socrates' discourse in *Oeconomicus* 4 is to convince Critobulus that the Persian king gives considerable attention to the administration and cultivation of the land. To this end, Socrates demonstrates that a civil administration, whose function is to see that the land and people flourish, exists parallel to, and is treated in an analogous fashion to, the military administration of the empire. The details given by Socrates, the doubts expressed by Critobulus, and the general tone of the passage all suggest that this predilection of the king for agricultural administration was not widely recognized in the Greek world, whereas Persian military preparedness was common knowledge.

Xenophon, through Socrates,[5] is obviously interested in and knowledgeable about the Persian system, for he could undoubtedly have used non-Persian examples to make his points about the value of careful management of agricultural resources. Xenophon's interest in Persia is also highlighted by the fact that he presents more details here than the argument strictly requires. Several items are mentioned for their intrinsic interest, including the distinction between regular troops and citadel garrisons, the exemption of citadel garrisons from muster, the satraps' exceptional control of both the civil and military branches of administration, the encomium of the younger Cyrus, and the details of his men's loyalty to him.

There is no denying that the tone of this passage is highly laudatory of the Persian king and of his administrative arrangements. In response to Critobulus' query about the kinds of pursuits to which he could devote himself most profitably, Socrates recommends the art of estate management and uses the Persian king as a paradigm of diligent concern and proper conduct in such matters. As Leo Strauss has pointed out, the Persian king, by virtue of being the wealthiest man and possessor of the largest "estate" in the world, is by definition the premier example of the *oikonomos* or estate manager.[6] In this passage he is depicted as an excellent administrator and a just master, who rewards good service and punishes negligence. He has a strong personal interest in the land and is personally active in the supervision of the agricultural resources of the empire. All these qualities are dear to the heart of a country squire such as Xenophon.

This chapter of the *Oeconomicus*, expressing enthusiastic approval of the Persian monarch, contrasts sharply with certain other passages in which Xenophon seems to be filled with scorn for the Great King of his day. One example is the ninth chapter of the *Agesilaus*, which accuses the king not only of crass materialism, self-indulgence, and enervating luxury, but also of remoteness and laxness in administrative matters. Similarly, the epilogue to the *Cyropaedia* (8.8) states that corruption is rampant in the Persian Empire and justice is no longer done; that the king rewards the craven rather than the brave; and that the empire is so weak militarily that an enemy can freely roam the land. The passage attributes this wholesale degeneracy to perversion of the old Persian morals and to the luxury to which the king and nobility have abandoned themselves.

One possible explanation of these apparent contradictions is that, in some passages, Xenophon is less concerned with either historical truth or the expression of personal views than with the achievement of a literary objective. In the *Agesilaus*, for example, he is anxious to eulogize his friend. To this end, he may use the Persian king, Agesilaus' lifelong foe, as a foil whose vices serve to highlight the virtues of the Spartan king. If truth has been subordinated to encomiastic needs, the portrayal of the Persian king in this passage is then an artificial construct. By the same token, it could be maintained that *Oeconomicus* 4 is a tendentious passage in which Xenophon, seeking to create an image of the model administrator, fancifully idealizes the king of Persia.

The passages from the *Agesilaus* and *Cyropaedia* are discussed in later chapters. The issue here is the extent to which the Persian administrative system depicted in *Oeconomicus* 4 is a faithful representation of facts or, alternatively, a philosophical conceptualization of an "ideal" system of estate management. If it can be established that Xenophon depicts circumstances actually to be found in contemporary Persia, it follows that his evident approval of this system reflects his attitude toward the real Persia.

Indicative of an idealizing tendency are the highly schematic presentation of the Persian system and the failure of some details to accord with evidence from patently historical sources. For instance, the rigid distinction claimed here between civil and military administration does not always seem to have been made in practice.

On the other hand, many of the details which Xenophon reports are confirmed by other testimony whose historicity is not in doubt. For instance, the claim that there was a *syllogos* or gathering place for military inspection or assembly prior to a campaign (*Oec.* 4.6) finds verification in the mention of the gathering point in the plain of Castolus in *Anabasis* 1.9.7 and *Hellenica* 1.4.3. The regular separation of civil and military commands (*Oec.* 4.9) is indirectly confirmed by the description of the dual mandate awarded to the younger Cyrus when he came down to Asia Minor in 407 (*Anabasis* 1.9.7). He was appointed *satrapes* or governor of Lydia, Great Phrygia, and Cappadocia, and *strategos* or general of all those who gathered at the plain of Castolus; that is, he held both the civil and military commands. Rewards for good service are abundantly attested; examples include the rewards given to Zopyrus after the capture of Babylon (Herodotus 3.154) and to Mordechai for reporting a conspiracy against the king (Esther 6).[7]

Xenophon's emphasis, in both the *Oeconomicus* and the *Cyropaedia*, on the Persian king's parallel concerns for military matters and for agriculture has received striking confirmation from the studies of Pierre Briant.[8] Briant has shown that these two spheres were vitally interconnected in the ideology and propaganda of the Achaemenid kings. The autocratic rule of the king and the tribute he collects from his subjects are justified by the services he performs in protecting the land and people and guaranteeing the fertility of both. There is a reciprocal relationship between the military activities of the ruling class and the productive functions of the tributary populations: the king must maintain a strong military force in order to provide the necessary protection, and the subject peoples are obligated to yield up the tribute which sustains the army and the administration. As might be expected, religion is also used to rationalize the existing social and political system. The peasantry are persuaded that hard work and procreation are religious duties[9] and that, in his capacity as guarantor of order and promoter of productivity, the king is the earthly representative of the god.

Thus it appears that Xenophon understood and accurately reflected the value system which both justified and gave impetus to the Persian kings' exploitation of the human and agricultural resources of the empire.[10] The evidence that much in *Oeconomicus* 4 is reliable enhances the credibility of other items of information for which there is no independent confirmation. It cannot be maintained that the whole chapter is an artificial construct in which Xenophon fancifully cloaks his own notions on *oikonomia* (estate management) in a Persian guise. At the least, there were elements in the Persian system which made it an acceptable choice for a paradigm.

This is not to deny that Xenophon has made the Persian system overly schematic, orderly, and smoothly functioning in order to increase the force of his point about proper estate management. It is not necessary to assume that the Persian king Artaxerxes II was the diligent, solicitous, personally involved administrator, and perfectly just master described in *Oeconomicus* 4. However, it is obvious that several elements of the Persian system have earned Xenophon's respect. And the fact that Xenophon is here so laudatory of the Persian king and the Persian administration requires at the least a careful evaluation of passages in which he seems to evince scorn and derision for Persia and her master.

Whether or not Xenophon really harbored such favorable feelings toward Persia as the passages discussed above seem to indicate, and even if he had some ulterior motive for taking such a stance, his adoption of such a positive tone in a published work is of some significance. It is commonly assumed that the attitude of fourth-century Greeks toward the Persians was one of hostility and scorn. Yet the positive references reviewed here indicate either that this attitude was not universally shared or that Xenophon exhibited great courage in defying the *communis opinio*.

In fact there are good reasons why Xenophon should have been able to assume a fair-minded attitude toward the Persians. In the first place, he had been to Persia, had fought against Persians in battle, and almost certainly had become personally acquainted with Persians in Cyrus' camp. Direct experience of a people and culture can be a strong antidote to inherited prejudice. Beyond that, Xenophon the country squire may have felt a bond with the Persian nobility, who shared his interests in the land, horses, hunting, and careful management of their estates.[11] David Lewis has recently pointed out that the Spartans had much in common with the Persians and that these two peoples ought to have had some understanding of each other.[12] Xenophon's description of the meeting between the Spartan king Agesilaus and the Persian satrap Pharnabazus on the grass near Dascylium in 395 (*Hellenica* 4.1.29–39) illustrates the workings of such a cross-cultural encounter. As one who had lived long in the Spartan orbit, first as a Spartan mercenary and then as master of a country estate in the Peloponnese given him by the Spartans, Xenophon would have been sensitive to the values and concerns of the Spartan and Persian nobility.

A story in Diogenes Laertius' *Life of Xenophon* (2.51–52) provides evidence of the extent to which Xenophon was affected by his sojourn in the East: "When he was in Ephesus [shortly before his return to Greece with Agesilaus in 394] and had a sum of money, he entrusted one half of it to Megabyzus, the priest of Artemis, to keep until his return, or if he should never return, to apply to the erection of a statue in honour of the goddess. . . . [Some years afterward] Megabyzus having arrived to attend the [Olympic] festival, Xenophon received from him the deposit of money and bought and dedicated to the goddess an estate with a river running through, which bears the same name Selinus as the river at Ephesus."[13] Of significance here are Xenophon's connections with Ephesus, of all the Greek towns of western Asia Minor the one most heavily pervaded by Oriental cultural influences; his relationship with and trust in a priest who has the Iranian title Megabyzus; and his devotion to Artemis, whose cult had strong Oriental affinities and who was equated with the Iranian goddess Anahita.[14]

Evidence such as this must at the least cast doubt on conventional pronouncements about Xenophon's hostility to the Persians. Nowhere in his references to Persia in the philosophical and technical works does Xenophon say anything which could be construed as disparaging or indicative of a sense of Greek superiority. At times his attitude toward Persia verges on respect and even outright admiration.

2

Trust and Deceit in the *Anabasis*

Aside from its popularity as a text for novice students of ancient Greek, the *Anabasis* is most often regarded only in terms of its historical value as a chronicle of the rebellion of the Persian prince Cyrus and the hazardous march home of his Greek mercenaries. Rarely is it taken seriously as a work of literature and its ideas scrutinized.

Over the last hundred years, a series of commentators have approached the *Anabasis* as an *apologia*. Some, who believe that Xenophon was exiled from Athens because of his collaboration with Cyrus, Athens' enemy in the latter stages of the Peloponnesian War, assert that Xenophon wrote the *Anabasis* in order to justify his conduct to the Athenian public.[1] Others view the *Anabasis* as a defense of his conduct on the march of the Ten Thousand against accusations by other members of the expedition.[2] Higgins has properly countered that these hypotheses do not begin to explain why Xenophon devotes so much space to matters unrelated to an apologia, such as details of topography and the customs of the barbarians.[3]

Still other commentators view the *Anabasis* as a piece of political propaganda, a vehicle for Xenophon's ideas about the policies which he felt the Greek states ought to be pursuing. Thus Morr and Luccioni maintain that, by narrating the successful escape of a relatively small force of Greek soldiers from the midst of the Persian enemy, Xenophon means to show the Greek world the fundamental weakness of the Persian Empire and to urge a panhellenic "crusade" against this Oriental colossus with feet of clay.[4] Delebecque detects the presence of a deep-rooted hostility to Persia and anger at Persian faithlessness, as well as disapproval of Sparta. In his view, Xenophon is protesting against the King's Peace, recently established between

Persia and Sparta, and is warning that one cannot expect the Persian "barbarians" to keep their word.[5] Robert is struck both by the abiding hatred for Persia which he perceives in the work and by the prominence which Xenophon gives to his own achievements as a military leader.[6] He thinks that the *Anabasis* was written in the mid-360s, when Athens and Sparta were pondering an attack on pro-Theban Persia, and that Xenophon is advertising his own qualifications for command of the prospective military expedition.

Fundamental objections can be brought against each of these attempts to see the *Anabasis* as a propagandistic political tract.[7] In the last analysis, none of the apology or propaganda theories is in itself able to account fully and satisfactorily for the form and content of the *Anabasis*.

In recent years several scholars have taken a different approach to the *Anabasis*, applying the techniques of literary analysis to its structure and to several prominent motifs. Nussbaum, whose primary concern is to investigate the social and political organization of the army of the Ten Thousand, notes that the *Anabasis* can be divided into four phases, marked by changes in the army's concerns and purpose.[8] In the first phase the contingent of Greek mercenaries, drawn from all over the Hellenic world, has no purpose of its own, having been assembled solely to help Cyrus achieve his aims. With the death of Cyrus and of the chief Greek mercenary commander, Clearchus, the army becomes an independent unit which must formulate its own purposes and develop a new organization. Until it reaches the sea at Trapezus that purpose is simple survival, a struggle to procure supplies, fight off the enemy, and find a way out of hostile territory. Once the army reaches the sea, its immediate danger subsides to some extent, and there begins a period of internal dissension as the mercenaries become increasingly concerned with enriching themselves along the way. Finally, when they reach Byzantium and the edge of the Hellenic cultural zone, they face the problem of reintegrating themselves into a Greek world dominated by Sparta, and they must again find an external patron and purpose. The Greek army on the move was a political and social unit akin to a *polis* or city-state, but because its "citizens" were drawn from all over the Greek world, the hybrid political organization which it evolved can be taken as a general reflection of the Greek political system of its time. Thus the *Anabasis* portrays the trials and triumphs of the common Greek ideals of life.

Higgins believes that the unifying theme of the *Anabasis* is men's self-deception as they pursue what they think is most important in life.[9] Xenophon's desire to leave his city and follow the dashing Cyrus arises from his infatuation with such heroic champions. Guile and deceit, as practiced by Cyrus, Clearchus, and others, are the hallmark of the march to Cunaxa. After the death of Cyrus, the Greeks deceive themselves about their situation, and only Tissaphernes' treacherous slaughter of their leaders brings them to their senses and enables them to understand their predicament. But Xenophon continues to dream impossible dreams—of founding a city in Asia, of holding the army together, of achieving great things. He is deceived about human nature and about his own nature and desires, and only gradually does he come to realize that he cannot keep everything as perfect as he would like. The dream fails and he returns to Greece an exile. But at Scillus, where he has been given an estate by the Spartans, he learns to be content with stability and with staying at home. In sum, the *Anabasis*, while presenting an unfictionalized account of a historical event, is patently one man's idiosyncratic view of that event and its meaning.

Wencis agrees that the artful and instructive arrangement of the *Anabasis* makes it more than a dry chronicle.[10] Employing the quadripartite division of Nussbaum, he traces Xenophon's use of the concept of suspicion—*hypopsia*—as a recurrent motif. In the first part tension develops because the Greeks suspect that Cyrus is leading them against the Persian king. This suspicion threatens the good order of the army, but Cyrus alleviates the Greeks' fears and wins them over because he inspires trust. After the death of Cyrus the narrative is dominated by mutual suspicion between Greeks and barbarians. Following Tissaphernes' seizure and execution of the Greek generals, distrust of the Persians becomes a recurrent theme in the speeches of the Greek war council. In the third section, as the Greeks traverse the southern edge of the Black Sea, Xenophon must repeatedly defend himself against the suspicions and accusations of his men, but he manages to retain the confidence of the majority. Finally, the themes of suspicion and the dangers of living without trust are linked in Xenophon's lengthy speech to the Thracian king Seuthes, in which he urges the latter to pay the Greek soldiers the money he owes them. Xenophon emphasizes that, unaccompanied by a reputation for trustworthiness, eloquence and wealth are valueless and power is insecure.

These students of the *Anabasis* have clearly established that it is a carefully crafted work of literature as well as a historical record. In the writing of history Xenophon was influenced by the example of his towering predecessor Thucydides. In fact his *Hellenica* was intended as a continuation of Thucydides' unfinished history of the Peloponnesian War. Thucydides' usual technique was to refrain from overt editorializing and to allow the narrative to make its own impression on the reader;[11] the dramatic effect of this approach is especially strong in his account of the ill-fated Sicilian expedition.[12] More than one commentator has recognized Xenophon's use of a similar technique in the *Anabasis*.[13] Yet despite widespread acknowledgment that Thucydides' history is of profound intellectual as well as historical value, Xenophon has not fared nearly as well. Most critics agree that the *Anabasis* is Xenophon's best and most vivid work, marked by dramatic intensity and power, but they have put little effort into discovering the source of that power.

Werner Jaeger has said that all of Xenophon's works were meant to educate.[14] Xenophon clearly had a strong interest in education, as any reader of the *Cyropaedia, Oeconomicus, Constitution of the Lacedaemonians*, or some of the technical treatises can testify. Thus it should not be surprising if the *Anabasis* had an instructional purpose. Learned commentators in antiquity, such as Dionysius of Halicarnassus, Dio Chrysostom, and Eunapius, already viewed the *Anabasis* as a source of lessons in military tactics and as a paradigm of the composed, resolute, and imaginative leader.[15] The posthumous character sketches of Cyrus and the murdered Greek generals, with their strong moral emphasis, must also be intended to serve a didactic purpose.

Some of the analytic techniques which have proved fruitful in recent studies of Thucydides—attention to recurrent motifs, to the occasional discontinuity between words and events, and to the way in which the speeches and actions of one part of the story may illuminate the meaning of another part[16]—can also provide insights into the *Anabasis*. This chapter explores Xenophon's use of the motifs of trust and deceit throughout the *Anabasis*. The primary purpose of this analysis is to extract one of the lessons implicit in his carefully contrived account. As will be seen, this lesson has a significant bearing on the question of Xenophon's attitude to Persia. His participation in the ill-fated expedition of Cyrus and the perilous return march of the Greek mercenaries was clearly a pivotal event in his life. Such a powerful experience must have had a permanent influence on his personality and values. It provided him with firsthand knowledge of the Persian Empire and with the opportunity to make the acquaintance of many Persians, and he later made use of the material which he had gathered not only in the *Anabasis* but also in the *Cyropaedia*.[17]

The complementary concepts of trust and deceit are pervasive in the *Anabasis*. Wencis has already pointed out that *hypopsia*—suspicion—poses a central problem for Cyrus, Clearchus, and Xenophon.[18] Higgins is struck by "how much guile and how much deceitful speech occur in the narrative of the march to Kounaxa."[19] Xenophon's use of trust, deceit, and related terms and concepts in the *Anabasis* goes far beyond what would be required in a mere chronicle. Through his recurrent treatment of these concepts in the work Xenophon explores a problem in human relations.

When analyzing the meaning of such a motif, it is particularly important to keep in view the entire work. After the execution of the Greek generals by Tissaphernes and the Persian king, a series of Greek speakers castigates the faithlessness and untrustworthiness of the Persians. This reproach against the barbarian became standard in the panhellenic rhetoric of the fourth century.[20] Probably largely on the basis of these indictments, the *Anabasis* is frequently cited as proof of Xenophon's profound hatred for the barbarian. Yet although the treachery of Tissaphernes is a turning point in the *Anabasis*, it is not the only instance of treachery and betrayal. Others besides the Persians (other barbarians, but particularly Greeks) are equally guilty but are not subjected to the same relentless accusations.

The issue of Persian treachery and faithlessness assumes extraordinary significance because "the Lie" was the central concept of evil in the Zoroastrian ethical code which underlay Achaemenid Persian culture.[21] To break an oath, to tell a lie, to prove untrustworthy were cardinal sins permitted under no circumstances, not even when one was dealing with an enemy.[22] The Avestan Hymn to Mithra, dated by its most recent commentator to the mid-fifth century, expressly states: "The knave who is false to the treaty, O Spitamid, wrecks the whole country, hitting as he does the Truth-owners as hard as would a hundred obscurantists. Never break a contract, O Spitamid, whether you conclude it with an owner of Falsehood, or a Truthowning follower of the good Religion; for the contract applies to both, the owner of Falsehood and him who owns Truth."[23] *Mithra*, taken as a common noun, means "contract" and includes all forms of engagements undertaken, including international treaties. It is formally indistinguishable from the name of the god Mithra, to whom the hymn is addressed and who guards the contract and punishes violators.[24] Mithra first appears in Old Persian inscriptions in the reign of Artaxerxes II,[25] against whom Cyrus and the Greek mercenaries fought; and Ctesias, who served at the court of this monarch, mentions the king's participation in the festival of Mithra.[26]

Thus one must conclude that Tissaphernes and Artaxerxes II operated within a religious and ethical system which expressly forbade lies, deceit, and the breaking of oaths. Herodotus was aware of this when he wrote that Persian youths were taught three things: to ride, to shoot, and to tell the truth (1.136). Considered in this context, the frequent Greek accusations of Persian treachery and faithlessness take on a special resonance. It would clearly be of value to determine whether Xenophon is aware of the centrality of the concept of the Lie in Persian culture and whether, in the *Anabasis*, he is knowingly accusing them of what is, in their own cultural terms, the ultimate sin.

In contrast, it appears that falsehood and deception were not necessarily considered as reprehensible in Greek culture as they were in the Persian ethical system. Odysseus in the *Odyssey* is admired for his clever lies, and Themistocles, with his deceptive message to the Persian king at Salamis in 480, serves as a historical example of a hero admired for his trickery. Likewise, one cannot help but smile at the bold lies and deceptions of the infant Hermes of the Homeric Hymn;[27] and Prometheus, who deceives the gods, is a benefactor of mankind. The chorus in Aristophanes' *Clouds* shamelessly employs deceit in order to punish the fatuous cheat Strepsiades, and this without any imputation of wrongdoing.[28] I know of no Greek legends predicated upon the negative consequences of lying. *Pseudesthai*, the nearest Greek approximation, did not have the sinful connotations which *lie* has for us or which *drauga* and its cognates had for the ancient Persians. Oath-breaking is another matter, for it involves improper conduct in relation to the gods; and *epiorkia* had a distinctly negative ethical value in Greek thought. But in extant Greek tragedy only Sophocles' *Philoctetes* shows a prominent concern for falsehood and the breaking of oaths, and even here the question whether the end justifies the means is left unanswered. It follows that lies and deceit were not major ethical concerns for the Greeks.[29]

Against this background of Greek ambivalence or disinterest, Xenophon's strong emphasis on *pistis*, trustworthiness, in the *Anabasis* and elsewhere becomes all the more noteworthy.[30] Might it not indicate that he was influenced by the strong and unambiguous stance of the Persian system of ethics?

Xenophon implicitly advertises the importance of the theme of trust and deceit by devoting considerable space to one particular incident on Cyrus' march inland: the intrigue, arrest, trial, and execution of the Persian noble Orontas (1.6). Intent on betraying Cyrus, Orontas writes to the Persian king and reminds him of his former fidelity (*pistis*) to the throne. He entrusts the letter to a man whom he believes to be faithful (*pistos*) to himself. This messenger betrays him and turns the incriminating letter over to Cyrus. Orontas is arrested and tried by Cyrus in the presence of seven Persian nobles and the Greek mercenary commander, Clearchus. It comes out in testimony that Orontas has repeatedly shown lack of *pistis*, for twice Cyrus has had him at his mercy and twice they have been reconciled and exchanged pledges of good faith (*pista*). Now Orontas has broken his word again, and even he admits that Cyrus is not likely to believe that he could again be a faithful friend (*philos kai pistos*). Condemned to death on the motion of Clearchus, he is led off and executed in secret by Cyrus' most faithful (*pistotatos*) attendant.

Clearly *pistis* is the reverberating motif of this story. There is abundant irony in the fact that Orontas advertises his *pistis* to the king at the very moment when he is violating his *pistis* to Cyrus. Moreover, the betrayer is betrayed by a man whom he considered to be *pistos* to himself, and he is executed by a servant who, unlike himself, is truly *pistotatos* to Cyrus. There is further irony in the fact that Clearchus, who proposes the death penalty as the price of Orontas' treachery, later suffers the same penalty on the same charge at the hands of the king. The episode also displays the leniency of Cyrus, who forgave the treachery of Orontas on several previous occasions, and it illustrates the real loyalty of others (Orontas' messenger, Clearchus and the seven Persian judges, the "most faithful" courtier who executes Orontas) to the young prince. Xenophon later emphasizes Cyrus' own personal trustworthiness in all matters and his distinctive talent for winning the trust of others (1.9). He adds that Orontas was the only one ever to defect from Cyrus to the king, whereas many of the king's partisans defected to Cyrus (1.9.29). Through the fullness of his coverage and the conspicuous repetition of words formed from the root *pist–*, Xenophon is manifestly announcing the importance of the *pistis* motif and setting a theme and tone for the rest of the *Anabasis*. In so doing, he is adopting a technique already used with great success by Herodotus. In the first book of the *Histories*, Herodotus focuses on a series of stories which articulate important themes and serve as paradigms for patterns which he sees operating in history. Sometimes these stories are anecdotal, chosen less for their intrinsic historical significance than for their exemplary value. An obvious example is the famous story of the meeting between Croesus, the opulent king of Lydia, and the Athenian wise man Solon. The narrative illustrates both the hubris of Croesus, who is excessively proud of his wealth and power, and the wisdom of Solon, who recognizes the instability of human affairs, the gods' jealousy toward those who are too fortunate, and the nature of real prosperity. Herodotus intends the reader to keep this story and the eventual collapse of Croesus' fortunes in mind throughout the *Histories*. Others, such as Polycrates, the tyrant of Samos, and the Persian king Xerxes, later fall into similar patterns of hubris and error and can be expected to suffer a like retribution.[31]

Xenophon has done something similar with the Orontas episode. Using an event of only limited importance in itself, he has delineated themes which will be operative throughout the *Anabasis*. Here he makes clear for the first time, in the downfall of Orontas, the wages of treachery.

Xenophon's development of the motif of trust and deceit can be divided into four stages.[32] In the first stage, which extends through the death of Cyrus in battle, the focus is on the deceptions practiced by three central figures: the rebellious Persian prince Cyrus, the Persian satrap (provincial governor) Tissaphernes, and Clearchus, the most influential of Cyrus' Greek mercenary commanders. In the second stage Clearchus and his successors in command of the Greek troops must contend with the treachery of Tissaphernes, the Persian king, and Persians who had been partisans of Cyrus. In the third stage the Greek army, while traversing the southern shore of the Black Sea, is repeatedly deceived by fellow Greeks. In the concluding section Xenophon delivers a climactic speech on the value of *pistis* and thereby wins the cooperation of the Thracian prince Seuthes.

The specter of treachery and suspicion is introduced on the first page of the *Anabasis*, in the statement that Tissaphernes "slandered" Cyrus before King Artaxerxes. The term used to describe Tissaphernes' action—*diaballei*—usually bears the sense of a false or distorted accusation.[33] In one sense, all the events in the narrative, and their often tragic consequences, follow from this action. For Artaxerxes becomes suspicious of Cyrus and arrests him. Eventually Cyrus is released, but he is so angry at his arrest that he plots revolt against his brother. Thus Tissaphernes' initial act of deceit sets in motion a chain of events which eventually brings Xenophon and the other Greeks to their predicament in the heart of Asia.

Tissaphernes is presented as a liar and deceiver both here and elsewhere in Xenophon's works. It is the cunning Tissaphernes, pursuing a policy of wearing down both sides in the Peloponnesian War, who fails to keep his promises to supply money and a Phoenician fleet to his Peloponnesian allies in the last book of Thucydides' history and whose continued machinations occupy the opening paragraphs of Xenophon's *Hellenica*. A decade and a half later he reneges on a truce with the Spartan king Agesilaus, taking advantage of the suspension of hostilities to gather new forces with which to attack the Spartan expeditionary army.[34] Perhaps Xenophon's portrayal of Tissaphernes as the epitome of the crafty, faithless Oriental is accurate.[35] In any case it is not the product of a stereotypical view of Persians, for Xenophon has obvious respect for the courage, trustworthiness, and noble spirit of the contemporary satrap of Dascylium, Pharnabazus. There is a distinct possibility that this image of Tissaphernes, whether based on fact or on the (possibly biased) testimony of Xenophon in the *Anabasis* and *Hellenica*, unduly colored the Greek conception of the Persians in the fourth century and helped to create the negative stereotype of the cunning and treacherous Oriental.

Xenophon's portrayal of Cyrus is admittedly problematic. Cyrus deceives his Greek troops about the true object of his expedition, fearing (with some justification) that they would be unwilling to march against the Great King. Yet Xenophon carefully avoids the use of language which would imply wrongdoing on Cyrus' part. Rather, Cyrus is said to offer the "explanation" (*prophasis*) that he intends to compaign against the recalcitrant Pisidians (1.2.1). *Prophasis* is an ambiguous term. In its most basic sense it refers to the reason one gives for doing something, but it can range in meaning from false pretext to true explanation.[36]

At a later stage of the march, when the Greek troops, suspecting the real objective of the expedition, refuse to budge from Cilicia, Cyrus and Clearchus contrive a scheme to induce them to march on. Clearchus, who feigns loyalty to the Greek troops, is sent along with others as an emissary to Cyrus. The Persian prince now claims that he is marching against his enemy Abrocomas in Syria, and the Greeks reluctantly agree to follow him (1.3). Once again Xenophon's terminology is neutral. Shortly thereafter occurs the incident in which Orontas is executed for treason.

Despite these several instances of Cyrus' active deception of his Greek troops, Xenophon repeatedly refers to the trust which Cyrus inspired. A faction of Milesian exiles had broken off their attack on Miletus and gladly followed Cyrus because they trusted him to fulfill his promise to restore them to their city after he had accomplished his own immediate object (*hoi de hēdeōs epeithonto; episteuon gar autōi*; 1.2.2); at 1.9.10 Xenophon mentions that Cyrus kept faith with these exiles through thick and thin. The testimony at the trial of Orontas illustrates that Cyrus had kept faith with Orontas despite the latter's multiple acts of treachery (1.6.6–8). At 3.1.9–10 Xenophon remarks that the reason the Greeks had continued to follow Cyrus, despite their suspicions, was that they were ashamed to betray him.

The motif of Cyrus' *pistis* or trustworthiness is hammered home in the encomiastic chapter which follows the account of his death in battle (1.9). Xenophon reports that, when Cyrus was sent down to Asia Minor as satrap.

> he showed, in the first place, that he counted it of the utmost importance, when he concluded a treaty or compact with anyone or made anyone any promise, under no circumstances to prove false to his word [*mēdamōs pseudesthai*]. It was for this reason, then, that the cities trusted him [*episteuon*] and put themselves under his protec-

tion, and that individuals also trusted him [*episteuon*]; and if anyone had been an enemy, when Cyrus made a treaty with him he trusted [*episteue*] that he would suffer no harm in violation of that treaty.³⁷

The deliberate repetition of the verb *pisteuō* in this passage is a clear indication that Cyrus is being set up as a model of *pistis*. Thus he is implicitly contrasted with the archdeceiver Tissaphernes. Cyrus and Tissaphernes are antithetical in more ways than one. Not only are they personal enemies³⁸ and fighting on opposite sides in the rebellion, but they also represent opposing principles: Cyrus is the epitome of truth and trust, Tissaphernes of treachery, cunning, and deceit. But why should Xenophon stress Cyrus' *pistis*? It has already been seen that trustworthiness, with its attendant virtues of truthfulness and the fulfillment of obligations, was a primary ethical and religious precept in ancient Iranian culture. Xenophon may be implying that, even in his own Persian cultural terms, Cyrus was an exemplary character.³⁹

It cannot be denied that there is a disturbing contradiction between Cyrus' alleged *pistis* and his deception of the Greek troops. However, the fact remains that neither Xenophon nor any other figure in the *Anabasis* ever accuses Cyrus of deceit, wrongdoing, or want of good faith. Nor does Xenophon make the slightest mention of Cyrus' lack of *pistis* in revolting from his brother the king and seeking to seize the throne. There seems to be a double standard in operation, with a blind eye turned to the sins of Cyrus. Perhaps Xenophon's intentions are at least in part ironic; he may expect the reader to recognize that Cyrus, for all his vaunted trustworthiness, did deceive his Greek allies and thereby helped to put them in mortal jeopardy. Be that as it may, *pistis* and its cognates appear so often in conjunction with Cyrus that it must be regarded as a deliberate and conscious motif.⁴⁰

Between the extremes of Tissaphernes and Cyrus, Clearchus, the most trusted of Cyrus' Greek mercenary commanders, is an ambiguous figure. Mention has already been made of the incident in Cilicia when Clearchus, in collusion with Cyrus, tricks the Greeks into continuing the march into the interior of Asia (1.3). At the time he claims to be ignorant of Cyrus' intentions and insists that, although he feels responsibility to Cyrus, he will never betray fellow Greeks and prefer the friendship of the barbarians. Yet that is precisely what he does, and Xenophon later maintains that Clearchus, alone of all the Greek commanders, knew Cyrus' plans from the beginning (3.1.10). Clearchus' primary loyalty is to Persian Cyrus, yet Xenophon does not explicitly disparage him for this, either in his account of the Cilician episode or in his obituary notice. Xenophon does not entirely disapprove of this stern but effective soldier, and the fact remains that he and the other Greeks on the expedition also felt a loyalty to Cyrus that kept them from deserting him despite their suspicions.

Thus the first stage of the *Anabasis* introduces three major figures, a bad Persian, a good Persian, and a Greek, all of whom practice deceit. It is clearly a vice which crosses ethnic lines.

The second phase in this drama of trust and deceit centers on the dealings between Greeks and Persians after the death of Cyrus. The main protagonists are Clearchus and Tissaphernes, whose story lines now intersect. After the news of Cyrus' death on the battlefield at Cunaxa has spread, Tissaphernes and a delegation of leading Persians, described as most faithful (*pistotatoi*) to the king, approach the Greek generals and ask why the Greeks have marched against the king. Clearchus explains that this had never been their intention but that Cyrus had used various pretexts (again the neutral word *prophasis*) to lead them on and they had been ashamed to abandon him (2.3.17–22). Clearchus is defending the conduct of the Greeks as based on *pistis*, a quality which the Persians should have been able to appreciate. Clearchus (and Xenophon) knew enough about Persian values to base this response on a motive which was calculated to appeal to Persian sensibilities.

When Tissaphernes returns to the Greek camp, he claims to have won over the king. He exchanges pledges (*pista*) with the Greek leaders and promises that there will be no treachery. This is a critical moment, and Xenophon describes it in great detail, giving Tissaphernes' words in direct speech and quoting the precise provisions of the agreement made by Persians and Greeks. In this way he ensures that the reader can determine who later broke the truce. Tissaphernes' speech, in which he claims to have argued vociferously before the king on the Greeks' behalf, is clever and disarming (2.3.25–28). Earlier he had predicated his goodwill for the Greeks on the fact that he was their neighbor in western Asia Minor and stood to benefit from their gratitude (2.3.18). The compact (what the Persians would have called *mithra*) is ratified on the Persian side by Tissaphernes and the king's brother-in-law, the latter presumably representing the king himself. Thus both the king and Tissaphernes are later implicated as liars and perjurers.

Xenophon does not describe other agreements (even those which are broken) in nearly as much detail. This instance clearly illustrates how Xenophon can influence the judgment of the reader by deliberate selection, emphasis, and treatment of material. Here Xenophon's purpose transcends mere historical reportage; he has a special case to make against Tissaphernes and the king. The same can be said for his presentation of the highly sophistic speeches of Tissaphernes. Although Xenophon may have been present at the actual interviews,[41] he almost certainly has exercised some literary license here.[42] He has sharpened the rhetoric and enhanced the irony of these speeches so as to create a portrait of the Persian satrap which verges on the diabolic.

Why is Xenophon so bitterly hostile to Tissaphernes and the king? It is probably because they were the paramount enemies of Cyrus, for whom he has so much esteem. In addition to continuing this sinister representation of Tissaphernes in his *Hellenica*,[43] Xenophon heaps scorn on Artaxerxes in the *Agesilaus* (9.1–5). But Xenophon does not express disdain for other Persians, either here or in other works.[44]

There follows a period of increasing mutual suspicion between Greeks and Persians. When these suspicions reach a critical point, Clearchus seeks an interview with Tissaphernes in the hope of averting trouble. This meeting of the Greek and Persian leaders is another pivotal moment in the drama of trust and deceit. In the interview, Clearchus insists that Tissaphernes is mistaken to mistrust the Greeks, for they would not dare incur the wrath of the gods by foreswearing their oaths. The moralizing tone of Clearchus' speech may strike many readers as naive, but it is possible that he is again trying to appeal to Persian belief in the imperative nature of *pistis* and the god's punishment of perjuries. In light of subsequent events, there is tremendous irony in Clearchus' insistence to Tissaphernes that he has nothing to fear from the Greeks.[45]

Tissaphernes' reply to Clearchus is a masterpiece of deception. He insists upon his own and the king's trustworthiness (*oud' an hymeis dikaiōs oute basilei out' emoi epistoiēte*), for perjury is impious and perjurers are rascals. They could easily destroy the Greeks at any time they choose, yet they will not.

The reason for this was my eager desire to prove myself trustworthy to the Greeks, so that with the same mercenary force which Cyrus led up from the coast in the faith of wages paid, I might go back to the coast in the security of benefits conferred. And as for all the ways in which you are of use to me, you also have mentioned some of them, but it is I who know the most important: the King alone may wear upright the tiara that is upon the head, but another, too, with your help, might easily so wear the one that is upon the heart.

(2.5.16–23)[46]

This speech of Tissaphernes is, in the words of Higgins, "irony perfected to vengeance." Read in the light of later events, it shows Tissaphernes to be a monster of cunning and treachery.[47] Most monstrous of all is the fact that he predicates his appeal on his own eager desire to prove himself trustworthy to the Greeks. He claims that he wants to succeed to Cyrus' place in their affections and baits the hook with a cryptic allusion to his own designs upon the throne. Surely the Greeks should have been put on their guard when, at the very moment that Tissaphernes is proclaiming his eagerness to win the Greeks' trust, he lets drop a hint that he is ready to betray his trust to the king. Tissaphernes is a master at winning false trust, and again the intended contrast (a comparison suggested by Tissaphernes himself) is with Cyrus, who ultimately deserved and proved worthy of the loyalty which he inspired. Tissaphernes' speech is so rhetorically effective and so barbed with irony that one must again assume that in composing it Xenophon has taken pains to create the most damning possible portrait.

The ironic conclusion of this interview is reported with chilling simplicity: "In these things that he said Tissaphernes seemed to Clearchus to be speaking the truth" (2.5.24). Clearchus is completely taken in and proceeds to step into the trap. He agrees to Tissaphernes' proposal that he bring the other Greek generals and captains to the Persian camp, so that the names of those on both sides who were sowing suspicion might be revealed. After a sojourn as Tissaphernes' dinner guest, Clearchus returns to his own camp, where he must threaten and cajole his fellows who are reluctant to send the Greek leaders to Tissaphernes. Some warn against trusting Tissaphernes (*mēde pisteuein Tissaphernei*), but Clearchus will have none of it. He suspects Menon of stirring up false rumors, because Menon has also met with Tissaphernes and Clearchus believes he is plotting to wrest the leadership of the Greek mercenaries away from him. Here, too, Tissaphernes has played his hand perfectly, manipulating the suspicions and ambitions of these two Greek leaders. The suspicion (*hypopsia*) and mistrust (*apistia*) between Clearchus and Menon have dire consequences. Once they have arrived at Tissaphernes' tent, the captains are killed on the spot, the generals seized and later executed. There follows a barbarian attack on the Greeks who are wandering in the plain between the camps (2.5.24–32).

Xenophon makes it abundantly clear that the truce is treacherously violated by Tissaphernes and the Persians. Moreover, Tissaphernes has violated the laws of hospitality by effecting the murder of his own dinner guest. But it is Xenophon's portrayal of Clearchus as utterly naive, foolish, and trusting that calls for an explanation.[48] Perhaps Clearchus was all of these things, although these qualities are not easily reconciled with his display of shrewdness on several occasions before this point (for example, at 1.3, 2.1.15–23, and 2.3.1–9) and with Xenophon's eulogy portraying him as a hard-bitten and experienced old soldier (2.6.1–15). It may be that Xenophon, embarrassed by the ease with which the Greeks were taken in, means to make Clearchus the scapegoat. In defense of Clearchus, it might be argued that he had come to believe that cooperation with Tissaphernes was the Greeks' only practical hope; that he need not so much have trusted Tissaphernes as seen that the Greeks could not afford to antagonize the one individual who offered them a way out of their desperate situation. But this is not how Xenophon represents the episode. Although he may respect Clearchus' qualities as a soldier, he is critical of the latter's self-serving ambition and poor judgment. On at least two occasions Clearchus imperiled the Greeks by preferring the friendship of a Persian to the best interests of his countrymen.

On the other hand, there is some reason to believe that in the fifth century the Persians had been famous for their fidelity to oaths (a quality which accords well with Zoroastrian precepts). In the epilogue to the *Cyropaedia* (8.8.2–3) the author insists that up to the time of the Anabasis the Persian king and his subordinates had always kept their oaths and promises, even with the worst offenders. He subsequently provides an alternative explanation for Clearchus' conduct, claiming that it was because of the Persians' reputation for trustworthiness that Clearchus and the Greeks relied on the king's oath after Cunaxa.[49] This reputation would account for Clearchus' conduct and for the surprise and outrage of the Greeks when they later found that Cyrus' Persian partisans, with whom they had exchanged oaths of fidelity, had deserted them.[50] It also goes far to explain the particular direction taken by some fourth-century antibarbarian rhetoric: those who were hostile to Persia must have taken special pleasure in subverting the old Persian reputation for *pistis* by accusing them of being the most faithless and untrustworthy of men.

The betrayal of the Greek generals is not the last act of Persian treachery. Immediately after the battle of Cunaxa, the Greek and barbarian contingents of Cyrus' army had sworn oaths of loyalty and alliance to one another (2.2.8). Yet even before the murder of the generals, the Greeks have become increasingly suspicious of their Persian allies. Agents from the Persian king have been repeatedly visiting the leading Persian partisans of Cyrus, bringing pledges of amnesty (2.4.1). In the immediate aftermath of the seizure and execution of the Greek generals, Ariaeus, Artaozus, and Mithridates are already operating in conjunction with Tissaphernes, and, given the timing, it is hard to avoid the conclusion that these former Persian supporters of Cyrus (ironically referred to as *pistotatoi*) have been privy to Tissaphernes' plan to seize the Greek leaders. They participate in a number of attempts, both diplomatic and military, to hinder the Greeks' escape (2.5.35–39; 3.3.1–7). What is particularly striking about this series of incidents is the evident surprise and disillusionment of the Greeks when confronted with the treachery of their barbarian allies. This is not to suggest that these experienced and battle-hardened Greek mercenaries were so naive as to put complete faith in barbarian oaths; indeed, during the march to Cunaxa Cyrus had warned them that his barbarian contingents could not be relied on if matters took a bad turn (1.5.16). However, if Xenophon is to be believed, the Greeks were caught off guard by these acts of betrayal, and they apparently saw no reason why barbarians should not be trusted to be reliable allies. This is another significant indication of Greek attitudes toward barbarians at the turn of the fourth century.

It remains to consider the Greek reaction to these Persian acts of treachery. On the night following the murder of the generals, Xenophon urges the Greeks to rouse themselves from despair and to choose new leaders. The ensuing assembly of Greek soldiers is one of the critical dramatic scenes in the *Anabasis*. It also furnishes the major evidence for those who believe that Xenophon hated the Persians and thought them innately treacherous and untrustworthy.

Xenophon presents three speeches in his account of the assembly. Cheirisophus the Lacedaemonian is first to speak. He complains that, on top of their other troubles, the Greeks have been betrayed by Ariaeus and his barbarian troops, their erstwhile allies. However, they must never yield and should fight to achieve either victory or an honorable death (3.2.2–3).

The second speaker is the Boeotian Cleanor. He first castigates "the perjury and impiety of the king"; then "the faithlessness [*apistia*] of Tissaphernes," whose crimes he catalogues; finally, the despicable conduct of Ariaeus, who has renounced his oaths, forgotten the memory of Cyrus, and defected to the enemy. He urges the Greeks never again to allow themselves to be deceived by these men, but to "fight as stoutly as we can and meet whatever fortune the gods may please to send" (3.2.4–6).

The third and last to speak is Xenophon himself, "arrayed for war in his finest dress." He alludes to the perjury and faithlessness (*apistia*) of the barbarians. Alas for the generals who trustingly (*dia pisteōs*) put themselves in Persian hands. But the Greeks should have high hopes for deliverance; for the gods will help them and will punish the Persians as perjurers and oath-breakers. Xenophon goes on to cite a variety of other considerations which, in his opinion, confirm the Greeks' favorable prospects should they choose to fight their way out of Persian territory. These include the standard appeals to famous Greek victories of the past as well as a reminder of the recent success of the Greek mercenaries over their barbarian opponents at Cunaxa. Some of his rationalizations ring hollow, as when he argues that their lack of cavalry is an advantage or that, should they threaten to stay in Persia, the king would give them anything in order to persuade them to leave (3.2.7–32).

What is the function of these three speeches in Xenophon's narrative? Although they may represent the essence of what was actually said, Xenophon has certainly taken the usual liberties with speeches allowed to the historian in antiquity. For it is unlikely that the real speeches, delivered in a moment of stress and high excitement, would be as concise, artfully arranged, and rhetorically effective as are those of Cleanor and Xenophon.

All three speakers express righteous indignation as they harp upon the recent treachery of the Persians. Xenophon repeatedly insists that this treachery will put the gods on the Greek side, although he is sensible enough to append other, more substantial, reasons for hope. Cleanor's speech is a carefully constructed rhetorical attack on the Persian king, Tissaphernes, and Ariaeus. He employs a series of morally tinged words in his accusation in order to drive home the point that these Persians have violated the most basic social and religious obligations.[51]

These three speeches operate in a complementary fashion. Cheirisophus first stresses the dangers of the situation and urges courage and resistance. Cleanor hammers home the point—emotionally, indignantly, rhetorically—that the Greeks should not trust these barbarians again. They are to make no more deals; rather, they must fight their way out. Finally Xenophon rises to speak, already outfitted for war, and explains why they ought to be of good hope. In response, the Greek assembly votes unanimously to fight (3.2.33).

These speeches are coordinated and delivered by the three Greek leaders for a specific purpose—to gain widespread support for their policy of resistance to the Persians.[52] Stranded as they were in the heart of a vast and hostile empire, it is probable that some fearful and despairing Greeks were still urging negotiations with the Persians or perhaps even a surrender on terms.[53] Xenophon and others wanted to fight for their freedom, and their speeches in the assembly are calculated to convince the army of the correctness of that policy. Thus they resort to rhetoric, hyperbole, and, in Xenophon's case, some rather dubious rationalizations. One need not assume that everything which Xenophon says in his speech about the faithlessness of the barbarians reflects his innermost convictions, any more than one has to believe that he welcomed the Greeks' lack of cavalry.[54]

In sum, this assembly is a dramatic high point. Speeches are delivered which aim at the adoption of a particular policy, and the critical decision to resist is made. The content of these speeches must be viewed both in their immediate context and in relation to what follows. It is a procedural error to excerpt antibarbarian statements from these speeches and to maintain that they represent the considered opinion of Xenophon, or of all fourth-century Greeks, concerning the trustworthiness of non-Greeks.[55]

Eventually, and with considerable difficulty, the Greeks outdistance Tissaphernes and the king's army, and after fighting their way through the mountain fastnesses of the Carduchians they descend into the Armenian plain. Soon they encounter Tiribazus, the satrap of Western Armenia. The Greek generals accept Tiribazus' invitation to a parley, and both sides agree to a truce (4.4.4–6).

Before long the truce with Tiribazus breaks down. Although Xenophon does not say so, a careful reading of his account reveals that it was the Greeks who first breached the agreement. The terms of the truce, as described by Xenophon, provided that Tiribazus would not harm the Greeks and that the Greeks could take whatever provisions they needed, so long as they did not burn the natives' houses (4.4.6). Yet some of the Greek mercenaries soon did burn the houses in which they were quartered (4.4.14), and this violation led to a resumption of hostilities. The Greeks, having learned from a prisoner that Tiribazus was preparing an ambush, struck first and sacked his camp (4.4.18–22).

Xenophon's treatment of this episode is equivocal. Although he does not state explicitly that the Greeks broke the truce, he supplies facts which make such an inference plausible. This impression of Greek responsibility is confirmed by the fact that no one accuses Tiribazus of treachery in preparing an ambush.[56] The cursory treatment of this episode contrasts strongly with the lengthy and elaborate portrayal of Tissaphernes' deception, replete with that satrap's sardonic speeches, details of the crime, and the repetitious Greek castigation of barbarian treachery. By his selection and treatment of material, by emphasis and de-emphasis, Xenophon is able to influence the reader's perception of events. His treatment of the Armenian incident, by its very brevity and straightforwardness, accentuates the dramatic significance of the Tissaphernes episode and confirms the necessity of inquiring into Xenophon's ulterior motives in attacking the king and Tissaphernes.

This Armenian episode, with its implications of the Greeks' own capacity for bad faith as they pass out of the area of Persian control, effects a subtle transition between the end of the second section of Xenophon's narrative, which focuses on Persian iniquity, and the third section. The latter sustains the motif of deceit, but this time Greeks practice deceit against fellow Greeks.

A rapid review of the major incidents will suffice. First, the people of Sinope and Heraclea, Greek communities on the southern shore of the Black Sea, promise a sum of money to two members of the Ten

Thousand, Timasion and Thorax, if they can arrange for the Greek army to sail away (5.6.21). Eventually the army does vote to depart, but when the Sinopeans and Heracleots learn that Xenophon had introduced the motion, they renege on their promise. In Xenophon's words, "they turned out to be deceivers" (*epseusmenoi ēsan*; 5.6.35).

As the Greeks approach the Bosporus, the Persian satrap Pharnabazus suborns Anaxibius, the Spartan admiral, to get the Greek army out of Asia. Anaxibius promises the Greeks regular pay if they will cross over to Byzantium. They readily comply, but Anaxibius then refuses to pay them and ejects them from the city. As the army marches out, the gates are shut and locked behind them, and he orders them to forage for themselves and march to the Chersonese. The angry mercenaries fight their way back into the city and threaten to go on a rampage. But Xenophon halts them and speaks to calm them. He admits that they are justifiably angry at having been so outrageously deceived (*exapatōmenoi*), but they will have to check their ire and withdraw, lest they make enemies of the Spartans, who now rule the Greek world. At least Anaxibius will know that they now leave, not because they are deceived, but because they are obedient (7.1.1–31).

Immediately thereafter a Theban named Coeratadas, who is eager to assume command of the Ten Thousand, promises to provide them with supplies in abundance if they will follow him. However, he repeatedly postpones distribution of the promised goods, and it is soon discovered that he has but a negligible stock of provisions. Once he has been unmasked as a fraud he quickly slips away (7.1.33–41).

Next, as soon as he learns that Anaxibius has been replaced as admiral, Pharnabazus refuses to pay him the promised reward. Instead he makes a similar deal with Aristarchus, the new Spartan governor of Byzantium (7.2.7). Aristarchus invites the Greek generals to a conference, intending to ignore his guarantee of safe-conduct and to arrest Xenophon, but Xenophon is alerted to the plot in time (7.2.12–16). There are striking similarities between this situation and Tissaphernes' treacherous seizure of the Greek generals.

Soon Xenophon calls an assembly and persuades the Greeks to enter the service of the Thracian prince Seuthes, for the Spartans block their passage over to Asia, sell them into slavery, cheat and deceive them (*exapatēsesthai*), and refuse to assist them in their desperate straits (7.3.2–6). In this speech Xenophon stresses the untrustworthiness of the Greek Aristarchus and recommends that the troops trust the promises of the barbarian Seuthes. Nobody any longer believes that Greeks are inherently more trustworthy than barbarians.

Throughout this section Xenophon avoids overt editorial criticism of the various Greek practitioners of deception, preferring instead, in the manner of Herodotus and Thucydides, to mold events and speeches to create the desired effect. In the previous section the Greek leaders used Persian faithlessness as an emotional issue to stiffen resistance and guarantee that a particular policy prevail. Xenophon has no such purpose here and so refrains from elaboration of material and speeches. This impression is confirmed by the fact that Xenophon does not revive the familiar refrain of "Persian treachery" when the satrap Pharnabazus cheats Anaxibius of the promised reward. That theme is no longer a concern. And it would appear all too hypocritical when seen in the context of so much Greek treachery.

The fourth and last act in this drama of trust and deceit covers the period during which the Ten Thousand are in the service of the Thracian prince Seuthes. Two speeches, both delivered by Xenophon, play a prominent role in the development of the action: the first deals with deceit, the second with trust.

The Greek mercenaries perform good service for Seuthes and help him to gain possession of a large expanse of new territory. But after the first month he is unable to pay the full sum of wages promised to them. That money was supposed to come from the sale of booty, a task entrusted to Seuthes' Greek aide Heraclides.[57] Xenophon soon begins to suspect that Heraclides has pocketed some of this money. Heraclides subsequently becomes Xenophon's enemy and seeks to discredit him with Seuthes (7.5.4–8). Apparently Xenophon does not regard the barbarian Seuthes as intent on defrauding the Greeks. He has been deceived by Heraclides, who is the last in a now long line of Greeks who have deceived their fellow Greeks.[58]

Now all parties are angry with Xenophon: Seuthes is annoyed because Xenophon has been constantly demanding the pay, and the Greek soldiers hold Xenophon responsible for Seuthes' default on their wages. They even accuse him of having been bribed by Seuthes

(7.5.7, 7.6.9–10). Xenophon rises to defend himself before the assembled Greek army, Seuthes, and a pair of Spartan agents. He marvels at the absurdity of his situation, at being blamed by the very men for whom he has made every sacrifice; denies that he has embezzled the money owed the Greeks; and asserts that he has received nothing from Seuthes. Later in the speech, conceding that he gambled on winning the friendship and gratitude of Seuthes, he concludes: "One might say, 'Are you not ashamed of being so stupidly deceived?' I certainly should be ashamed, by Zeus, if I had been deceived by one who was an enemy; but for one who is a friend, to deceive seems to me more shameful than to be deceived" (7.6.21).[59]

Does this statement represent Xenophon's own conception of correct conduct? One could argue that it is merely a response to the needs of the moment, a clever piece of rhetoric designed to get Xenophon off the hook with the troops. Nevertheless, it seems more likely that Xenophon envisions a wider didactic purpose for this speech which he puts into his own mouth. At this point in the expedition, when the Greeks have been deceived on so many occasions that most of them must have vowed never to trust anyone, Xenophon still insists on the importance of *pistis* between friends. One must be on one's guard against enemies, and it is a great dishonor to be deceived by an enemy, but there is no shame in being deceived by a friend, for between friends *pistis* is an obligation.

An earlier passage in the *Anabasis*—one of those rare editorializing passages which can be taken to represent Xenophon's own opinion—supports the contention that this speech reflects Xenophon's personal sentiments. In the obituary of Clearchus' fellow general and rival, Menon, Xenophon emphasizes the latter's consummate falseness:

> Again, for the accomplishment of the objects upon which his heart was set, he imagined that the shortest route was by way of perjury and falsehood and deception, while he counted straightforwardness and truth the same thing as folly. Affection he clearly felt for nobody, and if he said that he was a friend to anyone, it would become plain that this man was the one he was plotting against.... He thought he was the only one who knew that it was easiest to get hold of the property of friends—just because it was unguarded.... So Menon prided himself upon ability to deceive, the fabrication of lies and the mocking of friends. (2.6.22–26)

There can be no doubt that Xenophon despises Menon. His disdain is made clear by the way in which he contrasts, in back-to-back obituaries, the simple honesty and trustworthiness of his good friend Proxenus with the scurrility of Menon (2.6.16–30). Menon represents the type who is first to cheat or betray a friend lest he himself be taken advantage of. Consequently, Xenophon's claim, in the speech in Thrace, that it is less shameful to be deceived by friends than to deceive them—that is, that one has an obligation to keep faith with friends—ought to be regarded as an expression of his true sentiments.[60]

The climactic speech of the *Anabasis* soon follows. After his address to the Greek assembly, Xenophon is dispatched to demand from Seuthes the wages that he owes the Greek troops. Xenophon reports his speech to Seuthes at great length, as if to emphasize its importance in terms of both dramatic function and content. And *pistis* is the central and recurrent theme of the speech (7.7.20–47).

In Seuthes' presence Xenophon argues for the tremendous practical value of a reputation for *pistis*. Seuthes would be a fool to sacrifice his good reputation in exchange for a relatively small sum of money, when that reputation has already gained him so much and stands to bring him still more in the future. Because of Seuthes' refusal to pay, Xenophon has now lost his own influence and reputation for trust with the Greek army. Seuthes' venal agent Heraclides is a fool to value money more than a reputation for honesty. But Xenophon has been a true friend to the Thracian prince and still has confidence (*pisteuō*) that Seuthes will not fail the Greek troops who have served him so well.

Seuthes is persuaded by Xenophon's impassioned appeal. He claims that he never intended to defraud the Greeks and promises to pay them. He urges Xenophon to stay in his service and promises to bestow great benefactions upon him. Xenophon declines this offer but wins the right to be the agent through whom Seuthes will pay the Greeks, so that he may restore his own standing with the army (7.7.48–56). Clearly Xenophon is anxious to repair his own reputation for *pistis*, having just demonstrated his awareness of the value of such a reputation.

In this climactic speech Xenophon shows Seuthes why trust is important in human affairs.[61] Given that suspicion, deceit, and their consequences have plagued the Greeks throughout the narrative, both the location of the speech and its contents have significance. If Xenophon has a didactic purpose in the *Anabasis*, then this is precisely where one would expect to look for the lesson of the work. Xenophon has fashioned this speech to educate his readers on the value of *pistis* in human relations. The entire narrative to this point has shown clearly the consequences of deceit and the rewards of trust and good faith.[62] In this sense *pistis* has a pragmatic function. On the ethical plane, Xenophon suggests that *pistis* is related to virtue, nobility, and justice (7.7.4). It is characteristic of Xenophon to justify the right mode of conduct in terms of both practical and ethical value.

Civilizations habitually evolve customs and principles which regulate the relations between individuals and allow for the smooth and orderly functioning of human society. False conduct, that is, conduct which violates accepted norms, tends to erode those norms and poses a serious threat to the welfare of society. In the *Anabasis* Xenophon vividly depicts the ways in which false conduct threatened both the physical welfare and the social and political order of the Ten Thousand. It is most significant that the Thracian Seuthes, by conceding the truth of Xenophon's arguments and agreeing to pay the Greek soldiers, proves worthy of Xenophon's faith in him. After all the treachery, lies, deceit, and suspicion recounted in the *Anabasis*, and against a backdrop of repeated Greek deception of fellow Greeks, it is a "barbarian" who finally sees and accepts the importance of *pistis* in human affairs. This outcome should be seen as a rejection of the notion—exploited by the Greek leaders after the execution of the generals and seized upon out of context by modern historians—that the barbarians as a whole were inherently untrustworthy. Xenophon does not believe this, and the climactic moment of the *Anabasis* is the proof of it.

Contrary to the impression given by some previous discussions of the work, the *Anabasis* is not about Persian deceit, but about deceit in human affairs. All parties to the events narrated by Xenophon—Greeks and Persians, friends as well as enemies—practice deceit, with dire consequences for the Greek army. Xenophon's profound awareness of the role of trust and deceit in human affairs was engendered on the Anabasis and fortified by his meditation on the events of his time.[63] Strategically located in the finale of the *Ana-*

basis, his speech to Seuthes affirming the value of trust lays to rest the topic of deceit and its terrible consequences.

Xenophon's strong emphasis on *pistis* in the *Anabasis* also has a direct bearing on the question of his attitude toward Persia. Given that it was a much more powerful moral imperative in the feudal Persian culture than in Greek society,[64] it raises the distinct possibility that Xenophon was influenced by Persian values.

3

Agesilaus: The Making of a Panhellenic Hero

Xenophon's treatise on the life of Agesilaus, the king who dominated Spartan politics in the first half of the fourth century and who was also a close acquaintance of Xenophon, deserves to be included among the works in which Persia plays a central role. Of course, the campaigns of Agesilaus against the Persians were among the most celebrated events in his career, and one would expect them to figure prominently in any work which purported to commemorate his life. Even so, Persia plays so conspicuous a role in virtually every section of the *Agesilaus*, going far beyond the demands of simple historical accuracy, that some further explanation seems required.

The *Agesilaus* also merits attention for another reason. Commentators frequently point to it as proof of Xenophon's panhellenism and its inevitable concomitants, hostility to and contempt for Persia. Thus it will be necessary to investigate implicit and explicit attitudes toward Persia in the work. As in previous chapters, the procedure will be to analyze the relevant passages for their meaning and function, both in their immediate context and in the framework of the entire treatise, in order to avoid the serious distortions which often arise when a passage is interpreted out of context.

Previous studies of the structure of the work have produced the conventional division into three autonomous sections: a chronological Survey of Deeds (*erga*) of the Spartan king (1.6–2.31); a Catalogue of Virtues (*aretai*), illustrated by incidents selected from his long career (3.1–9.7); and a Summary of Virtues (11.1–16).[1] For the purposes of this investigation, the concluding section is of no account; on the other hand, in the Catalogue of Virtues a distinction must be made between anecdotes illustrating various virtues (3.1–8.8) and a point-by-point comparison of Agesilaus with the Great King of Persia (9.1–5).

The following discussion, then, examines the *Agesilaus* in terms of a series of ultimately interrelated problems. First, it analyzes the attitudes toward Persia expressed throughout the work. Next, it scrutinizes the detailed comparison of Agesilaus and the Persian king. Third, it demonstrates that Xenophon has given disproportionate coverage to Persian affairs. Finally, it offers an explanation of why he has done so, for in this lies the key to understanding Xenophon's primary purpose in writing this work.

In the year 395 Sparta, the dominant military and political power in Greece as a result of her victory over Athens in the Peloponnesian War, was locked in armed conflict with the Persian satraps of western Asia Minor. At issue was control of the Greek cities of that region. Agesilaus, who had only recently come to the throne, crossed over into Asia and entered into a compact with the Persian satrap Tissaphernes. (The king had rewarded Tissaphernes for his good service during the rebellion of Cyrus by appointing him the chief Persian officer in the western provinces.) Under the terms of the arrangement, both sides were to maintain a three-month truce while Tissaphernes sent messengers to the Persian king. The wily satrap insisted that royal approval was necessary before he could agree to the Spartans' terms for peace—a grant of autonomy to the Greek cities of Asia Minor. Instead, Tissaphernes violated his oath and spent the time gathering a larger army. Agesilaus, though aware of Tissaphernes' treachery, continued to abide by the terms of the armistice. "By showing up Tissaphernes as a perjurer, he made him distrusted everywhere; and, contrariwise, by proving himself to be a man of his word and true to his agreements, he encouraged all, Greeks and barbarians alike, to enter into an agreement with him whenever he wished."[2]

It is characteristic of Xenophon's aims and methods in the *Agesilaus* that he uses Agesilaus' deeds to illustrate his character. Here Xenophon presents a demonstration of Agesilaus' *pistis* or trustworthiness and the accrual of practical benefits from the exercise of this virtue. The necessity and value of *pistis* was one of the central themes of Xenophon's *Anabasis*, and it is no accident

Agesilaus: The Making of a Panhellenic Hero / 41

that Agesilaus' impeccable conduct is contrasted here with the villainy of Tissaphernes, for Tissaphernes had been the supreme example of faithlessness and oath-breaking in the *Anabasis*. But, while Tissaphernes' perjury is castigated, this reproach is directed against Tissaphernes personally. There is no suggestion that Persians or barbarians in general are by nature deceitful. In fact Xenophon specifically notes that, by his meritorious conduct, Agesilaus won the adherence of barbarians as well as of Greeks. The clear implication is that barbarians, too, valued trustworthiness.

The account of Agesilaus' subsequent military activities in Asia Minor is for the most part factual, with little explicit expression of sentiment concerning the barbarian foe. At one point Xenophon reports that Agesilaus urged his troops not to mistreat prisoners, presumably barbarians, because they were human beings (1.21).[3] On a later occasion Agesilaus had barbarian prisoners stripped naked and displayed for sale so that his soldiers could regard their pale complexion and soft bodies and thereby acquire contempt for the enemy (1.28). Although this act may be taken to mean that Agesilaus was scornful of the enemy, it is more important to focus, as Xenophon does, on the fact that he did this in order to inspire a feeling of superiority and confidence in his troops. Self-confidence was a vital ingredient of victory in ancient warfare, and the exposure of the prisoners is primarily a tactical ploy on the part of Agesilaus. In any case, one cannot maintain that the Hellenic forces lacked respect for their barbarian adversaries. Agesilaus clearly demonstrated his respect for the Persian cavalry when he decided that he must raise mounted forces of his own "if he was to avoid continually running away from the enemy" (1.23), and his allies were terrified of the forces led by Tissaphernes (1.13).

Xenophon devotes considerable space to Agesilaus' campaign in the vicinity of Sardis, which led to the defeat of the Persian forces and, ultimately, to the removal from office and execution of Tissaphernes by the Persian king (1.28–35). It is clear from his account that Agesilaus caught the enemy at a moment when they were vulnerable, with the cavalry unsupported by the infantry, and that the Persian horsemen put up a determined resistance. Agesilaus then invested the city of Sardis, but the enemy did not respond to his challenge to come out and fight. Xenophon goes on to say: ". . . he beheld the Greeks, compelled erstwhile to cringe, now honored by their oppressors; caused those who arrogantly claimed for themselves the honours paid to the gods to shrink even from looking the Greeks in the face; rendered the country of his friends inviolate, and stripped the enemy's country so thoroughly that in two years he consecrated to the god at Delphi more than two hundred talents as tithe" (1.34). Here Xenophon echoes the resentment felt by the Greeks of Asia Minor for the strange customs and offensive demands of their Persian overlords.[4]

However, there is no warrant in any of this for asserting that Xenophon or the Greeks in general looked with contempt upon the barbarians. The Greeks of Asia, who now held their heads high, had not themselves turned the tables on their former masters but rather owed their good fortune to Agesilaus. The Persians had fought bravely in the battle and were overcome by Agesilaus' astute generalship. Xenophon's account of the investment of Sardis is perhaps a little disingenuous. True, the Persians did not respond to the challenge to come out from the safety of the walls to fight, but it was rare in the ancient world for a recently defeated army to do so.[5] In any case, Agesilaus did not take Sardis,[6] and the Persians' refusal to emerge could be justified on these grounds alone. In sum, there is no explicit imputation of cowardice to the Persians. It is Agesilaus' strategic brilliance that has guaranteed a Greek victory here, not the inferiority of the Persian opponent. After all, what is the value of a victory over an unworthy opponent? In a patent encomium such as this,[7] any party which is compared with the hero of the work will necessarily come off second best, but owing to the hero's conspicuous superiority rather than the innate inferiority of the opponent.

In the Catalogue of Virtues, Xenophon analyzes the character of Agesilaus in terms of various abstract qualities, including the canonical four virtues, wisdom, justice, courage, and self-control, as well as piety, foresight, and urbanity. Under the heading of patriotism (*philopolis*), he refers to the fact that Agesilaus was a "Greek-lover" (*philhellēn*) and a "Persian-hater" (*misopersēs*; 7.4–7).[8] As a "Greek-lover" he was unwilling to sack conquered Greek cities and even looked upon victory over fellow Greeks as a disaster. He lamented the death of a large number of Greek enemies in battle at Corinth because the deceased could have assisted in the conquest of the barbarians. Xenophon then gives the reasons why Agesilaus was a "Persian-hater":[9] "because in old days he [the Persian king] set out to enslave Greece, and now allies himself with the side which offers him the prospect of working the greatest mischief, makes gifts to those who, as he believes, will injure the Greeks most in return, negotiates the peace that he thinks most certain to produce war among us...." This rationale echoes the motives attributed to Agesilaus for undertaking the invasion of Asia Minor in the mid-390s—"to pay back the Persian in his own coin for the former invasion of Greece" (1.8)—and for embarking upon his last campaign in Egypt in 362—to "chastise the Persian for his former hostility, and for demanding now, when he professed to be an ally of Sparta, that her. claim to Messene should be given up" (2.29).

These motives are a mixture of traditional vengefulness for the depredations of the Persian Wars and contemporary Spartan hostility to a Persia which had transferred her support from Sparta to Thebes in the 360s. It is unnecessary here to belabor the point that the Spartans had not considered it "mischief" when the Persians had backed them. What is of immediate importance is that the reasons for Agesilaus' hatred of Persia are practical ones. "It is honourable to hate the Persian," not because he is a barbarian, or innately inferior, or intrinsically and inevitably at odds with the Greeks, but because in the past Persia has pursued a hostile policy toward Greece and continues to do so. It is not a case of ethnic prejudice but a reaction to a real or perceived threat. For that matter, hostility often implies respect for the enemy.[10]

Other anecdotes in the Catalogue of Virtues involve individual Persians, and there is never a hint of disrespect for these Eastern nobles. Spithridates and Pharnabazus clearly are proud and dignified men (3.3, 3.5), and it is assumed that there is nothing shameful in Agesilaus' love for the young Megabates (5.4–5). Only in the comparison of Agesilaus with the Persian king is a barbarian cast in an unflattering light.[11] Even here Xenophon derides the Persian king as an individual, without suggesting that these reproaches should be extended to all Persians.

This crucial passage deserves to be considered in greater detail. It involves a series of explicit contrasts between Agesilaus and the Great King of Persia, and, of course, Agesilaus proves to be superior on all counts. The Persian king is said to have been addicted to luxury, driven by an insatiable thirst for wealth, remote, unjust, and deceitful. Agesilaus, on the other hand, led a moderate, self-controlled existence, was just and open in his dealings, and ultimately was the happier man because he could accommodate himself to the natural order of the world.

This comparison of Agesilaus with the Persian king forms the climax of the Catalogue of Virtues. Xenophon's choice of a foil is deliberate. In the first place, it is somehow fitting to compare one king with another. Insofar as many Greeks regarded the Persian king as the greatest and happiest man in the world[12] the choice of foil serves to exalt Agesilaus. Moreover, the Spartan and Persian kings had at several times been enemies (and were so at the end of Agesilaus' life); thus their rivalry could conveniently be extended into the moral sphere, and they are seen to represent opposing principles in a struggle which begins to take on cosmic ramifications. It is important to recognize the schematic nature of this contrast. Xenophon's primary aim is to praise Agesilaus; any denigration of the Persian king is secondary. In this sense, his technique is analogous to the one employed for the Sardis campaign, where glorification of Agesilaus rather than disparagement of his Persian opponents is the goal.

Some readers may still feel that the attacks on the character of the Persian king are more than incidental and go beyond what is strictly necessary to accomplish the exaltation of Agesilaus. But Xenophon's whole treatment in this section is a kind of philosophical *topos*. The terms of the comparison of Agesilaus and the Persian king are revealing. The Persian king is guilty of hubris and excessive luxury; Agesilaus is praised for his moderation and self-control, for his pursuit of the simple life, and for living according to nature. Xenophon's eloquence about Agesilaus' ability to sleep anywhere and to endure extremes of heat and cold is reminiscent of Plato's portrait of Socrates (for example, in *Symposium* 219E–220D). This sort of contrast must have been commonplace in Socratic circles, and Xenophon has simply adapted it to his encomium of Agesilaus.[13]

Some of Xenophon's criticisms of the Persian king are manifestly tendentious, as when he seizes upon the remoteness of the king and the slowness of the Persian administration as signs of shameful conduct and faithless dealing. Even without detailed knowledge of the Persian court, common sense should have told him that the differences in scale between Sparta and the Persian Empire made the situation of the two monarchs vastly different. Xenophon is unfairly drawing moral conclusions from bureaucratic practice. In this case he is probably aiming at rhetorical effect, for several passages in the *Cyropaedia* reveal that he knew better. There he states that, after conquering Babylon, Cyrus coerced his friends into allowing him to conduct himself in a more remote and kingly fashion (7.5.37,

Agesilaus: The Making of a Panhellenic Hero / 45

7.5.55–56). The whole scene implies Xenophon's understanding of why the ruler of an empire must be remote. Later in the *Cyropaedia* he discourses on the value of pomp for a ruler (8.3.1). This discrepant treatment makes the criticism of the Persian king in the *Agesilaus* appear tendentious.

Furthermore, Xenophon may have derived both the notion and the form of a comparison of a Greek with a Persian king from the *Evagoras* of Isocrates, written in about 370. Although the tone and the terms of comparison in the two works are quite different, there is widespread agreement among the experts that Xenophon modeled his encomium of Agesilaus on, and borrowed many stylistic and organizational features from, Isocrates, who virtually originated the concept of a prose encomium of a contemporary figure with the *Evagoras*.[14] In chapters 37 and 38 Isocrates undertakes a point-by-point comparison of the deeds and character of his hero, the king of Cypriot Salamis, with those of Cyrus the Great, founder of the Persian Empire. Isocrates regarded Cyrus as an admirable historical figure but insisted that he came off second best when compared with Evagoras.

All these considerations—the suitability of the Persian king as a foil; the stereotypical, philosophically based terms of comparison; the tendentious nature of some of the criticisms; and the precedent offered by Isocrates—tend to point in the same direction. This passage of the *Agesilaus*, in which Xenophon compares the Spartan and Persian kings to the discredit of the latter, is motivated by the demands of the encomiastic genre. The argument seems to indicate that denigration of the Persian king is essentially secondary, a means to an end, and one need not assume that Xenophon is motivated to a very large degree by scorn or hatred for the Persian king.[15]

Xenophon devotes a disproportionate amount of space to Agesilaus' activities against Persia in the historical Survey of Deeds, which comprises the first two chapters. This tendency continues in the Catalogue of Virtues, where a majority of the incidents used to illustrate various aspects of Agesilaus' character involve Persians, and reaches a climax in the elaborate comparison of Agesilaus with the Persian king. The disproportion is most easily grasped in mathematical terms. In the Survey of Deeds, over 57 percent of the narrative concerns his anti-Persian activities, that is, the Asia Minor campaign of 395–394, the last campaign in Egypt around 362, and brief mention of activities in support of rebel satraps in Asia Minor at some time in the 360s. Another 27 percent deals with the march home from Asia Minor in 394, culminating in the battle of Coronea. Thus, 84 percent of the Survey concerns a period of little more than three years, with only 16 percent devoted to the remaining thirty-two years of Agesilaus' career (394–362), all of which were spent in Greece. There is an even more striking disproportion in the Catalogue of Virtues. Many of the virtues attributed to Agesilaus are illustrated by one or more anecdotes drawn from the Spartan king's career. Of the twelve anecdotes related in this section, ten involve the Persians, and this figure excludes the comparison of Agesilaus with the Persian king. Clearly Xenophon gives extraordinary coverage to Agesilaus' activities against the Persians. An inevitable corollary is that he neglects more than three decades of activity in Greece.

A comparison of the Survey of Deeds with Xenophon's history of the same period in the *Hellenica* makes the significance of this discovery even more apparent.[16] For the period up to and including the battle of Coronea, Xenophon omits from the *Agesilaus* matters which he must have felt did not reflect well on his hero and which would therefore be inappropriate in an encomium. Accordingly, he makes no mention of Agesilaus' discreditable schemes to acquire his nephew's throne (*Hellenica* 3.3.1–4); instead, he alleges that the Spartans chose Agesilaus because of his superior qualifications (*Agesilaus* 1.5). Nothing is said of Lysander's role in getting Agesilaus dispatched to Asia Minor (*Hell.* 3.4.2); instead, Agesilaus is given full credit for the plan in a passage replete with panhellenic rhetoric (*Ages.* 1.6–8). No mention is made of Boeotian opposition to Agesilaus at Aulis (*Hell.* 3.4.4), nor of how Agesilaus ultimately turned against his benefactor Lysander (*Hell.* 3.4.7–10). Finally, there is no mention of the setbacks suffered by Agesilaus in his first Phrygian campaign (*Hell.* 3.4.13–15). In place of these last two incidents Xenophon substitutes digressions on Agesilaus' fidelity to compacts (*Ages.* 1.12) and his merits as a military commander (*Ages.* 1.17–22).

Xenophon does not hesitate to discuss the Corinthian War, in which, as he tells it, virtually all Greece was up in arms against Sparta, and the Coronea campaign is recounted at length. Naturally, nothing is said about the reasons for hostility to Sparta. However, he is obviously extremely selective in his treatment of the crucial

Agesilaus: The Making of a Panhellenic Hero / 47

decades after the battle of Coronea, a period which receives little coverage in any case. For the period from the King's Peace (387/6) to the battle of Leuctra (371) Xenophon mentions only four events in which Agesilaus was involved: (1) when the enemy sought peace in 387/6, Agesilaus insisted on the restoration of pro-Spartan exiles to Corinth and Thebes (*Ages.* 2.21); (2) Agesilaus restored pro-Spartan exiles to Phlius (*Ages.* 2.21); (3) Agesilaus went to the rescue of Lacedaemonians besieged in Thebes (*Ages.* 2.22); and (4) Agesilaus undertook another expedition to Thebes in the following year (*Ages.* 2.22).

Examination of the corresponding sections of the *Hellenica* shows that Xenophon has omitted many items of considerable historical significance. He has failed to mention the participation of Persia in the peace of 387/6, often known as the King's Peace because it was in essence an edict of the Persian king. His silence conceals the fact that the Spartans sought the peace and that they collaborated with the Persians to enforce the peace upon the cities of Greece for their own benefit. One must also turn to the *Hellenica* (5.1.25–34) to discover that Agesilaus presided over the signing of the peace treaty and that he used the threat of Spartan and Persian force to coerce the Thebans into leaving the Boeotian cities independent and the Argives into evacuating Corinth.

Although Xenophon does briefly mention two Theban campaigns of Agesilaus, he does not explain why the Thebans were hostile to Sparta. He says nothing about the treacherous seizure of the Theban acropolis by a Spartan officer named Phoebidas or about Agesilaus' indirect defense of Phoebidas when the latter was brought to trial at Sparta (Agesilaus maintained that the essential concern was not whether what Phoebidas had done was right or wrong, only whether it had helped or harmed Spartan interests; *Hell.* 5.2.25–35). Xenophon himself, as he reveals elsewhere, strongly disapproved of this action and attributed Sparta's eventual fall from power to the injustice of the deed (*Hell.* 5.4.1). Eventually the Thebans managed to eject the Lacedaemonian garrison and depose the pro-Spartan oligarchy (*Hell.* 5.4.2–12). It is in this context that Agesilaus undertook the two Theban campaigns mentioned in the *Agesilaus*; here, however, Xenophon is misleading insofar as he implies that Agesilaus' mission was to rescue fellow Lacedaemonians who were under attack in Thebes. The Lacedaemonian garrison had actually been driven out before Agesilaus set out on the march, and his campaign was merely punitive.

Finally, Xenophon makes no mention in the *Agesilaus* of the Spartan king's involvement in the acquittal of Sphodrias, a Spartan commander who, without provocation, had attempted a surprise attack on Athens (*Hell.* 5.24–33). By ignoring Agesilaus' involvement in the affairs of Phoebidas and Sphodrias, Xenophon suppresses his responsibility for antagonizing both Athens and Thebes and thereby setting in motion the forces which ultimately led to the battle of Leuctra and the humiliation of Sparta.

Xenophon's account of the period between the campaigns of Leuctra (371) and Mantinea (362) reveals the operation of a similar tendency. For this momentous decade, in which Sparta lost both her reputation for military invincibility and her hegemony in Greece, he can bring himself to mention only a few events: (1) an expedition led by Agesilaus against the pro-Theban alliance in Arcadia at a time when supporters of Sparta were being murdered in the Arcadian cities (*Ages.* 2.23); (2) the defense of Sparta against enemy attacks and a Helot revolt (*Ages.* 2.24); and (3) the dispatch of Agesilaus as an envoy to the Persian rebel Ariobarzanes (*Ages.* 2.26–27). A comparison of this account with the parallel passages of the *Hellenica* reveals that Xenophon has omitted all mention of the peace conference of 371, at which Agesilaus, by refusing to allow the Thebans to ratify the treaty, purposefully laid the groundwork for an attack on Thebes (*Hell.* 6.3.19). This led directly to the disastrous Spartan defeat at Leuctra. He has also neglected to report the dispatch of Agesilaus to Mantinea to prevent the restoration of that city, which had earlier been broken up into villages by Sparta. The mission failed and Agesilaus departed in anger (*Hell.* 6.5.4–5). Xenophon does discuss Agesilaus' subsequent invasion of Arcadia in 370, but his account is misleading: he implies that the powerful Theban army was present at the time, when in reality it was not, and he drops no hint that the Spartans were forced to withdraw (*Hell.* 6.5.10–21). Finally, there is no word of the fact that, in the military maneuvers before the battle of Mantinea in 362, Agesilaus was badly outfoxed by the Theban Epaminondas and was barely able to save Sparta from destruction (*Hell.* 7.5.9–10).

In sum, not only does Xenophon devote minimal space in the *Agesilaus* to the Spartan king's activities in Greece in the period 394–362, but he also omits all mention of most of the important

Agesilaus: The Making of a Panhellenic Hero / 49

events in which Agesilaus was involved and misrepresents the few which he does mention.

The foregoing demonstration of Xenophon's concentration on Persian affairs throughout the *Agesilaus* has a significant bearing on the question of his purpose in writing the *Agesilaus*. The traditional view is that the work is an encomium pure and simple, intended to glorify the deeds and character of the late Spartan king.[17] There is general agreement that Xenophon has neglected the historian's duty to assess the historical impact and contribution of his subject[18] and that he is more interested in depicting an ideal type of man than in penetrating to the essence of Agesilaus' individual personality.[19] Beyond these areas of fundamental agreement, certain scholars claim to have detected additional levels of meaning in the work. Luccioni thinks the encomium of Agesilaus evolves into a celebration of Sparta as well as an idealization of monarchy.[20] Dihle sees the work as the portrait of an ideal military commander.[21] And everyone has had something to say about the panhellenic sentiment which pervades the work.

Delebecque develops a characteristically elaborate scheme to explain the date of composition and Xenophon's purpose in writing the *Agesilaus*.[22] His starting point is the significant observation that the panhellenic sentiment which is so palpable in the *Agesilaus* is absent from the *Hellenica*, even though Xenophon adapted much of the historical content of the *Agesilaus* directly from the *Hellenica*. He feels that in later years Xenophon's memory transformed the *Anabasis* and the campaigns of Agesilaus and Dercyllidas in Asia Minor (in all of which he had participated) into crusades against the infidel Persians. Caught up in dreams of Agesilaus' liberation of the Greek cities of Asia Minor, and perhaps even in dreams of the conquest of Persia, Xenophon gave these events an epic, legendary flavor in the *Agesilaus*. Moreover, the work is suffused with Xenophon's anger and fear of Persia. As Delebecque sees it, all these features are most easily accounted for by the assumption that Xenophon wrote the *Agesilaus* circa 355 and that his purpose was to warn the Greek states to stand up to the threats of the new Persian king, Artaxerxes III Ochus. Xenophon is anxious for the Greek reading public to know that Greece now needs a man like Agesilaus to lead the crusade against Persia. Thus, for Delebecque, the element of panhellenism which Xenophon has superimposed on the

50 / *Agesilaus*: The Making of a Panhellenic Hero

historical foundation borrowed from the *Hellenica* is called forth by Xenophon's panhellenic fantasies late in life and by fear of a resurgent Persia.

This thesis is open to various objections. In the first place, the complicated argument for the date of composition is unconvincing. It is much more likely that Xenophon wrote an encomium soon after Agesilaus' death (circa 360), and the Persian king with whom Agesilaus is compared is certainly Agesilaus' sometime foe, Artaxerxes II, rather than Ochus, who came to the throne only in 358. There is also ample reason to doubt the presence of that intense anger and fear of Persia which is central to Delebecque's thesis. The analysis earlier in this chapter of attitudes in the *Agesilaus* toward Persians indicates that Xenophon despised the lies and treachery of Tissaphernes but otherwise respected the Persian nobility. The heavy-handed criticism of the Persian king is put in excessively rhetorical terms, and he is seen to be more pathetic than formidable. However, although most of the elements of Delebecque's theory do not carry conviction, he has made an important point in stressing the presence of a panhellenic sentiment which is absent in Xenophon's other writings.

More recent work has tended to draw less extreme conclusions than Delebecque. Breitenbach maintains that the panhellenism of the *Agesilaus* is a romantic ideal rather than a political program, and he recognizes that it is employed as a rhetorical device to popularize Agesilaus.[23] Higgins develops an idea first put forth by Luccioni.[24] As he sees it, Xenophon is concerned with the nature of true royalty. In answer to the question "What is a king?" he demonstrates, in the person of Agesilaus, that true royalty is based on moderation and a sense of natural limitations, not on license and self-indulgence. The Persian king, for all his power and wealth, is an impostor, an enslaver of men, and himself enslaved by luxury. Agesilaus, thanks to his self-control, is a free man and is committed to bringing freedom to other Greeks. The *Agesilaus* is therefore neither political propaganda nor an exhortation to launch a crusade against Persia. Xenophon has a loftier philosophical intent—to demonstrate that those who seek renown and true nobility should emulate the self-mastery of Agesilaus.

It is unlikely that any of these exponents of one or another "program" of the *Agesilaus* would deny that Xenophon intended the work primarily as an encomium of Agesilaus. There is room for

Agesilaus: The Making of a Panhellenic Hero / 51

more than one aim in a work of this kind. However, earlier commentators have considered the panhellenic element from the wrong perspective and have paid insufficient attention to the apologetic nature of Xenophon's narrative.[25] The disproportionate coverage of Agesilaus' anti-Persian activities at the expense of his activities in Greece, which gives the *Agesilaus* its peculiar tone and content, is best explained by the operation of a pervasive slant or bias. Xenophon resolved to defend his old friend against the spate of accusations which either first arose or were revived upon the occasion of Agesilaus' death, when the Greek world paused to evaluate his life and achievements. The core of these accusations will have been that Agesilaus was *philobarbaros*—a "barbarian-lover"—that he had repeatedly collaborated with the Persians and had spent the better part of a lifetime engaged in aggressive activity against the cities of Greece. Xenophon relies on two closely connected tactics to defend Agesilaus against these indictments. He inverts the charge of collusion with the barbarian by insisting that Agesilaus was a lifelong foe of Persia and a tireless advocate of a crusade against the national foe. And by concentrating on Agesilaus' activities against the Persians, he hopes to divert attention from three decades of collaboration with Persia and infringements on the autonomy of the Greeks.

There can be no doubt that Xenophon had ample information on Agesilaus' activities in the neglected period 394–362 yet chose to suppress it. And it is not enough to attribute his choice of material to the demands of the encomiastic genre. Obviously an encomiast is going to pass over matters which reflect badly on the reputation of his subject. But the material which Xenophon does include has too particular a slant. It is meant to elevate Agesilaus to the role of a panhellenic hero engaged in a lifelong struggle against the barbarian who threatens the welfare and freedom of Greece. However, the panhellenism which is so prominent in the *Agesilaus* does not stem from a concern to give credit where credit is due, nor from any strong panhellenic and antibarbarian sentiments on Xenophon's part, but rather from the pressing need to defend Agesilaus against charges of collaboration with the Persians and hostility to fellow Greeks. The panhellenism of the *Agesilaus* is motivated primarily by the unpanhellenic character of much of Agesilaus' activity.

Evidence of the tenor of the accusations leveled against Agesilaus by contemporaries is available from two other ancient sources on the career of Agesilaus, Plutarch's *Life of Agesilaus* and the universal history of Diodorus Siculus. Diodorus (15.19.4) represents the other Spartan king, Agesipolis, as blaming Agesilaus for the fact that "Sparta was in ill repute for having surrendered the Greeks of Asia to the Persians and for organizing the cities of Greece in her own interest, although she had sworn in the common agreements that she would preserve their autonomy."[26] Diodorus also contrasts Agesipolis, "who was peaceful and a just man" and a champion of autonomy for the Greek city-states, with Agesilaus, who "was fond of war and yearned for dominance over the Greeks." If, as is commonly assumed, Diodorus derived his information and bias from Ephorus, who was a contemporary of Agesilaus, then this passage is indicative of the accusations made against Agesilaus in his own lifetime.

In his *Life of Agesilaus* Plutarch cites, besides Xenophon, seven other literary sources and two contemporary documents.[27] Even though he seems to have derived much of his information about the career of Agesilaus from Xenophon, his very different interpretation of the motives and character of the Spartan king must come from his other sources.[28] Plutarch's biography of Agesilaus is a rich source of accusations against the Spartan king. They can be summarized as follows:

1. Throughout his career Agesilaus was motivated by personal hatred for Thebes. As a result, in pursuing this private vendetta he often acted against Sparta's best interests and ultimately caused her downfall.

2. Agesilaus actively supported Phoebidas' seizure of the Theban Cadmeia and urged Sparta to retain control of the citadel.

3. Agesilaus was accused of serving the Persian king by enforcing the King's Peace upon Greece.

4. Agesilaus supported the tyrants at Thebes.

5. Agesilaus and Sparta always considered self-interest before justice.

6. The Peloponnesian allies complained that Agesilaus was exploiting them, and all of Greece for that matter, in order to satisfy a personal resentment against the Thebans in 371. Thus he purposely kept Thebes out of the peace of that year and pushed for war.

7. Agesilaus was blamed at Sparta for the Leuctra debacle.

Agesilaus: The Making of a Panhellenic Hero / 53

8. Agesilaus was blamed at Sparta for the loss of Messenia in his reign.

9. Agesilaus' impractical refusal to accept the loss of Messenia in 362 led to the Mantinea campaign of that year.

10. The same obstinacy kept Sparta, alone of all the Greek states, out of the common peace that was concluded after the battle. Moreover, Agesilaus tried in every way to sabotage and undermine this peace. He was headstrong, obstinate, insatiable of war.

11. In a sense, Agesilaus was responsible for the loss of the whole Spartan empire.

12. Agesilaus' adventures in Egypt at the end of his life were undignified and marked by treachery to his Egyptian allies. He served the barbarians so that he could get money with which to make war on Greeks.

It is probable that most, if not all, of the accusations concerning Agesilaus' activities in Greece in the period 387–362 (excluding 12) were leveled against him in his lifetime. It is also safe to assume that all or most of the information available to Plutarch and Diodorus was known to Xenophon. In light of these circumstances, it is not surprising that Xenophon chooses to treat this period in so cursory a manner in the *Agesilaus*.[29]

A careful reading of the *Agesilaus* confirms its apologetic nature. Certain passages, when reconsidered in light of the accusations now known to have been made against Agesilaus by contemporaries, take on a new significance, and in some of these Xenophon's tone is perceptibly defensive.[30] For example, it is presumably because he is anxious to counter accusations that Agesilaus was *philobarbaros*, a "barbarian-lover," that Xenophon excludes from the *Agesilaus* several incidents which linked Agesilaus with the Persians, such as the story, found in the *Hellenica*, of the guest-friendship of Agesilaus and the son of Pharnabazus.[31] Likewise, no mention is made of the Persian king in connection with the peace of 387/6. Xenophon may also be concealing the fact that Agesilaus was a mercenary commander in the service of the Persian Ariobarzanes.[32]

In the preceding examples, Xenophon accomplishes his apologetic purpose primarily by careful selection of material. Elsewhere he meets accusations head on. Chapter 4, which deals with Agesilaus' justice in money matters, has a peculiarly defensive tone, as if

54 / *Agesilaus*: The Making of a Panhellenic Hero

Xenophon is defending Agesilaus against accusations of theft, bad faith, embezzlement, and taking bribes. At the end of the chapter he refers to the episode in which the Persian royal agent Tithraustes, after executing Tissaphernes, offered Agesilaus gifts if he would agree to leave his country. Agesilaus is said to have delivered a stinging rebuke: "Among us, Tithraustes, a ruler's honor requires him to enrich his army rather than himself, and to take spoils rather than gifts from the enemy" (4.6). At this point the account breaks off, and the reader is led to believe that Agesilaus refused to be influenced by Persian gold. But the corresponding passage in the *Hellenica* (3.4.26) shows that Tithraustes gave Agesilaus thirty talents "for provisions," whereupon Agesilaus evacuated the Sardis satrapy and moved off into Pharnabazus' territory. This account does not necessarily prove that Agesilaus was bribed in this case. He may have had strategic reasons for departing. But it does suggest that Agesilaus was accused in Greece of having been bought off by the Persians and that Xenophon is anxious to dispel this notion by expounding on his justice in money matters and his utter lack of avarice.

Similarly, Xenophon goes to great lengths to convince his audience that Agesilaus exercised perfect self-control over his sexual impulses. He never allowed himself to succumb to the blandishments of the Persian youth Megabates and always kept himself untainted by scandal.

> . . . but we all know this, that the greater a man's fame, the fiercer is the light that beats on all his actions; we know too that no one ever reported that he had seen Agesilaus do any such thing, and that no scandal based on conjecture would have gained credence; for it was not his habit, when abroad, to lodge apart in a private house, but he was always either in a temple, where conduct of this sort is, of course, impossible, or else in a public place where all men's eyes became witnesses of his rectitude.   (5.6–7)

Xenophon's protestations here are excessive, and the reader may plausibly suspect that some rumor of scandal underlies his impassioned appeal.

A later story involves certain letters sent to Agesilaus by the Persian king. In Xenophon's account Agesilaus delivers a sharp reprimand to the royal envoy, instructing him to tell his master that "'there is no need for him to send me private letters, but, if he gives proof of friendship for Lacedaemon, and goodwill towards Greece, I on my part will be his friend with all my heart. But if he is found plotting against them, let him not hope to have a friend in me, however many letters I may receive'" (8.3). Of course the content of the royal letters and Agesilaus' reply would not have been public knowledge. But awareness of the existence of the letters may well have sparked rumors, and again Xenophon is anxious to prove that Agesilaus was not a Persian collaborator.[33]

There can be little doubt that Agesilaus was stigmatized as an agent of the Persian king and was accused of working for the interests of Persia and Sparta to the detriment of the rest of Greece. In the Catalogue of Virtues Xenophon confronts these accusations and rejects them. In the Survey of Deeds he concentrates almost exclusively on Agesilaus' hostile actions against Persia so as to dispel charges of collaboration. As for the period after 387, in which Agesilaus and Sparta enforced the King's Peace upon the rest of the Greek world, the less said the better.

When all is said and done, the primary function of the *Agesilaus*, contrary to the view of earlier scholars, is neither encomiastic nor propagandistic, but apologetic.[34] This interpretation makes sense of the peculiarly unbalanced coverage of Agesilaus' career. It takes account of other traditions about Agesilaus found in later writers such as Plutarch and Diodorus. It also sheds light on the panhellenism of the work, for there is little reason to believe, on the basis of Xenophon's other writings, that he was a particularly committed panhellenist, and such sentiments are lacking in the *Hellenica*,[35] from which most of the historical data of the *Agesilaus* derive. The panhellenism and hostility to Persia of the *Agesilaus* are a device, meant to divert attention from the less appealing aspects of Agesilaus' historical activities. Consequently, it would be a mistake to regard this work as representing Xenophon's own feelings about Persia, especially insofar as it conflicts with other evidence for Xenophon's attitudes. It may, however, reflect to some extent the sentiments of the average Greek, for one must assume that Xenophon expected his strategy to strike a responsive chord in his readers.

APPENDIX A.
The *Hellenica* and the Composition of the *Agesilaus*

It has long been recognized that extensive passages of the *Agesilaus* are virtually identical with passages in the *Hellenica*. On the other hand there are, as has been seen, a number of discrepancies between the two accounts. This has led to a vexed and, as yet, unresolved dispute over the order of composition and the relationship of the two works. The traditional view has been that Xenophon, anxious to compose an encomium for his friend Agesilaus shortly after the latter's death in 360, quarried the already written *Hellenica* for the material which he needed in the section devoted to Agesilaus' career and deeds.[36] However, on the basis of highly detailed and subtle examinations of the divergences between the two works—divergences in style, phraseology, organization, and content—scholars have proposed various modifications to the traditional view of the composition question as well as diverse explanations for the differences between the two works.[37]

This is not the place to undertake a comprehensive reconsideration of the composition question. But it is necessary to discuss briefly the recently advanced theory of Bringmann, whose ideas about the treatment of certain matters in the *Agesilaus* have points of contact with the position taken in this chapter.[38] Bringmann maintains that Xenophon took material from the *Hellenica* for the *Agesilaus* up to the battle of Coronea, but that the account of Coronea was written first for the *Agesilaus*. It follows that Xenophon had not yet composed the corresponding section of the *Hellenica* and that he later transferred to it his account of the battle of Coronea (with minor changes). When Xenophon composed that part of the *Agesilaus* which concerns itself with events after the battle of Coronea, he had not yet written the later books of the *Hellenica* and he had only summary and imprecise information on Agesilaus' activities after that battle. This theory would explain the marked differences between Xenophon's two accounts of Agesilaus' activities in the period after Coronea, and it is along these lines that one is to understand the omission of major events in Agesilaus' career from the pages of the *Agesilaus*. Later, after acquiring more and better information, Xenophon was in a position to compose the fuller account of the *Hellenica*.

It is clear that Bringmann is disturbed by the sketchy coverage of the period after Coronea in the *Agesilaus*, by the glaring discrepancies between the two works, and by the frequent omission from the *Agesilaus* of material which is to be found in the corresponding sections of the *Hellenica*. But his explanation of these phenomena fails to persuade. His thesis hinges on his claim of priority for the version of the battle of Coronea which is found in the *Agesilaus*, but this rests upon very fragile foundations. His major argument concerns the Greek phrase διηγήσομαι δὲ καὶ τὴν μάχην, which initiates the account of the battle in both versions. Bringmann insists that because of the sense of καί here, equivalent to "also," the phrase is better suited to its context in the *Agesilaus*, which must therefore be the original locus. But this is a subjective matter, and de Sanctis was equally convinced that these words were better suited to the *Hellenica*'s context.[39] Bringmann also maintains that certain passages concerning Agesilaus' virtues as a military commander in the *Agesilaus* version of the Coronea campaign were deliberately omitted from the *Hellenica*. But one could as easily argue that they were inserted in a later *Agesilaus*.

Bringmann points to omissions and divergences from the *Hellenica* in the *Agesilaus* narrative of events in the period after Coronea as evidence for the prior composition of the *Agesilaus*. But his explanation—that when Xenophon wrote the *Agesilaus* he did not yet have the fuller and more accurate information which he used in the *Hellenica*—rings hollow. In the first place, it is extremely unlikely that Xenophon, who lived in the Peloponnese for most of the period concerned and was probably often in the company of Spartans, if not of King Agesilaus himself, did not know about such public matters as Agesilaus' participation in and enforcement of the King's Peace or his support for Phoebidas and Sphodrias. In the second place, Bringmann is not consistent in his explanation of divergences and omissions. For the period before Coronea he makes a perfectly good case for the thesis that Xenophon, when composing the *Agesilaus*, omitted or distorted historical data derived from the manuscript of the *Hellenica* which did not contribute to the glorification of Agesilaus. There is no compelling reason not to apply the same explanation to the omissions and distortions of the *Agesilaus* narrative for the period after Coronea. The greater divergences between the two works for the later decades are most easily explained by the more deplorable character of Agesilaus' activities in this period.

Ultimately, for the purposes of the thesis advanced in this chapter, it matters little whether the *Hellenica* or *Agesilaus* was composed first, as long as it is conceded that Xenophon was well aware of Agesilaus' activities in the period 394–362 and that he purposely chose not to mention most of them in the *Agesilaus*.

APPENDIX B.

Xenophon and Isocrates

Most commentators on the *Agesilaus* agree that Xenophon was influenced by Isocrates' *Evagoras*, which was published circa 370, or about ten years before the *Agesilaus*.[40] Isocrates claims to have been the first to write a prose encomium of a contemporary figure (in this case, the late ruler of the Cypriot city of Salamis). According to the conventional interpretation, Xenophon derived not only the concept of a prose encomium from Isocrates but also certain features of organization and style.[41] However, a case can be made that the influence of Isocrates was even more profound than has been hitherto suspected, and that Xenophon derived other ideas from the *Evagoras* which have a direct bearing on the thesis of this chapter.[42]

Despite Isocrates' repeated claims in the *Evagoras* (10, 21, 39) to be reporting only the facts, the work is full of extravagant and artificial rhetoric. Eventually Isocrates admits that part of his purpose in writing such an encomium is to mold the character of young men (in this case Evagoras' son and successor, Nicocles) by giving them an example of virtue to imitate (76–77). Xenophon expresses a similarly pious hope that the *Agesilaus* may serve as a paradigm for those who wish to cultivate virtue (10.2).

Commentators have noted that Isocrates reports only Evagoras' successes, never his setbacks. Here, too, there are obvious parallels with the *Agesilaus*. Scholars would probably also agree that not all the personal and moral characteristics ascribed to Evagoras by Isocrates are historically accurate; a similar consensus prevails regarding Xenophon's treatment of Agesilaus.[43] The multiple parallels between the specific virtues attributed to Evagoras and to Agesilaus are easily understood as standard categories for moralizing encomia.

These correspondences prove only that Xenophon was operating in the same genre as Isocrates. Of far greater significance is the correspondence between the *Tendenz*—the consistent overall slant or bias—of the *Evagoras* and the agenda of the *Agesilaus*. Isocrates consistently plays down Evagoras' aggressive expansion of his power on Cyprus. He achieves this by omitting virtually all mention of such activities and by insisting long and loud that Evagoras never acted unjustly (43), never took what was not his, and attacked only after being attacked (28). Isocrates also minimizes Evagoras' subjection to and collaboration with Persia. Although he is forced to admit that Evagoras and Conon cooperated with Persia to defeat Sparta in the war of the 390s, he insists that they were motivated by a desire to liberate Athens and restore her naval hegemony (54–56, 68).[44] Again, Isocrates is at pains to prove that Evagoras was not a tyrant. Thus he devotes an inordinate amount of space to Evagoras' ancestry in order to establish that he belonged to the legitimate ruling family at Salamis, and he neglects to mention Evagoras' death by assassination, lest anyone think that Evagoras had been unjust or oppressive.[45]

Sykutris has pointed out that Isocrates devotes seven Teubner pages to Evagoras' rise to power but only three lines to his conquests.[46] This treatment closely resembles Xenophon's disproportionate and uneven coverage of the career of Agesilaus. Isocrates has carefully glossed over Evagoras' conquest of other cities on Cyprus and in the eastern Mediterranean. He inverts the charge of *pleonexia*—of having a greedy or grasping nature—which must have been leveled at Evagoras in his lifetime, by insisting that Evagoras never took what was not his and never attacked unless provoked. Furthermore, Isocrates claims that the Persian king so feared Evagoras' military prowess that he launched a preemptive attack against the ruler of Salamis (57–60).[47] Yet modern historians are almost certainly correct in their contention that the Persians were forced to act in order to check Evagoras' expansion at the expense of other Persian clients on Cyprus.[48] If Isocrates is to be believed, Evagoras had minded his own business and been in possession only of his own city, but once forced to go to war he conquered far and wide (62). So successful was he that he compelled the Persian king to leave him in possession of all he had before the war (63–64). This is a curiously misleading rendition of the fact that Evagoras was driven out of the other cities, besieged in Salamis, and ultimately forced to abandon his claims to everything other than Salamis.

Isocrates' treatment of Evagoras' attitude toward Persia is equally tendentious. As portrayed by Isocrates, Evagoras is a champion of Hellenism, who saved Salamis and all Cyprus from barbarism, made the island accessible to Greeks, and brought to the natives the benefits of Greek civilization. In the words of Jaeger, Isocrates presents Evagoras "as the champion of Greek areté and Greek character on the most easterly outpost of Hellenism against the Asiatic power of Persia."[49] He is a lifelong foe of Persia, and when he does cooperate with Persia in the 390s it is for the sake of Athens.

Again, this is not the story revealed by the best modern historical work on Evagoras. Evagoras was a Persian vassal for decades. As Costa points out, even though Isocrates is eager to depict Evagoras as panhellenic and anti-Persian, he cannot produce a single example of friction between Evagoras and the Persian king between 411 and 394. Costa demonstrates that Evagoras was loyal to Persia until 391, and makes a convincing case that even then he did not plot against Persia but simply miscalculated in expecting that, in return for his help in the war with Sparta, Persia would tolerate the expansion of his power on Cyprus.[50]

The *Tendenz* of the *Evagoras* is manifest. Isocrates has minimized Evagoras' aggressions against other cities on Cyprus and his longtime collaboration with Persia. Evagoras is transformed into a champion of Hellenism and a formidable enemy of the Persian king.

There are, as should now be apparent, multiple correspondences between this view of Isocrates' *Evagoras* and the interpretation of the *Agesilaus* advocated in this chapter. Just as Isocrates set out to exculpate Evagoras, Xenophon labors to vindicate Agesilaus, who had been accused of aggression against the Greek cities and collaboration with Persia, by magnifying the Spartan king into a panhellenic hero. There is some reason to believe that Xenophon and Isocrates were familiar with and influenced by each other's literary works. Therefore, it is perfectly conceivable that Xenophon was familiar with the *Evagoras*, that he understood the tactics employed by Isocrates, and that he made them his own in his defense of Agesilaus.[51]

4

The *Cyropaedia* and History

The *Cyropaedia*, which purports to be the story of Cyrus the Great, founder of the Persian Empire, is crucial to an understanding of Xenophon's attitudes toward and knowledge of Persia. The work is the primary repository of sentiment favorable to Persia in the Xenophontic corpus. And the so-called epilogue is the most frequently cited locus of hostility to Persia.

The preceding chapters have shown that the scholarship on Xenophon and his works has been marked by an obsession with finding anti-Persian motives and sentiments.[1] This tendency is primarily a reflection of the commentators' assumptions about what Xenophon must have or ought to have felt, believed, and championed. These assumptions can be traced to a number of causes. They are, in part, a product of the way in which the panhellenic, antibarbarian harangues of Isocrates have colored the modern view of attitudes in fourth-century Greece. They are also triggered by the compulsion of scholars to systematize and simplify. In this case, the attitudes expressed in a few key passages, such as the Greek commanders' call for resistance in the *Anabasis* or the comparison of the Spartan and Persian kings in the *Agesilaus*, have been generalized into a single, rigid mentality to which Xenophon was allegedly shackled.

Not surprisingly, a similar approach has been tried even with the *Cyropaedia*, despite the latter's Persian setting and seemingly favorable attitude. Schwartz and Prinz claimed to have discovered an elaborate allegorical system at work in the *Cyropaedia* according to which Cyrus stood for Agesilaus, Old Persia for Sparta, while Assyria represented the fourth-century Persian enemy, so that the work was actually a call for a panhellenic crusade, led by Sparta, against the Persian Empire.² This perverse view was demolished by Scharr.³ If the panhellenic, anti-Persian interpretation was misguided in the case of the *Anabasis* and *Agesilaus*, it is simply absurd when applied to the *Cyropaedia*.

The tendentiousness of so many of the interpretations of Xenophon's works is an important factor to keep in mind when considering the scholarship on the *Cyropaedia*. It is probably fair to say that the majority of classicists regard the *Cyropaedia* as a thoroughly Greek work which has been transferred to a fairy-tale "Persian" setting. They assume that Xenophon simply invented most of the alleged events in the career of his Cyrus. Consequently, they consider the work to be worth little as a source of information on Persian history, culture, or institutions, or of insights into the attitude of fourth-century Greeks toward Persia.⁴ According to one recent study: "Xenophon's choice of subject need not, therefore, be taken as an indication of some new cosmopolitanism, nor a reflection of his own travels abroad, especially since a Persian ingredient in the *Kyroupaideia* is little more than a flavoring."⁵ This is a *petitio principii*, a product of the same sort of thinking that has been so prevalent in studies of the *Anabasis* and *Agesilaus*. It is based on unexamined assumptions about the attitude of Xenophon and leads, in the case of the *Cyropaedia*, to a quite paradoxical conclusion.

On the other hand, many Orientalists who are primarily concerned with the civilization of ancient Iran have taken a very different view. For them the *Cyropaedia* has long been a major source of information for the history and institutions of the Persian Empire.⁶ Given these two fundamentally antithetical approaches, it is clearly a matter of importance to determine the true character of the *Cyropaedia*. The following discussion will show that the role of Persia in the work is the key to understanding the nature of the *Cyropaedia* and the purposes of the author, for it raises the question whether it is history, fiction, or something in between. The answer to this question will dictate the extent to which, and the way in which, the historian is entitled to make use of the *Cyropaedia*. And insofar as the *Cyropaedia* was widely read in antiquity⁷ and had considerable impact on the evolution of a number of literary genres, a determination of the character of the work should be a matter of interest not only to historians of ancient Persia but also to students concerned with the development of Greek thought.

There are a number of reasons for questioning the traditional view of classical scholars about the Persian elements in the *Cyropaedia*. In the first place, it begs the question simply to assert that the authentically Persian features are few and trivial and that Xenophon's choice of a Persian setting is of no great significance. This issue needs to be examined. One must ask why Xenophon has chosen a Persian king and allegedly Persian models of education, ethics, leadership, and administration to express his ideals. The question takes on added importance if the Greeks of the fourth century were really as hostile to and contemptuous of Persia as is commonly assumed, for this was the audience for which Xenophon wrote. And it becomes even more perplexing if one accepts the conventional wisdom which says that Xenophon personally harbored an irrevocable hatred toward Persia.

In the second place, the *Cyropaedia* contains numerous facts about the Persian Empire, its history, culture, institutions, and peoples. Some can be confirmed elsewhere, in Greek and Oriental sources; others are at least quite plausible. Xenophon claims that many of the customs and institutions of the elder Cyrus' day are still in force in his own time. He also claims to have done research and to have had access to Oriental songs and legends. Orientalists have detected stories and motifs in the *Cyropaedia* which recur in different contexts in the *Shahnama* and other Persian literature based on oral tradition. Some of the romantic digressions in the work, such as the story of Panthea and Abradatas, have an Oriental feel to them. The career of Cyrus as conqueror, founder of empire, and lawgiver and his deathbed political testament conform to characteristic Iranian story patterns. The historicity and factuality of the *Cyropaedia* are examined in detail below. For now it will suffice to have raised a critical question: Why does Xenophon go to the trouble of discovering and reporting this wealth of data about Persia?

In the next place, there are a number of significant connections between the *Cyropaedia* and other more obviously "factual" works of Xenophon. These connections need to be examined; for in some cases, by establishing the authenticity of an item in another context, one demonstrates the validity of the corresponding information in the *Cyropaedia* and contributes to the case for the value of the *Cyropaedia*, taken as a whole, as a source of information on Persia. Each of the following connections will be examined later in this chapter:

1. The significant correspondences between the education of the younger Cyrus as described in the *Anabasis* (1.9.2–6) and the Persian educational program outlined in the *Cyropaedia* (1.2.2–12)

2. The striking similarities between the personality, character, and conduct of the younger Cyrus as depicted in book 1 of the *Anabasis* and the portrayal of Cyrus the Great throughout the *Cyropaedia*

3. The many parallels between the administrative arrangements of the Persian king in the military and agricultural spheres, as described in highly laudatory terms by Xenophon in chapter 4 of the *Oeconomicus*, and the administrative institutions allegedly created by Cyrus shortly after the conquest of Babylon and reported in *Cyropaedia* 8.1.2

Finally, it must be realized that the *Cyropaedia* is about the acquisition and administration, not of a *polis*, but of an empire.[8] In the first pages of the *Cyropaedia* Xenophon expresses his concern to discover how it might be possible to rule over men (1.1.1–3). Some commentators explain that Xenophon was deeply disturbed by the instability of city-state governments and the incessant warfare within and between Greek communities during his lifetime, and that this concern prompted him to a discourse on government in the *Cyropaedia*.[9] Thus, the *Cyropaedia* is to be seen as espousing some sort of solution to the problems of the Greek *polis*.

Indeed, many of Xenophon's contemporaries were concerned with the problems of the Greek city-state. Plato in the *Republic* and the *Laws* and Aristotle in the *Politics* gave much deep thought to the nature of the *polis*, and each offered his vision of the ideal community. In both cases the emphasis is on the structure of the state. However, the comparison with Plato and Aristotle serves only to point up the differences in Xenophon's approach. He addresses the problem of rule by focusing on the individual ruler: thus he intends to investigate "who he [Cyrus] was in his origin, what natural endowments he possessed, and what sort of education he had enjoyed, that he so greatly excelled in governing men" (1.1.6).[10] Not only is Xenophon talking about a much larger and more complex political entity, that is, an empire extending over vast distances and comprising many different peoples, with all the problems of administration that this must entail; but he also focuses less on political structures than on the character of the individual ruler. Could he really have been prompted to this meditation by a desire to solve the problems of, say, contemporary Athens? In the Greek world, too, the idea of monarchy was enjoying currency. In this era Isocrates was seeking a champion to unite the Greek world under his rule and to lead a panhellenic crusade against the Persian "infidel." Plato had taken a personal interest in the powerful tyrants of Syracuse. Xenophon himself was aware of the wide-ranging ambitions of Jason of Pherae (*Hellenica* 6.4.27, 32), and in his last years the growing might of Philip of Macedon was casting its shadow over the Greek world. If Xenophon is prescribing for the Greek world, he has taken what was, for a Greek, a giant intellectual step by conceding that the solution to the political problems of the Greek world meant transcending the level of city-state organization and accepting incorporation into a larger, imperial structure. Xenophon would then stand with Isocrates, who advocated some form of political unification for Greece, rather than with Plato and Aristotle, who could not or would not see beyond the city-state.

It should also be recognized that things were not going well for the Persian Empire in the fourth century, racked as it was by revolts (by Evagoras of Cypriot Salamis circa 391–380, by the Phoenicians circa 350, and by the western satraps in the 360s and 350s), attempted coups d'état (Cyrus in 401), and Egypt's secession from the empire in the period 405/4 to 343. Given that the subject matter of the *Cyropaedia* is the conquest and rule of an empire, one should not exclude the possibility that Xenophon has been prompted to these reflections by the difficulties faced by contemporary Persia. If he is indeed contemplating the problems of the Greek world, there is no reason why this concern cannot be complementary to, rather than an exclusive alternative to, his interest in Persia.

In sum, one must ask why Xenophon has concerned himself with the problems facing an individual who seeks to rule, not a city-state, but an empire. Whichever specific situation Xenophon may have had in mind, it is clear that, in the search for a solution to the problem of administering an empire, the authentic historical experience of Persia would be of the utmost instructional value.

All the aforementioned considerations raise doubts about the prevailing assumption that the authentically Persian elements of the *Cyropaedia* are superficial and of little real moment. Xenophon had both a keen interest in and ample knowledge of Persia, based in large part on his experiences during the rebellion of the younger Cyrus. To establish that the *Cyropaedia* contains much more that is authentically Persian than is usually thought, this chapter examines the subject matter, genre, and purpose of the *Cyropaedia*, as well as Xenophon's sources and methods. This survey will lead to a consideration of the validity of his information on the history, culture, and institutions of Persia and to a reexamination of the problems associated with the epilogue, which reverses the trend of the rest of the work and expresses a very negative view of fourth-century Persia.

Despite the fact that many readers in antiquity regarded the *Cyropaedia* as a historical work,[11] there is little agreement among modern scholars about such fundamental issues as the genre of the *Cyropaedia*, Xenophon's purpose in writing it, the sources he used, and how he used them.[12] Perhaps it is unreasonable to hope for a single, simple answer. Xenophon was not afraid to cross traditional genre lines, and indeed he assisted in the creation or early development of several new genres.[13] When all is said and done, the *Cyropaedia* is an enigma and probably will remain so.

Nevertheless, certain things can be said. In the preface Xenophon makes a revealing statement about his intentions.

> Thus, as we meditated on this analogy, we were inclined to conclude that for man, as he is constituted, it is easier to rule over any and all other creatures than to rule over men. But when we reflected that there was one Cyrus, the Persian, who reduced to obedience a vast number of men and cities and nations, we were then compelled to change our opinion and decide that to rule men might be a task neither impossible nor even difficult, if one should only go about it in an intelligent manner. . . . Believing this man to be deserving of all admiration, we have therefore investigated who he was in his origin, what natural endowments he possessed, and what sort of education he had enjoyed, that he so greatly excelled in governing men. Accordingly, what we have found out or think we know concerning him we shall now endeavour to present. (*Cyropaedia* 1.1.3, 6)

From this it follows that the *Cyropaedia*, although it may contain much historical and biographical material, is neither history nor biography. Xenophon is intrigued by the question of how one may govern that most problematic of creatures—man—and feels that Cyrus' success in this enterprise makes him a fruitful sub-

The *Cyropaedia* and History / 67

ject for study (1.1.1–6). Thus, on Xenophon's own testimony, the *Cyropaedia* is to be an investigation of how Cyrus conquered and ruled his empire. This choice of focus accounts for the fact that Xenophon concentrates on certain periods of Cyrus' life—his boyhood, the early years of his reign, and his last days—for this approach allows him to expatiate upon the early signs of Cyrus' outstanding nature, the program of education which molded his character, the manner in which he carried out his conquests, his initial provisions for administration of the new empire, and his deathbed political testament. He disregards other aspects of Cyrus' career—his years as a teenager and young adult, other campaigns of conquest, and most of his adult reign—as not providing further insight into the issues of character, conquest, and rule. A comprehensive and continuous treatment of the full career of Cyrus, such as would be expected in either a history of old Persia or a biography of Cyrus, is not attempted and was surely never contemplated. Perhaps one can safely describe the *Cyropaedia* as a didactic work on the subjects of education, values, military science, and political administration, with Cyrus used as a paradigm. Xenophon may also have recognized the importance of providing a cohesive and entertaining framework for the instructional material.

Yet, if it is conceded that the *Cyropaedia* is not history or biography and that Xenophon's primary purpose is didactic, it must also be denied that it is pure invention on Xenophon's part. Some classical scholars do regard the work as largely or entirely fictional.[14] But this interpretation disregards Xenophon's claim that he is concerned to study the career of the historical Cyrus for the illumination which it may provide on the problem of good government, and that he is going to relate what he has found out (1.1.6).[15] He repeatedly refers to stories and songs about Cyrus to be found among the barbarians,[16] and he also mentions paintings of Persians (1.2.13). These are evidently being cited as sources for his inquiry. Given these explicit statements of Xenophon's intentions in writing the work, of the research which he undertook, and of the sources to which he had access, the common allegation that he fabricated most or all of the content of the *Cyropaedia* is perverse. In most cases this position is merely asserted, with little or no effort made to substantiate it with argumentation and evidence. The burden of proof should be on those who maintain such views in the face of the explicit contrary testimony in the text. In order to override such allegations

68 / The *Cyropaedia* and History

once and for all, the following paragraphs advance several arguments which tend to confirm the essential veracity of Xenophon's claim that he uses true information about Cyrus and Persia.

Xenophon's sources of information on Cyrus and Persia fall into three major categories. One is books written by fellow Greeks. Xenophon was clearly familiar with the *Persica* of Ctesias,[17] for in the *Anabasis* (1.8.26) he refers to Ctesias' account of the battle of Cunaxa. It is reasonable to assume that he made some use of Ctesias for the *Cyropaedia*, and it is very likely that his account of the death of Cyrus the Elder is derived in part from Ctesias.[18]

Since he does not cite Herodotus by name anywhere, it is impossible to prove that Xenophon was familiar with the *Histories*, but it remains a quite probable supposition. There are strong similarities between Xenophon's and Herodotus' accounts of Cyrus' capture of Sardis and Babylon. And Xenophon's story of the interview between Cyrus and Croesus (7.2.9–28) is not only reminiscent of the parallel scene in Herodotus (1.86–90); it assumes familiarity with the Herodotean version.[19] In addition, Xenophon's frequent citation of oral tradition among the barbarians is reminiscent of Herodotus.[20]

The case of Antisthenes is more problematic. It is known that this disciple of Socrates wrote one or more dialogues titled *Cyrus*.[21] But the extant fragments are too meager to permit an appraisal of its nature or contents and thus to evaluate Xenophon's debt to Antisthenes. Gigon makes the plausible observation that it would be remarkable if Xenophon had not been familiar with the treatise of his fellow Socratic.[22] On the other hand, Xenophon's depiction of Antisthenes in the *Symposium* indicates that he had little respect for him.[23]

Barbarian oral tradition constitutes a second category of source material. As has already been noted, Xenophon occasionally cites the stories and songs about Cyrus to be found among the barbarians. Clearly Cyrus had become a figure of legend among the peoples of the Near East.[24] Xenophon would have picked up such stories during his travels in the interior of the Persian Empire, first as a member of the entourage of the younger Cyrus and later as a commander of the Greek mercenaries.

His experiences in the Persian Empire are also integral to the third category of evidence. Obviously he could draw upon what he had seen and learned firsthand in the course of his travels. There is ample evidence that Xenophon tended to retroject into the past certain Persian practices of his own day. He frequently marks this in the *Cyropaedia* by employing some variant of the phrase *eti kai nun*—"and still today."²⁵

In sum, it is fair to say that Xenophon was familiar with and used the written works of Herodotus and Ctesias, that he also had access to contemporary oral traditions among the barbarians, and that he could draw upon his own experiences in Asia. One may with justification entertain doubts about the historicity of Herodotus' and Ctesias' accounts of the career of Cyrus or about the veracity of the oral traditions circulating among the barbarians. And, in some cases, Xenophon may be mistaken in assuming that a contemporary institution or custom was already in existence in Cyrus' day. But what is most important for present purposes is that Xenophon drew upon sources which he considered, and had every reason to consider, to be of some value.

Insofar as most of the source material available to Xenophon is not extant today, only a little can be inferred about his methods and his criteria for using this material. Sometimes he takes over a version of a story found in Herodotus or Ctesias.²⁶ These cases present no problem. At other times he gives an account which is at variance with that of Herodotus or Ctesias and which is not attested elsewhere.²⁷ Critics tend to point to these cases as examples of Xenophon's tendency to fabricate stories. But it is methodologically unsound to presume that Xenophon has simply invented any story for which independent confirmation has not chanced to survive to modern times. The possibility must remain open that he has preferred an alternative tradition.²⁸ Already by Herodotus' day Cyrus had become a figure of legend among Greeks as well as among barbarians. Herodotus claimed to be aware of four different versions of the birth of Cyrus and many tales of his death, and by Xenophon's day this process of mythifying would have gone further. It is fair to assume that Xenophon, like Herodotus before him, often had several versions of a story from which to choose.²⁹

Why, then, does Xenophon choose a particular version in a given case? This question relates to the problems of the genre and purpose of the *Cyropaedia*. It has been maintained above that the work is neither pure history or biography on the one hand nor pure invention on the other, but a didactic work which draws upon the lessons of the past. One should not expect Xenophon to have submitted his source material to the kind of rigorous critical scrutiny which a

Thucydides would have demanded; a precise reconstruction of the past was not his primary objective. Rather, he would have favored traditions about Cyrus which best enabled him to illustrate those qualities of character and intellect which he felt were most important in a leader and ruler. Xenophon is concerned with truth, but (to put it in Aristotelian terms) philosophical or general truth is to be preferred to strict historical accuracy. The closest parallels in Greek literature may be the Socratic dialogues of Plato and of Xenophon himself. These treatises are philosophical and didactic, but they are placed in a historical setting. Real historical personalities are employed, and they often espouse a point of view which they actually held or could plausibly have held. Xenophon's Cyrus serves a similar function. With numerous traditions about Cyrus in circulation, Xenophon was in a position to choose the one which best suited his didactic purposes. It should be recognized that there is a meaningful difference between spontaneous invention of stories, of which Xenophon is so frequently accused, and the selective use of authentic traditions.[30] That having been said, it should not be denied that occasionally he may have invented episodes when the traditions failed him.

So far, the discussion of Xenophon's sources and methods has pertained largely to the historical framework of the *Cyropaedia*, that is, to the sequence of events which make up the career of Xenophon's Cyrus. But the reader of the *Cyropaedia* soon discovers that there is a great deal more to the work than a mere series of incidents. At this point it is helpful to draw a distinction between the historical framework and what one might call the didactic core of the work—the extended dialogues, speeches, and excursuses of all sorts which form the bulk of the *Cyropaedia* and which contain the essential didactic matter which Xenophon wishes to present. Much of this material is obviously of Greek origin. After all, Xenophon is a Greek writing for Greeks. It has been said that Xenophon meant to present the fruits of a lifetime of experience in the *Cyropaedia* and that the figure of Cyrus is a device which allows him to lecture on all manner of subjects, including education, administration, warfare, leadership, hunting, ethics, oratory, and cooking. Often, when Cyrus speaks, one feels the presence of Socrates.

In one sense, then, the *Cyropaedia* may be said to comprise a Greek didactic core set into a Persian historical framework. Such a formulation is proper insofar as it acknowledges that Xenophon has fused Greek and Persian elements.³¹ However, one must keep in mind that the distinction between Persian framework and Greek core is, at most, a convenience. As a literary strategy, the framework and core are obviously interdependent. The dialogues and speeches must be set in a plausible historical context, one which is conducive to their content. Moreover, as will be shown later, the content of the dialogues and speeches is not exclusively Greek. In his own thinking on a wide range of subjects Xenophon has been influenced by Persian concepts. Other scholars have demonstrated the extent to which the *Cyropaedia* is pervaded by ideas and attitudes which are ultimately of Greek origin; but they have tended to overlook or even to deny the presence of authentic Oriental material. In what follows, this neglected aspect of the *Cyropaedia* will be emphasized.

The Persian setting of the *Cyropaedia* must be accounted for. Xenophon set out to write a treatise which, among other things, explored the problem of leadership by portraying an ideal military commander and ruler. There are some similarities with Plato's *Republic*, which also depicted an ideal system of society, government, and education. Since Xenophon's aims were primarily philosophical rather than historical, he was free to choose any setting he wished. He could have selected a time and place from the Greek past, as he did in the *Hiero*, or have followed Plato in postulating a purely hypothetical context. Instead he chose to set his story in Old Persia in the time of Cyrus the Great, founder of the vast and mighty Persian Empire, which by Xenophon's day had cast its shadow over the affairs of the Greek city-states for the better part of two centuries.

This choice of setting ought to constitute an embarrassment for that majority of scholars who claim that Xenophon was a lifelong panhellenist and a bitter foe of Persia. Yet most have ignored the problem. Some remark that Xenophon is following a well-established Greek tradition about Cyrus which can be seen in Aeschylus, Herodotus, and, more recently, Antisthenes. For them the Persian setting is merely a veneer and need not be taken seriously.³² Others explain that the distance in space and time of Cyrus' Old Persia allowed Xenophon to disregard the hard facts of history and to concentrate on his literary and didactic goals.³³ Delebecque, who maintains that Xenophon is lecturing to the fickle Athenians on the critical issues of the day, argues that it was safer for him to present his message in a Persian guise.³⁴

All these positions fail to approach with sufficient seriousness the significance of Xenophon's choice of setting. At the very least, he should be credited with the capacity for making a deliberate and meaningful choice. Clearly he had respect for Cyrus and Old Persia. And why should he not? The greatness and capacity of Cyrus and the Persians as builders and rulers of a vast empire were self-evident. In a relatively short period Cyrus and his immediate successors had conquered an empire which, in modern geographic terms, stretched from Turkey to India, from Russia to the Sudan. For almost two centuries the Persian Empire had dominated most of the world as the Greeks knew it. For one who was in search of a solution to the age-old problem of how to rule mankind successfully, the authentic historical experience of Persia would clearly be of considerable relevance. Indeed, Xenophon was not the first Greek to express publicly his admiration for the founder of the Persian empire. Aeschylus, Herodotus, Antisthenes, Plato, and even Isocrates had all had occasion to praise the achievements and character of Cyrus.[35] This fact may make Xenophon's choice of subject less surprising, but it does not make it less significant.

Any analysis of Xenophon's sources of information and inspiration must take one other factor into consideration. Xenophon had marched into Asia in the company of Cyrus the younger, and it is clear that he was impressed by this brave and rebellious Persian prince.[36] In *Anabasis* 1.9 he follows his account of the death of Cyrus in battle at Cunaxa with a stirring encomium in which he extols Cyrus' character and achievements. The encomium opens with a suggestive evaluation of Cyrus as ἀνὴρ ὢν Περσῶν τῶν μετὰ Κῦρον τὸν ἀρχαῖον γενομένων βασιλικώτατός τε καὶ ἄρχειν ἀξιώτατος—"a man who was the most kingly and the most worthy to rule of all the Persians who have been born since Cyrus the Elder." Xenophon is signaling a clear connection between Cyrus the Great, founder of the Persian Empire, and the young prince who aspired to rule the same empire a century and a half later.

There is reason to believe that the younger Cyrus himself may have suggested the comparison to Xenophon. When Cyrus set out to organize a rebellion against his brother, Artaxerxes II, he must have known that he would need some sort of justification, that is, a propaganda theme which he could use both to attract support for his cause and to vindicate his usurpation of the throne. Indeed, it is readily apparent from the first book of the *Anabasis* that Cyrus was anxious about the loyalties of his barbarian troops and therefore tended to rely heavily on his Greek mercenaries.[37] Several extant sources preserve traces of the theme of Cyrus' propaganda, in which he apparently took advantage of his famous name to summon up memories of a former period of greatness, the Old Persia of Cyrus the Great. Plutarch (*Artaxerxes* 6.3) preserves a remark of the younger Cyrus to the effect that Artaxerxes, because of his faintheartedness and softness, could neither keep his horse on the hunt nor his throne in a crisis. Cyrus must have argued that Artaxerxes was not worthy of the Persian throne. Cyrus the Great had won an empire on account of his excellence, and the younger Cyrus, who, as Xenophon says, was most like his namesake in kingliness and worthiness to rule (*Anabasis* 1.9.1), deserved to sit on the throne of empire and would revive the customs and qualities that had made Persia great.

Admittedly this reconstruction of Cyrus' program of propaganda is, in part, conjectural, but it can be confirmed by the counterpropaganda which issued from Artaxerxes' camp. If Cyrus was invoking the legendary Cyrus, it was to Artaxerxes' advantage to belittle this claim. One can detect this process at work in the *Persica* of Ctesias, a Greek who served as physician to Artaxerxes' family and lived at the Persian court during Cyrus' rebellion. Whereas Herodotus and Xenophon agree that the elder Cyrus was the son of Cambyses, the vassal king of Persia in the Median Empire, Ctesias makes him a commoner, son of a lowborn cutthroat named Atradates and his goatherd wife Argoste, who began his career as a servant at the Median court.[38] This account is tantamount to a denial that Cyrus was an Achaemenid, a member of the legitimate line of Persian kings.

The tendency of Artaxerxes' counterpropaganda receives further confirmation from a pair of Old Persian inscriptions on gold tablets found at Ecbatana. These inscriptions carry the names of Ariaramnes and Arsames, addressing each as "the great King, King of Kings, King in Persia."[39] It is known from Darius I's monumental inscription at Behistun that Ariaramnes and Arsames were his great-grandfather and grandfather in the line of Achaemenes, the eponymous ancestor.[40] Around 522 Darius, a member of a junior branch of the Achaemenid clan, took possession of the throne which had belonged to the then extinct line of Cyrus. Darius does not claim that his progenitors were kings of Persia, and, for that matter, they could not have been, for the Cyrus Cylinder states that Cyrus' royal predecessors and ancestors were Cambyses, Cyrus, and Teispis.[41] Moreover, the terminology of the inscriptions from Ecbatana, "King of Kings," is wrong for the period of vassalage to Media. Orientalists feel that the orthography of these inscriptions is appropriate to the time of Artaxerxes II in the fourth century, and R. G. Kent has suggested that they were erected as part of an anti-Cyrus propaganda campaign during or shortly after the revolt of the younger Cyrus.[42] This hypothesis makes perfect sense. By erecting these inscriptions, Artaxerxes is claiming that the ancient Cyrus was a commoner and usurper, and that the legitimate royal line is that of Darius. In this way he counters his brother's pretensions to revive the Old Persia of Cyrus the Great.[43]

Xenophon would have been exposed to the propaganda of the younger Cyrus while he was traveling with the prince, for this propaganda was directed primarily at the Persians in Cyrus' camp. It encompassed a picture of Cyrus the founder which the new Cyrus undertook to emulate, and a concept of Old Persia which he promised to restore. Viewed in this light, Xenophon's choice to idealize the elder Cyrus and Old Persia in the *Cyropaedia* takes on a new meaning. Xenophon may well have been inspired by the hopes, dreams, and self-serving claims of the younger Cyrus.[44]

The link between the younger Cyrus and Xenophon's vision of Old Persia is seen to be even stronger when one considers the striking similarities—often remarked upon by the commentators—between the younger Cyrus of the *Anabasis* and the elder Cyrus of the *Cyropaedia*.[45] There are a fair number of passages in the *Cyropaedia* in which Xenophon describes a trait or habit of the elder Cyrus in terms similar or identical to those used for the younger Cyrus in the *Anabasis*. They undergo comparable educations,[46] show a remarkable aptitude and enthusiasm for its basic features—riding, shooting, hunting—and excel over all other boys in their age-group (*Cyropaedia* 1.2.2–1.3.1, 1.4.5; *Anabasis* 1.9.2–6). Each is prone to reckless daring—the elder Cyrus in killing a boar on his first hunt and in his first battle in Media (*Cyr.* 1.4.8, 1.4.21), the younger Cyrus in confronting a bear during a hunt and in his fatal assault on his brother at Cunaxa (*Anab.* 1.9.6, 1.8.24–27). Each has the habit of exercising before meals (*Cyr.* 8.1.37; *Oeconomicus* 4.29), each sends food to friends as a gesture of affection (*Cyr.* 8.2.3, 8.4.6;

Anab. 1.9.25–26), and each proclaims his desire to surpass friends and enemies at doing good and harm respectively (*Cyr.* 5.3.32; *Anab.* 1.9.11). Finally, there are multiple correspondences, sometimes in virtually identical phraseology, between Xenophon's description of the younger Cyrus' conduct as satrap in Asia Minor (*Anab.* 1.9.7–31) and his account of the elder Cyrus' efforts to guarantee the security of his person by winning popularity among friends, potential rivals, and subjects (*Cyr.* 8.2 passim).

It is hard to resist the conclusion that Xenophon's portrayal of the character, conduct, and personal relations of the elder Cyrus is based largely on the personality of his one-time patron Cyrus the prince.[47] Some scholars have suggested that the *Cyropaedia* is a kind of fantasy or projection of how things might have been if Cyrus had survived at Cunaxa and gone on to seize control of the empire.[48] While there may be some truth to their claims, none of them makes the essential point that Xenophon is not operating purely out of his own imaginings. He had received a particular vision of Cyrus the Great and Old Persia from the younger Cyrus. So powerful was this impression that Xenophon could not easily disassociate the younger Cyrus from the ancestor whom he claimed to imitate and, in a sense, to reincarnate.

To maintain that Xenophon modeled the figure of Cyrus the Great on the personality of the younger Cyrus is not necessarily to accuse him of lack of concern for historical accuracy or of willful distortion of the truth. By Xenophon's day Cyrus had already been dead for one hundred and fifty years, his story encrusted with layer upon layer of legend. Where was Xenophon to turn for insight into the personality of the founder of the empire or for a picture of conditions in sixth-century Iran? There is no reason to believe that in ancient Iran there existed a historical tradition, written or oral, that would have made possible an accurate recreation of the events, personalities, and conditions of the age of Cyrus. Xenophon worked with what he had, and the fullest and most vivid picture of Cyrus and Old Persia available to him came from the camp of the younger Cyrus. To the extent that the *Cyropaedia* violates history, it does so not as a result of bald invention on Xenophon's part, but as a result of the fact that he had to rely on available sources, written and oral, with the younger Cyrus prominent among the latter, and on the practices of contemporary Persia, for his picture of the Old Persia of Cyrus the Great.

76 / The *Cyropaedia* and History

From this it follows that the traditions about Old Persia embodied in the *Cyropaedia*, however anachronistic, may also represent, in some degree, a different sort of truth. They may reflect some of the Persians' own conceptions about their past and thereby provide precious insights into the traditions and values of the aristocracy in fourth-century Persia. The *Cyropaedia* would then be analogous, in certain respects, to the early books of the Roman historian Livy, which may preserve little that is historically accurate about Rome in the era of the kings and the earliest days of the Republic but nevertheless constitute a priceless treasury of the conceptions held by Romans in the late Republic and early Empire concerning their past.

The preceding discussion has attempted to show that Xenophon's uses of the material available to him were tailored to his purpose in writing the *Cyropaedia*. His criteria for selection between competing versions would often have been conditioned by his didactic agenda. But he would probably have regarded his role as largely one of showing how the record of the past confirmed certain important lessons.

It is now necessary to assess the reliability of the historical information embedded in the *Cyropaedia*. Yet such an assessment is not easily made. For one thing, many aspects of Cyrus' career are still subjects of dispute among experts. Although the Nabonidus Chronicle and the Cyrus Cylinder, a pair of cuneiform documents contemporary with the reign of Cyrus, provide valuable evidence, the major source is still Herodotus, and, as was shown earlier, the realities of Cyrus' career were already obscured by an accretion of legends in Herodotus' day. Nevertheless, it is possible to establish that the *Cyropaedia* has more historical validity than is usually allowed.

Xenophon reports that Cyrus was the son of Cambyses, king of Persia, a principality within the Median Empire (*Cyr.* 1.2.1). This information is confirmed by the Cyrus Cylinder, a propaganda tract in Akkadian cuneiform thought to have been composed at Cyrus' behest after the capture of Babylon and giving his lineage as "son of Cambyses, great king, king of Anshan; grandson of Cyrus, great king, king of Anshan; descendant of Teispis, great king, king of Anshan, of a family (which) always (exercised) kingship."[49] Thus Xenophon is shown to be correct, in contrast to Ctesias, who made Cyrus a commoner and child of the unknown brigand Atradates and his goatherd wife Argoste,⁵⁰ and Herodotus, who accepted the folklore motif of Cyrus' exposure as a baby and made his Persian father Cambyses "well born and of a quiet temper . . . much lower than a Mede of middle estate" (1.107).⁵¹

As Xenophon's Cyrus is poised to attack Assyria,⁵² he gains the allegiance of the Assyrian vassal Gobryas (4.6.1), who later plays an important part in the capture of Babylon and kills the wicked Assyrian king (7.5.24–30). This time confirmation comes from the Nabonidus Chronicle, a contemporary cuneiform document which describes, among other events of the reigns of Nabonidus and Cyrus, the fall of Babylon: "[Seventeenth year:] . . . The 16th day, Gobryas (Ugbaru), the governor of Gutium and the army of Cyrus entered Babylon without battle. . . . Till the end of the month the shield (-carrying) Gutians were staying within Esagila. . . . In the month of Arahshamnu, the 3rd day, Cyrus entered Babylon. . . . Gobryas, his governor, installed (sub-) governors in Babylon."⁵³ So Xenophon is right to claim that Cyrus enlisted the support of one Gobryas, a Babylonian vassal who was instrumental in the capture of Babylon.⁵⁴ This detail is absent from Herodotus' account and from the extant portions of Ctesias' *Persica*.

Xenophon never names the Babylonian king, but he insists that he is young (4.6.2). Here he may have been misled by the fact that, during the last eleven years of his reign, the real Babylonian king, Nabonidus, was in residence at the Oasis of Tema', while his son Belshazzar ruled in Babylon as co-regent for his absent father. Belshazzar would be the young king who Xenophon thinks was killed by Gobryas during the assault on Babylon.⁵⁵ Chapter 5 of the Book of Daniel also mistakenly refers to Belshazzar, who sees the ominous handwriting on the wall just before the Persian onslaught, as king of Babylon, and insists that he was killed during the capture of the city.

Xenophon's account of the campaign which culminated in Cyrus' capture of Sardis has much in common with the narrative of this event in Herodotus. One must presume either that Xenophon drew upon Herodotus or that Xenophon and Herodotus had a common source. After a hard-fought battle at Thymbrara, in the vicinity of Sardis, Croesus' army retreats within the walls of Sardis, but the city is taken by a party of daring Persians who scale the wall at its most precipitous, and therefore undefended, point (*Cyropaedia* 7.1.4–2.4; cf. Herodotus 1.79–81, 84). Following this passage is the report of an interview between Cyrus and the captive Croesus which assumes familiarity with Herodotus' account of the meeting of these two kings and amounts to a conscious elaboration of the Herodotean material (*Cyr.* 7.2.9–28; cf. Herodotus 1.87–91).[56] As in Herodotus, Xenophon's Cyrus spares the life of Croesus and keeps the Lydian king in his entourage (*Cyr.* 7.2.29; cf. Herodotus 1.153).

There are also differences between the two accounts. Xenophon does not report an initial battle in Pteria, east of the Halys River (Herodotus 1.76). He regards Croesus as commander of a coalition which included, besides nearly all the peoples of Asia Minor, the Assyrians, Phoenicians, and Egyptians (*Cyr.* 6.2.10). Certain elements in Xenophon's description of the battle of Thymbrara have appeared to some scholars to reflect the circumstances of the fourth century.[57] And Xenophon makes no mention of any attempt by Cyrus to immolate Croesus on a pyre (Herodotus 1.86–87). Scholars have proposed various explanations for these divergences, including outright invention on Xenophon's part, but there is no reason why such variant items could not have been present in oral tradition or in a written history such as that of Ctesias.[58]

In a similar fashion, Xenophon's account of Cyrus' conquest of Babylon shows a clear relationship to the tradition in which Herodotus worked. Both have the city taken when water is diverted from the riverbed at the point where it enters the city, although the mechanism by which the water is diverted is not identical in the two accounts. And both have the city taken during a festival (*Cyr.* 7.5.1–34; Herodotus 1.190–92).[59] However, there is a problem with both Herodotus' and Xenophon's accounts of the fall of Babylon. The contemporary Nabonidus Chronicles insists that the city fell without a fight: "On the 16th day, Gobryas, the governor of Gutium, and the troops of Cyrus entered Babylon without battle." In this instance Xenophon shares Herodotus' misconception.[60]

None of these cases warrants the conclusion that Xenophon has fabricated incidents. Rather, he seems to be drawing upon existing traditions about the career of Cyrus. Furthermore, these examples should serve as a warning against the simplistic assumption that Xenophon's depiction of the career of Cyrus is correct only when it is in agreement with the account of Herodotus and inevitably mistaken whenever it conflicts with that account. In some instances Xenophon's alternative version has proved to be correct, and in at least one case in which their accounts tally, both are in error.

The *Cyropaedia* and History / 79

Three important incidents in the *Cyropaedia*, which are regularly cited as among the most flagrant examples of Xenophon's alleged liberties with the known history of Cyrus, both strengthen the argument made here for the work's historical reliability and provide further insights into the way Xenophon handles his historical materials. In each case it is commonly assumed that Xenophon simply invented his version because it suited his literary purposes, that is, the glorification and idealization of Cyrus, although he knew the truth full well from reading Herodotus. These three incidents are Cyrus' conquest of Egypt, his peaceful acquisition of the Median throne, and his tranquil death at home in bed. In all three cases it can be shown that Xenophon had some authority for his version.

It is well known that in Herodotus' *Histories* it is Cambyses, the son of Cyrus, who brings Egypt into the empire (2.1, 3.1–13). But Xenophon has a different story. Early in the *Cyropaedia* (1.1.4) he concludes the list of Cyrus' conquests with the assertion that ἐπῆρξε . . . καταβὰς δ'ἐπὶ θάλατταν καὶ Κυπρίων καὶ Αἰγυπτίων— "and, descending to the sea, he added both Cyprus and Egypt to his empire." But Xenophon does not narrate Cyrus' Egyptian campaign. After Cyrus has settled his affairs in Babylon, he *is said* (*legetai*) to have gathered a large army around him (8.6.20–22).

> ἐπεὶ δὲ ταῦτα συνεσκεύαστο αὐτῷ, ὥρμα δὴ ταύτην τὴν στρατείαν ἐν ᾗ λέγεται καταστρέψασθαι πάντα τὰ ἔθνη ὅσα Συρίαν ἐκβάντι οἰκεῖ μέχρι Ἐρυθρᾶς θαλάττης. μετὰ δὲ ταῦτα ἡ εἰς Αἴγυπτον στρατεία λέγεται γενέσθαι, καὶ καταστρέψασθαι Αἴγυπτον.

> And when these [military preparations] had been ready for him, he started out on that expedition on which he is said to have subjugated all the nations that fill the earth from where one leaves Syria even to the Indian Ocean. His next expedition is said to have gone to Egypt and to have subjugated that country also.

Xenophon goes on to say: "From that time on his empire was bounded on the east by the Indian Ocean, on the north by the Black Sea, on the west by Cyprus and Egypt, and on the south by Ethiopia. The extremes of his empire are uninhabitable, on the one side because of the heat, on another because of the cold, on another because of too much water, and on the fourth because of too little. Cyrus himself made his home in the center of his domain. . . ."

It is clear from his double use of *legetai* in this passage that Xenophon is only reporting a tradition which he has heard. Apparently there were legends of Cyrus' worldwide travels and conquests, perhaps similar to the later legends about Alexander. It should come as no surprise if oral tradition attributed to Cyrus conquests made by his immediate successors. Xenophon makes a special point of qualifying his report here with *legetai*. This is not his usual practice elsewhere in the *Cyropaedia*; for the most part, he simply reports events as established fact. Here he is reporting a tradition, but he does not, as a historian, affirm it. Nor does he pursue it in any detail. His caution may be due to his awareness of the discrepancy between this tradition and the account of Herodotus.

His report of the tradition about the Egyptian conquest is followed directly by a description of the vast extent of the empire, bounded as it was by uninhabitable regions. Cyrus chose to establish himself at Babylon, Susa, and Ecbatana, in the center of his domains. Breitenbach regards this conception of the Persian Empire as a world-spanning empire, with the Iranian heartland in the very center, as an authentic ethnocentric Persian conception.[61] In the *Anabasis* the younger Cyrus describes the extreme limits of the empire which he sought to gain in nearly identical terms (1.7.6). These considerations strengthen the case for Xenophon's reliance upon a Persian oral tradition when he credits Cyrus with the conquest of Egypt.

It may be that Xenophon derived this notion from the propaganda of the younger Cyrus. At the time of the latter's revolt, Egypt had broken away from the Persian Empire. Although the precise date of this secession is not known, most modern scholars place it circa 405/4, that is, shortly before or after Artaxerxes II's accession to the throne.[62] Cyrus could easily have used this military and political setback as one more piece of ammunition in his efforts to prove the incapacity of his brother to rule the empire. Egypt, the richest province of the empire, had broken away, and Artaxerxes could do nothing about it. In such a context it would be to the further advantage of the younger Cyrus, who promised to emulate the example of Cyrus the Great and revive the glories of Old Persia, to assert that Cyrus had conquered that Egypt which the weakling Artaxerxes had now lost. If so, then Xenophon may have heard the tradition from Cyrus. This speculation is made more plausible by the near identity between the younger Cyrus' description of the extreme limits of the empire in the *Anabasis* (1.7.6) and the corresponding description adjoined to the report of Cyrus' conquest of

The *Cyropaedia* and History / 81

Egypt in the *Cyropaedia*. Obviously, this is not an argument for the correctness of Xenophon's version as against that of Herodotus. Still, it is important to recognize that Xenophon drew upon preexisting traditions about Cyrus, and these traditions, regardless of their accuracy, are of interest to the historian.

The second great historical "error" which has disturbed many critics involves the way in which Cyrus acquires the Median throne. In all other versions (Herodotus, Ctesias, the Nabonidus Chronicle) Cyrus overcomes Astyages by force and seizes control of Media and its dependencies. In the *Cyropaedia*, however, the Median king is not Astyages but his son, Cyaxares.[63] And, according to Xenophon, Cyrus remains nominally loyal to Cyaxares, marries his daughter, and, on the death of Cyaxares, ascends the Median throne by legitimate right of succession. Thus Xenophon has transformed the rebellion of Cyrus against the Median king into a peaceful inheritance of the kingdom. Unfortunately, Xenophon's sources for his version of Cyrus' acquisition of the Median kingdom are unknown.[64] But what is often overlooked is that Cyrus, in the *Cyropaedia*, does effectively execute a coup against his Median overlord.[65]

Cyrus persuades virtually the entire Median army to join him in an attack on the Assyrians, leaving Cyaxares and his retinue behind in the process (4.2.9–11). When he receives an order from the angry Cyaxares demanding that he return (4.5.10), Cyrus persuades the Medes and other allies to stay with him (5.1.19–29). Perhaps this incident is to be connected with the tradition, found in Herodotus and the Nabonidus Chronicle, that Astyages' Median troops rebelled against him and went over to Cyrus.[66]

Although he is nominally in the service of Cyaxares, Xenophon's Cyrus regards the lands conquered by him as his own. After his initial successes he sends messengers to Persia to "ask them to send reinforcements with the utmost dispatch, if the Persians desire to have control of Asia and the revenues accruing therefrom" (4.5.16).[67] After the capture of Babylon, "Cyrus desired to establish himself as he thought became a king . . ." (7.5.37). He has now become master of an empire: ". . . he began at once to organize the rest of his court. And . . . he considered his own situation, that he was undertaking to hold sway over many people . . ." (7.5.58).

Cyaxares, who is jealous and humiliated, is pawned off with gifts and fine phrases (5.5.5–40). Afterward he is treated with courtesy and empty honors, but the real power resides with Cyrus. Cyaxares, in turn, offers Cyrus the hand of his daughter and the Median kingdom as a dowry (8.5.17–19). This account is reminiscent of the tradition in Herodotus 1.130 that Cyrus spared the conquered Astyages and kept him with him till he died, and the story in Ctesias (frags. 9, 9a) that Cyrus honored the vanquished Astyages as a father, married his daughter, and made him ruler of the Barcanians in eastern Iran.

In sum, the differences between Xenophon's account in the *Cyropaedia* and the narrative of Herodotus are not as great as is commonly made out. In Xenophon's pages Cyrus has effectively staged a coup against Cyaxares, although it is never called that. He has usurped command of the Medes against the will of the Median king.

Xenophon attributes this transfer of power to the voluntary act of the Medes, who recognized the manifest excellence of Cyrus in contrast to the lassitude of Cyaxares. These exceptional qualities of Cyrus, by which he attracts followers and wins their loyalty and devotion, call to mind Xenophon's description of the younger Cyrus in the *Anabasis* encomium (1.9 passim), and the self-indulgence and weakness of Cyaxares find their parallel in the younger Cyrus' low estimation of his brother Artaxerxes. There is a suggestive parallelism between the situation of the elder Cyrus, who gradually wrests power from his overlord, and that of the younger Cyrus, who means to take the place of his brother. It is easy to see how an explanation of Cyrus' acquisition of power along the lines of the story in Xenophon might have proved useful to the rebel prince. He would have cited his superior virtue as legitimation for his attempt on the throne, pointing to the precedent of Cyrus the Great.[68] He may even have expressed the hope that his brother's forces would come over to him and that no fighting would be necessary.[69] In this instance, as in the previous one, the possibility exists that Xenophon's account of the career of Cyrus the Great has been colored by the claims of the younger Cyrus in 401.

The third major historical crux involves the death of Cyrus. In Herodotus' pages Cyrus dies a sudden and violent death in battle against the Massagetae. His body is captured, and the bloodthirsty nomad queen sticks his head in a sack of blood and taunts him (1.214). All too often it is forgotten that Herodotus goes on to say: "Many stories are related of Cyrus's death; this, that I have told, is the worthiest of credence."[70]

The *Cyropaedia* and History / 83

The final pages of the *Cyropaedia* furnish a very different account. Cyrus, now far advanced in years, has returned to the Persian homeland. A dream informs him that he is soon to die, and shortly thereafter he becomes weak and bedridden. Summoning his sons, his friends, and the Persian officials, he proclaims his last will and testament. Cambyses, the elder son, is to be king; Tanaoxares is to receive the satrapies of Media, Armenia, and Cadusia. Both are urged to love each other and to treat all men fairly. He also gives instructions for his burial (8.7).

Much of the content of Cyrus' deathbed oration is invented by Xenophon. Cyrus' declaration that he has always avoided hubris, knowing that misfortune could strike at any time and that no man can be truly accounted blessed until he is dead (8.7.7–8), is a thoroughly Greek sentiment which calls to mind the lecture of Solon to Croesus in Herodotus 1.30–33. His discourse on the immortality of the soul (8.7.17–22) is reminiscent of the speeches of Socrates in Plato's *Apology* and *Phaedo*.

But the historical framework of the scene is manifestly not the invention of Xenophon. There is a strikingly similar account of the last moments of Cyrus in Ctesias' *Persica* (frag. 9). Here Cyrus is wounded in battle against the Derbici, an obscure central Asian people. He is carried back to his camp, where he lingers for several days. Before dying he must have summoned his friends and family, for he appoints Cambyses to succeed him as king and makes the younger son, Tanyoxarkes, master of Bactria, Choramnia, Parthia, and Carmania. He urges his friends and family to show love for one another, praying for blessings on those who abide in mutual good fellowship and cursing those who foment trouble.

It is clear that Xenophon has drawn upon either Ctesias or the tradition from which Ctesias derived.[71] Both have a deathbed scene in which the moribund monarch summons his family and associates in order to deliver his last will and testament. Both refer to the younger son by an essentially identical name Tanaoxares or Tanyoxarkes, whereas he is known in other sources by some variant of Persian Bardiya;[72] and in both accounts this son is given a command comprising several regions in central Asia. In both versions Cyrus urges concord upon those who survive him, and he dies in the presence of his family and friends. If the full text of Ctesias' account of this event had survived, rather than Photius' brief epitome, it might be possible to point to further correspondences.

Thus it appears that Xenophon had a legitimate source for his version of the death of Cyrus, a version which contradicts the supposedly historical version of Herodotus. Herodotus admitted that numerous other accounts of the death of Cyrus were in circulation, and this will have been one of them.

Any decision as to which version is to be preferred must take into account an additional factor, the tomb of Cyrus. In Xenophon's dramatic deathbed scene, Cyrus discusses arrangements for his burial. It is known that Cyrus was buried in a stately tomb at Pasargadae.[73] This tomb was visited and restored by Alexander the Great and is described by the historians of that era. From their reports it is clear that the structure was not a cenotaph, but rather housed the body of Cyrus.[74] This circumstance can easily be accounted for by Xenophon's and Ctesias' versions of the death of Cyrus; Xenophon has him expire in Persia, and Ctesias maintains that Cambyses had the body of Cyrus returned from the land of the Derbici to Persia, where it was buried (frag. 13). But it is hard to reconcile the existence of the tomb of Cyrus at Pasargadae with Herodotus' account, in which Cyrus' body is captured and dismembered by the vengeful Massagetae.

There is yet another reason for believing in an ultimate Iranian origin for Xenophon's account of the passing of Cyrus. Christensen has shown that the overall conception of Xenophon's account of the death of Cyrus is firmly rooted in Iranian tradition. In the *Shahnama* of Ferdowsi, which preserves the cultural concepts and story patterns of ancient Iranian oral tradition, the life of the ideal king ends with a scene in which the dying king summons family, friends, and advisers, arranges the succession, makes known his last wishes, and communicates to his successors a political testament. The conclusion of the *Cyropaedia* fits this mold precisely.[75]

This survey is not an attempt to argue for the historicity of the *Cyropaedia* as a whole. Certain episodes, as well as numerous conversations, speeches, and private encounters, must have been invented by Xenophon, for there could have been no possible source for such material. However, it should now be acknowledged that, in constructing the historical framework of the *Cyropaedia*, Xenophon had access to a number of credible sources of information—Greek written sources, Greek and barbarian oral tradition, and the example of Persian customs and institutions of his own day. It is clear that the *Cyropaedia* contains a greater quantity of valuable infor-

The *Cyropaedia* and History / 85

mation about Persian history than is generally recognized; and even where one is inclined to doubt the historicity of a given event, it should be conceded that Xenophon may have preserved an authentic Greek or barbarian tradition—however false or distorted—about Persian history.

So far, the discussion has been concerned primarily with the historical framework of the *Cyropaedia*. It remains to be demonstrated that even in the didactic heart of the work, where the patently Greek elements of thought, speech, and values are most prevalent, there is a strong Persian element. Not only does Xenophon provide much valuable information about Persian culture and institutions, but, what is of even greater significance, in his own thinking on a wide range of topics Xenophon has been influenced by Persian concepts.

The basic structure of the *Cyropaedia* reveals the central didactic concerns of the work. Book 1, which relates the education (in the fullest sense) of the young Cyrus, begins with the formal Persian *paideia* or program of training for boys; follows Cyrus through a youthful sojourn in Media, where he acquires experience and knowledge of many things; and culminates in a lengthy dialogue in which Cyrus is given instruction in the general's craft by his father, Cambyses.[76] From 2.1.1 through 7.5.36 the focus is Cyrus' campaigns and the problems of military command; 7.5.37 through 8.7 are concerned with the administration of empire.[77] Thus the primary themes of the *Cyropaedia* are education, military command, and administration of an empire.[78]

A substantial body of evidence indicates that Xenophon was influenced by Persian conceptions in these three areas. A clear connection can be made in the matter of education. In the *Anabasis*, Xenophon begins his encomium of the younger Cyrus with a description of his education (1.9.2–6). This passage is, in a literal sense, a *Cyropaedia*; that is, it concerns the education of Cyrus and therefore prefigures the title and content of the *Cyropaedia*. There are clear parallels between the program of education of the younger Cyrus in the *Anabasis* and that of the elder Cyrus in the *Cyropaedia* (1.2.2–12). Both involve education of boys in the vicinity of the royal court. It is, in large part, a moral education,[79] emphasizing instruction by observation of examples. Stress is placed on moderation, modesty, and obedience. The boys and youths are trained in the use of bow and javelin, they master horsemanship (although Cyrus in the *Cyropaedia* must learn this skill in Media, since the Persians have not yet taken up riding), and they hone their martial skills on the hunt. Since there is no reason to doubt that the account in the *Anabasis* is authentic—that is, an accurate report of what Cyrus or some other noble Persian told Xenophon—then to the extent that the education of the elder Cyrus in the *Cyropaedia* is similar, it is permeated by authentic Persian educational concepts. Moreover, in his description of the Persian educational system in the *Cyropaedia*, Xenophon speaks throughout in the present tense, indicating that the system was still in force in his time.

Herodotus provides confirmation of certain aspects of the educational program described in the *Cyropaedia*. He says that Persian boys were taught three things only: to ride, to shoot, and to tell the truth (1.136). Perhaps one should not take "only" too literally, since this statement is an apothegm designed to gain force from the starkness of the expression. But there is significance in the fact that Herodotus describes an education which has two major components, one military and the other ethical. This is precisely the situation described in the *Cyropaedia*.

Strabo, who also describes the Persian educational program (15.3.18), appears to derive some of his information from Herodotus and Xenophon, but he has other sources as well.[80] Again the training is partly military (riding and shooting, with practice acquired on the hunt) and partly ethical (instruction in truth-telling and endurance). As in the *Cyropaedia* (1.2.5), the boys assemble early in the morning and are divided into companies. But Strabo introduces several new elements. The boys are instructed by wise men who incorporate myth and song into the program.[81] They are also taught agricultural skills, the planting of trees and the gathering and utilization of plant products. This report calls to mind *Oeconomicus* 4, where Xenophon reports on the Persian king's attention to agricultural matters on his estates and in the provinces and concludes with the famous story of the younger Cyrus' tree-planting activities in his paradise at Sardis.[82]

In sum, Herodotus and Strabo both seem to describe a mode of education which, in its emphasis on ethical and military training, is much like that of the *Cyropaedia*. If these three descriptions do not correspond in every particular, they are all infused with a similar spirit.

It has often been claimed that the allegedly Persian *paideia* of the *Cyropaedia* is modeled on that of Sparta. But a comparison of *Cyropaedia* 1.2 with Xenophon's treatment of Spartan education in his treatise the *Constitution of the Lacedaemonians* does not support this view. Higgins points out that, unlike the Spartan system of education, the Persian system is open to all.[83] Furthermore, military training is neither the sole nor the main object of the Persian system, and, insofar as it was concerned to inculcate justice in its pupils, it would not condone the thievery which was encouraged in the Spartan *agogē*. In general, the openness of the *paideia* of the *Cyropaedia* is foreign to the Spartan temperament. Therefore, there are no cogent reasons for doubting that the description of the Persian educational system in the *Cyropaedia*—a system which Xenophon is obviously recommending to his readers—reflects actual Persian practice.[84]

Military science is another of Xenophon's significant concerns in the *Cyropaedia*, and here one naturally presumes that much of the didactic material in the *Cyropaedia* is based on Xenophon's own ample military experience. Some of this experience was gained in the service of Persian Cyrus, some in fighting against Persian forces. Rahe has argued convincingly that Xenophon learned from the younger Cyrus on the plains of Asia about the coordinated use of cavalry and heavy infantry.[85] Such tactics play a crucial role in Xenophon's reconstructions of the elder Cyrus' battles in the *Cyropaedia*. Xenophon includes among the weapons of a Persian ephebe a short slashing sword (*kopis*) and two stout javelins (*palta*), one to throw, the other to be used for self-defense (*Cyr.* 1.2.9). At the battle of Cunaxa the younger Cyrus had been armed with two *palta* (*Anabasis* 1.8.3). Xenophon had also witnessed a cavalry skirmish in Asia Minor in which the Persian cornel-wood *palta* proved superior to Greek spears (*dorata*; *Hellenica* 3.4.14). It is probably as a consequence of this experience that, in the treatise *On Horsemanship*, he recommends the use of Persian offensive armament to the Greek cavalryman (12.11–12).[86] Thus it seems clear that, in the military sphere, Xenophon was influenced to some degree by Persian practice.

Finally, there is the problem of imperial rule. The *Cyropaedia*, as was noted earlier, is not about government of a *polis* but about administration of an empire. It should be apparent that, when it came to the problems of running an empire, the Persian historical experience was infinitely more relevant than the situation in Greece, and that Xenophon very likely took some of his ideas on this subject from Persian practice. Xenophon claims on more than one occasion that many of the administrative features which he attributes to the elder Cyrus were still in effect in the fourth century.[87] At the beginning of book 8 he gives a detailed exposition of Cyrus' comprehensive provisions for the administration of his newly conquered empire, concluding with an explicit declaration to the effect that these institutions had been preserved unchanged to his own day (8.1.7):

ὡς δ' ἐν τῷ λόγῳ δεδήλωται Κῦρος καταστησάμενος εἰς τὸ διαφυλάττειν αὑτῷ τε καὶ Πέρσαις τὴν ἀρχήν, ταὐτὰ καὶ οἱ μετ' ἐκεῖνον βασιλεῖς νόμιμα ἔτι καὶ νῦν διατελοῦσι ποιοῦντες.

And the institutions which Cyrus inaugurated as a means of securing the Kingdom permanently to himself and the Persians, as has been set forth in the foregoing narrative, these the succeeding kings have preserved unchanged even to this day.

Many of the administrative provisions found in the *Cyropaedia* can be confirmed elsewhere.[88] Xenophon notes that no satraps were sent to Cilicia, Cyprus, or Paphlagonia because these countries had voluntarily gone over to him (*Cyr.* 8.6.8). This statement finds confirmation in Darius' Behistun inscription, which includes none of these places in the list of subject countries.[89] In a memorable scene early in the *Cyropaedia*, the boy Cyrus protests against the power of Sacas, cupbearer to his grandfather Astyages, the Median king (*Cyr.* 1.3.8). The political importance of the royal cupbearer at the Iranian court is attested in the biblical book of Nehemiah. As royal cupbearer Nehemiah was able to persuade the Persian king to entrust him with the task of rebuilding Jerusalem (Nehemiah 2:1–6).[90]

A number of the assertions about Persian provincial administration in the *Cyropaedia* have parallels in chapter 4 of the *Oeconomicus*. Both works state that the governor of each region is required to provide maintenance for the troops in his district (*Cyr.* 8.6.3, *Oec.* 4.5). The *pistoi* or trusted agents sent out to inspect the civil and military condition of the provinces (*Oec.* 4.8) must be equivalent to the *ephodoi* or circuit commissioners who go out annually with an army and attend to problems in the provinces (*Cyr.* 8.6.16). The separation of civil and military commands and the civil governor's sphere of duties (*Oec.* 4.9) correspond to the arrangements of the elder Cyrus (*Cyr.* 8.6.1, 8.6,3, and 8.6.9). This separation of powers enables the civil and military officials to watch over and inform on each other (*Cyr.* 8.6.1, *Oec.* 4.10). The king's solicitude for the care and cultivation of paradises (*Oec.* 4.13) is paralleled by Cyrus' instructions to his satraps to keep such paradises (*Cyr.* 8.6.12). Insofar as *Oeconomicus* 4 has proved to be a reliable source of information about the situation in the Persian Empire,[91] it provides confirmation of those administrative provisions which are also found in the *Cyropaedia*.

A solid body of evidence seems to indicate that, as regards the three primary didactic topics of the *Cyropaedia*—education, military command, imperial administration—Xenophon has taken over general concepts and specific practices from Persia. The *Cyropaedia* is also a valuable source of information on other features of Persian civilization. Xenophon's purpose in reporting this information may at times be didactic; at other times he may simply be catering to the Greek reading public's curiosity about Persia.[92]

Many of the Persian practices described by Xenophon in the *Cyropaedia* find confirmation in Herodotus or other written sources. Both Xenophon and Herodotus maintain that the Persians do not indulge certain bodily functions in public (*Cyr.* 1.2.16; cf. Herodotus 1.122); that men of comparable status greet and take leave of each other by means of a kiss on the lips (*Cyr.* 1.4.27; cf. Herodotus 1.134); that the Persians regarded Cyrus as a father (*Cyr.* 8.1.1, 44; cf. Herodotus 3.89); that the Persians adopted Median dress (*Cyr.* 8.1.40; cf. Herodotus 1.135); and that the Persians had a postal relay system to provide rapid communications throughout the empire (*Cyr.* 8.6.18; cf. Herodotus 1.98).[93] In one passage Xenophon describes "shoes of such a form that without being detected the wearer can easily put something into the soles so as to make him look taller than he is" (8.1.41) and later describes a public appearance of Cyrus in curious terms that seem to hint at the use of this device (8.3.14). Strabo may be referring to such "elevator shoes" when he says that Persian leaders wear a *hypodēma koilon diploun*—"hollow double shoe" (15.3.19).

Boyce has recently discussed Xenophon's treatment of Persian religion in the *Cyropaedia* and the *Anabasis*.[94] She points to many facets of religion and conduct in the two works which reflect authentic Zoroastrian precepts—the keeping of oaths, the emphasis on impartial justice, the concern for purity, a single daily meal, respect for physical labor and hardihood, the pitching of tents to face east, the functions of the Magi, various religious observances and sacrifices,[95] festivities and communal meals after sacrifices, the particular deities who are invoked (in their Greek equivalencies), and the absence of temple worship. Boyce concludes that Xenophon is a reliable observer and reporter of Zoroastrian practices.

These examples, while far from exhaustive, provide ample proof that Xenophon has incorporated in the *Cyropaedia* a large quantity of valid information about Persian culture and institutions, and the student of ancient Iran would be foolish to neglect it or to reject it out of hand. It should now be apparent that any consideration of Xenophon's sources of information and purpose in composing the *Cyropaedia* must take into account the quantity and quality of information it contains about Persia. There is simply too much good information for it to be mere cosmetic adornment. This important point is too often denied by commentators who regard the Persian setting of the *Cyropaedia* as little more than a facade for a Greek discourse. The real question is not whether the *Cyropaedia* is Greek or Persian in inspiration, but the more subtle issue of where the Persian matter ends and the Greek begins. Xenophon has been influenced in his thinking on a wide range of topics by Persian ideas and Persian practices, and, in particular, he has created an ideal of education, military command, and government which is a personal synthesis of Greek and Persian concepts.[96] Thus the Persian context is entirely fitting, an acknowledgment of Xenophon's debts and a measure of his respect for Persia.[97]

How did Xenophon conceive of the role of the factual and historical elements in the *Cyropaedia*? Any formulation of his conception of his mission must necessarily be tentative. But an understanding of the role of Persia in the *Cyropaedia* points the way. In considering this issue it is important to recognize that, whereas people in the modern world tend to treat the boundary between truth and fiction as absolute, as clearly separating two different and irreconcilable orders of things, this boundary was a shifting and permeable one for the people of antiquity.[98] Xenophon's situation might be compared to that of two modern writers who are usually classified as historical novelists. Both Robert Graves and Gore Vidal have written stories set in the ancient world, and each has on occasion protested against the classification of these works as fiction. Each insists in his own way that, although he is not a professional historian, his work is based on historical research and represents a reconstruction of the past.⁹⁹ Obviously Xenophon lacked the self-awareness of these modern writers, and the genres of history and novel were only in process of formation in his time. But he might have seen himself in a similar light and have claimed that the *Cyropaedia* offered both particular truths to be garnered from the record of the past and the higher truths which he superimposed by artistic license.

In contrast to the main body of the *Cyropaedia*, which manifests Xenophon's respect and positive feelings toward Persia, the so-called epilogue (8.8) is the most extreme expression of hatred and hostility toward Persia in the Xenophontic corpus. In this epilogue the claim is made that, after the death of the elder Cyrus, everything began to deteriorate. As a result, in contemporary Persia all the admirable old customs and values have been debased, corrupted, and perverted, and the Persians of the present day are far inferior to their ancestors. So abrupt is the change of tone, so awkward the sudden shift in attitude, that many have been led to question whether this postscript could have been written by the same person who produced the rest of the *Cyropaedia*. Consequently, no study of Xenophon's attitudes toward Persia can be complete without a reconsideration of the authenticity of the epilogue.

In the nineteenth century classical scholars tended, for the most part, to deny the authenticity of the epilogue. The most succinct expression of their view comes from H. A. Holden: "It is not easy to comprehend how Xenophon, after rounding off so well his epic narrative, could have so deliberately defeated his own object, by representing the institutions which their heroic founder had spent his life in establishing, as destitute of all organic bond of cohesion, and falling to pieces on removal of his personal influence."¹⁰⁰ In other words, the epilogue undercuts the previous eight books of the *Cyropaedia*, depriving the bulk of the work of significance and value. These scholars pointed to a number of instances in which the epilogue flatly contradicts the testimony of the main body of the work. Some thought the epilogue to be the work of an interpolator; others entertained the possibility that Xenophon added it to the text at a later time, either because he had by then become hostile to Persia¹⁰¹ or because public outrage at praise of the Persian foe compelled him to write a retraction.

More recent scholarship has inclined toward acceptance of the epilogue as the authentic work of Xenophon and as an organic part of the whole work, not a later addition.[102] The most influential formulation of this position has been that of Delebecque,[103] who makes the following points:

1. The occasional contradictions in detail between the main body of the text and the epilogue are only to be expected in a work of this length.

2. Xenophon had already prepared the way for the final section on contemporary Persia. At frequent intervals in the text he points out that "still today"—*eti kai nun*—such and such a custom or institution prevails in the Persian Empire.

3. The epilogue has all the marks of Xenophon's style and personality.

4. There is an analogy with Xenophon's *Constitution of the Lacedaemonians*, in which, after praising the Spartan system as established by Lycurgus, Xenophon concludes with an indictment of the degeneration of modern-day Sparta.

5. The epilogue is essential. Xenophon had to anticipate the objection that the Persian system which he had so lavishly praised was now, in the mid-fourth century, in a serious state of decline. Xenophon countered that the decline was due to the faulty character of the present-day Persian king and ruling class, not to the institutions themselves as established by Cyrus.

It will be argued here that Delebecque is mistaken on all five points and that the epilogue cannot be an original and intrinsic part of the *Cyropaedia*.

In the first place, his claim that one should not be surprised by occasional contradictions in detail in a work of this length is dubious. These are not minor inconsistencies, but flagrant contradictions of points made in the main body of the text. For instance, in 1.2.16 Xenophon says, in reference to the Persians' habit of exercising in order to work off bodily moisture and food: καὶ νῦν δ' ἔτι ἐμμένει μαρτύρια καὶ τῆς μετρίας διαίτης αὐτῶν καὶ τοῦ ἐκπονεῖσθαι τὴν δίαιταν—"There remains even unto this day evidence of their moderate fare and of their working off by exercise what they eat." But in the epilogue this information is flatly contradicted (8.8.8): νῦν δὲ . . . τὸ δ' ἐκπονεῖν οὐδαμοῦ ἐπιτηδεύεται—"But now ... they never give themselves the trouble to work off the moisture in some other direction." In 8.1.34–36 Xenophon describes how Cyrus trained his retinue for war by taking them on the hunt. He concludes by saying: καὶ νῦν δ᾽ ἔτι βασιλεὺς καὶ οἱ ἄλλοι οἱ περὶ βασιλέα ταῦτα ποιοῦντες διατελοῦσιν—"And even to this day the king and the rest that make up his retinue continue to engage in the same sport." But the epilogue asserts that, although this was the case in the past, ἐπεὶ δὲ Ἀρταξέρξης ὁ βασιλεὺς καὶ οἱ σὺν αὐτῷ ἥττους τοῦ οἴνου ἐγένοντο, οὐκέτι ὁμοίως οὔτ᾽ αὐτοὶ ἐξῆσαν οὔτε τοὺς ἄλλους ἐξῆγον ἐπὶ τὰς θήρας—"But since Artaxerxes and his court became the victims of wine, they have neither gone out themselves in the old way nor taken the others out hunting" (8.8.12).

Other flagrant contradictions between the epilogue and the main body of the text are to be found.[104] It is hard to believe that these are mere oversights, the more so since no such striking internal contradictions surface within the body of the work. All the discrepancies are clustered in the handful of pages which constitute the epilogue. And the contradictions most frequently concern passages in which Xenophon has made a special point of insisting that *eti kai nun*— "and still today"—these practices are maintained in contemporary Persia. If the phrase *eti kai nun* were not there, one might argue that there is no inherent contradiction, but rather a contrast between the virtuous practices of Old Persia and the corruption of the fourth century. However, the presence of *eti kai nun* vitiates this possibility. The contradictions are there, they are glaring, and they are unparalleled elsewhere in the work. They cannot be glossed over.

Delebecque boldly maintains that these very *eti kai nun* passages prove that Xenophon was thinking about the Persia of his own day and paving the way for the epilogue. But if this were the signal function of these passages, it would only make the fact that they are frequently in conflict with the epilogue more embarrassing. In fact the *eti kai nun* passages are equivalent in function to the epilogue and obviate the need for the latter. They constitute Xenophon's reflection on the connections between Old Persia and the empire of his own day. Taken as a whole, they amount to a proclamation that many of the fine old customs and institutions of Cyrus' Persia were maintained into the fourth century.

Next, Delebecque contends that the epilogue has all the marks of

Xenophon's style and personality. Even if, for the sake of argument, one ignores the large degree of subjectivity inherent in considerations of matters such as style and personality, there are still substantial grounds for disagreement with Delebecque's assertion.[105] The tone of the epilogue is sarcastic, abusive, sometimes even vulgar; it stoops to gratuitous insults and puerile humor, and it takes perverse delight in demonstrating how the Persians have fallen from their former greatness, thus reflecting the intense hostility of the writer toward Persia. Furthermore, much of the censure is leveled against an ambiguous "they," whom one must assume to be Persians in general. The sarcasm and the undignified tone of the criticism are not typical of Xenophon. And there is no other place in the extant corpus of Xenophon's writings where the author wallows in hatred for the Persian people. In the *Anabasis* and *Agesilaus* his anger or scorn is reserved for the Persian king and a handful of nobles.

It is just this fact—that the abuse of the epilogue is directed, in large part, against all Persians—that is most disturbing. One would have expected Xenophon to attribute the decline of contemporary Persia to the personal failings of the king himself.[106] For it cannot be the institutions and values of Old Persia which were at fault. The entire *Cyropaedia* is a testament to that. Surely, if all Xenophon was interested in and regarded as the key to Cyrus' success was the individual personality of the latter, he would not have spent so much time describing the customs and institutions which Cyrus had established.[107] An earlier passage in book 8 offers a glimpse of the approach Xenophon would probably have chosen if he had sought to criticize contemporary Persia. He has just finished reporting that "the institutions which Cyrus inaugurated as a means of securing the kingdom permanently to himself and the Persians, as has been set forth in the foregoing narrative, these the succeeding kings have preserved unchanged even to this day" (8.1.7). He continues: "And it is the same with these as with everything else: whenever the officer in charge is better, the administration of the institutions is purer; but when he is worse, the administration is more corrupt" (8.1.8).[108] Here Xenophon praises the institutions of Persia and only raises the possibility that the character of a leader can affect their efficacy. It is clear from this passage that Xenophon, if he were going to complain about the decline of the Persia of his day, would have laid the blame at the feet of the current Persian king. This is precisely what he does in the *Agesilaus* (8.6–9.5). Furthermore,

Xenophon, who had been to Mesopotamia and back, and had fought alongside, as well as against, Persians for a number of years, knew that the Persians were better and more formidable than the author of the epilogue is willing to concede.[109] Delebecque is also mistaken in claiming that the epilogue allows Xenophon to defend the institutions described in the main body of the *Cyropaedia* against the objections of contemporary Greeks by restricting his criticism to the Persian king and his entourage. This is precisely what the author of the epilogue has not done. Xenophon had already shown his willingness to confront contemporary antibarbarian prejudices by setting his treatise on government in Old Persia, since this necessarily entailed a glorification of that same Persia.

Finally, there is the oft-cited parallel with the so-called epilogue to Xenophon's treatise on the *Constitution of the Lacedaemonians*. This epilogue is also at variance with the rest of its text, containing harsh criticisms of Sparta, which is praised throughout the rest of the work.[110] However, the epilogue of the *Constitution* is as much an object of dispute as the epilogue of the *Cyropaedia*. It appears in all manuscripts as the next-to-last, rather than the last, chapter. It may be out of place, but there is no agreement about where it actually belongs.[111] In the second place, the epilogue of the *Cyropaedia*, insofar as it undercuts a clear and carefully structured work, creates a more disturbing problem than the epilogue of the *Constitution*, for the latter is an ill-organized, incomplete, and in many ways perplexing work. Moreover, because of the many explicit *eti kai nun* passages in the *Cyropaedia*, its epilogue creates more inescapable contradictions with the main body of the work than does the epilogue of the *Constitution*.

All the arguments about the date of the *Constitution*'s composition, the meaning of the work, and the position of the epilogue in the manuscripts are highly subjective. The work is still too poorly understood and too seriously in dispute for much to be said with certainty. Ultimately the epilogue of the *Constitution* contributes little to the resolution of the problems surrounding the epilogue of the *Cyropaedia*. Indeed, the strongest parallel between the two epilogues is that both are claimed by some to be late additions or interpolations—hardly an argument for authenticity. It is possible that both are a product of the tendency of a later age to supplement or improve upon Xenophon.

In sum, each of the five points advanced by Delebecque to prove the authenticity of the epilogue of the *Cyropaedia* and to see it as an integral part of the work is open to serious question. There is one further consideration which raises doubts about the authenticity of the epilogue. It has long been acknowledged that Plato, in book 3 of the *Laws*, is probably reacting to Xenophon's *Cyropaedia*. As will be argued in the appendix to this chapter, the relationship between that section of the *Laws* and the *Cyropaedia* is even greater than hitherto realized. Xenophon had described a covenant habitually contracted between Persian kings and people wherein the king pledges to preserve the laws of the Persians, while the people promise to remain loyal to the king (*Cyr.* 8.5.24–27). In *Laws* 3.697C–698A Plato attributes the decline of Persia to the excessive despotism of the kings, which destroyed the bonds of friendliness and fellowship in the state. This should be seen as a rejoinder to Xenophon. Apparently Plato had read this passage of the *Cyropaedia* and was so exasperated by Xenophon's insistence that many admirable features of Cyrus' program, including this covenant between king and people, were maintained into the fourth century, that he felt compelled to respond and to demonstrate the perversion of that idyllic state of affairs reported by Xenophon. Yet, if Plato's text of the *Cyropaedia* had contained the epilogue which appears in our manuscripts, there would have been no need for a rebuttal in the *Laws*. For the epilogue accomplishes precisely the same purpose, pointing up the corruption of the old Persian institutions which had been panegyrized in the main body of the *Cyropaedia*. It follows that the epilogue could not have formed part of the edition of the *Cyropaedia* which came into Plato's possession.

It seems clear, from this reexamination of all the issues surrounding the authenticity of the epilogue, that it could not have been an original and integral part of the *Cyropaedia*. It is possible that Xenophon added it at a later time. But it is more likely that the epilogue was written by someone who, like Plato, was provoked by the idealization and glorification of Persia in the *Cyropaedia*.[112]

However, the most important gain for the purposes of the present study is the discovery that the epilogue—the most extreme example of hostility and hatred for Persia in the Xenophontic corpus—either is not by Xenophon at all or is a late and tendentious addition. The *Cyropaedia*, minus the discredited epilogue, is extraordinary among fourth-century Greek writings precisely because

Appendix / 97

of its highly sympathetic stance toward the Persian Empire, and it must be regarded as the major document for an evaluation of Xenophon's attitude toward Persia.

APPENDIX
Plato and the *Cyropaedia*

Although scholars from antiquity to the present day have recognized that Plato, in a famous passage in the *Laws*, is leveling criticism at the *Cyropaedia* of Xenophon, the extent of his reaction to the *Cyropaedia* has not been fully appreciated. The oft-cited passage is *Laws* 3.694C:

μαντεύομαι δὴ νῦν περί γε Κύρου τὰ μὲν ἄλλ' αὐτὸν στρατηγόν τε ἀγαθὸν εἶναι καὶ φιλόπολιν, παιδείας δὲ ὀρθῆς οὐχ ἧφθαι τὸ παράπαν οἰκονομίᾳ τε οὐδὲν τὸν νοῦν προσεσχηκέναι.

Respecting Cyrus, then, I thus divine; that in other respects he was a good general, and a lover of his country, but that he had not laid hold at all of a correct education, nor applied his mind to the regulation of his household.[113]

This is tantamount to a rejection of the portrait of Cyrus presented in the *Cyropaedia*, which focuses, above all else, on Cyrus' experiences and accomplishments in the spheres of education, military command, and administration of empire. While Plato does not mention Xenophon by name, it is hard to resist the conclusion that this rebuke, which juxtaposes the figure of Cyrus and the issues of education and administration, is aimed directly at Xenophon and the *Cyropaedia*.[114] To prove his point, Plato proceeds to explain that Cyrus' mistake was to have his sons brought up by women and eunuchs in the harem and that this practice has been responsible for the degeneracy of subsequent Persian kings (*Laws* 3.694D–695E).

Diogenes Laertius interpreted the passage to mean that Plato was denouncing the *Cyropaedia* as a fiction, because the real Cyrus did not answer to Xenophon's description of him.[115] If so, it is interesting to note that for Plato, at least, the *Cyropaedia* was intended to be historical in some sense.[116] And he is sufficiently aroused by what he has read in the *Cyropaedia* to feel the need to issue a written protest.

But the influence of the *Cyropaedia* upon Plato is still more extensive. The passage in *Laws* 3 starts from a surprising premise. Plato has been discussing the two mother-forms of constitution, monarchy and democracy, and notes that Persia represents the former carried to an extreme, Athens the latter. His own feeling is that it is best for a polity to partake of both forms in a mixed type of constitution. He then proceeds to say:

> When the Persians, under Cyrus, maintained the due balance between slavery and freedom, they became, first of all, free themselves, and, after that, masters of many others. For when the rulers gave a share of freedom to their subjects and advanced them to a position of equality, the soldiers were more friendly towards their officers and showed their devotion in times of danger; and if there was any wise man amongst them, able to give counsel, since the king was not jealous but allowed free speech and respected those who could help at all by their counsel,—such a man had the opportunity of contributing to the common stock the fruit of his wisdom. Consequently, at that time all their affairs made progress, owing to their freedom, friendliness and mutual interchange of reason. (694A–B)

Where did Plato get this conception of an Old Persia in which the monarch allowed his subjects a due measure of freedom and free speech, thereby engendering an atmosphere of friendliness and cooperation in the exercise of empire? The most likely source is the *Cyropaedia*. In Xenophon's picture of the Persia of Cyrus' father, Cambyses, the king's authority is limited by the existence of an assembly (*koinon*), a council of elders, and a body of peers (*homotimoi*; 1.5.4–5). After he has conquered an empire, Cyrus is still anxious to secure the approval of his friends and supporters in creating the institutions of empire (7.5.37, 71). He encourages those around him to offer their advice (7.5.47). He is anxious to secure the best people to serve under him and is not afraid to delegate power and responsibility (8.1.10, 12, 14–15, 43). Potential rivals are won over to friendship by generosity and attentions, rather than summarily disposed of (8.1.48–2.26). Moreover, he corrects his subordinates by example rather than by fiat (7.5.85; 8.1.12, 21–33). When he returns to Persia, his father, Cambyses, arranges a covenant between Cyrus and the Persian people, whereby Cyrus pledges to preserve the constitution and act in the public interest, while the Persians promise to maintain the monarchy and to serve the ruler loyally (8.5.24–25).

The *Cyropaedia*'s portrayal of Persian institutions, which is so much at variance with stereotypical Greek conceptions of Persian absolute despotism, has obvious affinities with the depiction of Old Persia in Plato's *Laws*.[117] It is a reasonable inference that Plato's conception of the Persia of Cyrus as a place where a proper balance had been struck between monarchy and democracy is derived from the *Cyropaedia*. If not, then the Platonic passage can be taken as confirmation of the independent existence of the tradition about Old Persia found in the *Cyropaedia*.

There is a third, equally striking, connection between Plato's *Laws* and

Appendix / 99

Xenophon's *Cyropaedia*. In an episode described toward the end of the *Cyropaedia*, Cyrus has returned to Persia after his extraordinary string of conquests. Cambyses assembles the Persian elders and magistrates in Cyrus' presence, recalls the great things which have been achieved through the cooperation of Cyrus and the Persians, and urges continued cooperation in the future.

> If, therefore, you continue to be of the same mind also in the future, you will be the cause of much good to each other. But, Cyrus, if you on your part become puffed up by your present successes and attempt to govern the Persians as you do those other nations, with a view to self-aggrandizement, or if you, fellow-citizens, become jealous of his power and attempt to depose him from his sovereignty, be sure that you will hinder one another from receiving much good. And that this may not befall you, but the good, it seems best to me for you to perform a common sacrifice and to make a covenant, first calling the gods to witness. You, Cyrus, on your part, must covenant that if any one sets hostile foot in Persia or attempts to subvert the Persian constitution, you will come to her aid with all your strength; and you, Persians, on your part, are to covenant that if any one of his subjects attempts to revolt, you will come to your own rescue as well as Cyrus's in whatsoever way he may call upon you. . . . And as they then covenanted, with the gods as their witnesses, so the Persians and their king still continue to this day to act toward one another.
> (8.5.24–27)

Most commentators feel that this covenant between Cyrus and the Persians is an anachronism, for it bears a very strong resemblance to the covenant made at intervals between the Spartan king and the city of Sparta, as described in Xenophon's *Constitution of the Lacedaemonians* (15). On the other hand, the compact—*mithra*—is a distinctive feature of Iranian culture and the Zoroastrian religion, and the god Mithra claims the right to bestow kingship.

Setting aside the question of historicity, what matters in the present context is Plato's reaction to this passage. When he summarizes the reasons for the degeneration of Persia from the earlier ideal mixture of monarchy and democracy, he says:

> We find that they grew still worse, the reason being, as we say, that by robbing the commons unduly of their liberty and introducing despotism in excess, they destroyed in the state the bonds of friendliness and fellowship. And when these are destroyed, the policy of the rulers no longer consults for the good of the subjects and the commons, but solely for the maintenance of their own power; . . . and

thus they both hate and are hated with a fierce and ruthless hatred. And when they come to need the commons, to fight in their support, they find in them no patriotism or readiness to endanger their lives in battle. . . . (*Laws* 3.697C–E)

Plato is saying that the Persian kings have succumbed to the very temptation against which Cambyses had warned Cyrus—giving in to greed and despotism—and as a result they have lost the goodwill and cooperation of their people. Plato seems to be responding directly to the passage of the *Cyropaedia* quoted above. He is asserting that the arrangement guaranteed by the compact between king and people, which Xenophon insists was renewed into his own day, has broken down.

5

The King's Eye

Xenophon claimed to be an expert on Persian affairs, and his works have served as a major source of information for the history, culture, and institutions of the Persian Empire of the sixth, fifth, and fourth centuries. But how much did Xenophon really know about the Persian Empire? The previous chapter discussed the problems surrounding the historicity of the *Cyropaedia* and the authenticity of its information about Persia and concluded that the work contains much valuable information about Persian history and civilization. This chapter buttresses those general conclusions through an examination of a passage in the *Cyropaedia* in which Xenophon seems to contradict the testimony of all other surviving Greek sources. The issues involved are complex, and the investigation will raise the broader question of the reliability of Greek sources regarding the institutions of the Persian Empire. This question has great importance insofar as students of the history and institutions of the Achaemenid Empire, for lack of extensive Oriental materials, tend to rely to a large extent on the testimony of the Greek sources.

Cyropaedia 8.2.10–12 is a passage whose implications have not been fully appreciated. The elder Cyrus, the hero of the work, was concerned about his personal security, for he was surrounded at court by many powerful and ambitious nobles, and he determined that the best way to guarantee his own safety was to win their friendship. Xenophon describes the various ways in which Cyrus endeavored to make himself popular. Chief among them was the giving of gifts: "It was Cyrus, therefore, who began the practice of

102 / The King's Eye

lavish giving, and among the kings it continues even to this day" (8.2.7). This is the context for *Cyropaedia* 8.2.10–12:

κατεμάθομεν δὲ ὡς καὶ τοὺς βασιλέως καλουμένους ὀφθαλμοὺς καὶ τὰ βασιλέως ὦτα οὐκ ἄλλως ἐκτήσατο ἢ τῷ δωρεῖσθαί τε καὶ τιμᾶν· τοὺς γὰρ ἀπαγγείλαντας ὅσα καιρὸς αὐτῷ εἴη πεπύσθαι μεγάλως εὐεργετῶν πολλοὺς ἐποίησεν ἀνθρώπους καὶ ὠτακουστεῖν καὶ διοπτεύειν τί ἂν ἀγγείλαντες ὠφελήσειαν βασιλέα. ἐκ τούτου δὴ καὶ πολλοὶ ἐνομίσθησαν βασιλέως ὀφθαλμοὶ καὶ πολλὰ ὦτα. εἰ δέ τις οἴεται ἕνα αἱρετὸν εἶναι ὀφθαλμὸν βασιλεῖ, οὐκ ὀρθῶς οἴεται· ὀλίγα γὰρ εἷς γ᾽ ἂν ἴδοι καὶ εἷς ἀκούσειε· καὶ τοῖς ἄλλοις ὥσπερ ἀμελεῖν ἂν παρηγγελμένον εἴη, εἰ ἑνὶ τοῦτο προστεταγμένον εἴη· πρὸς δὲ καὶ ὅντινα γιγνώσκοιεν ὀφθαλμὸν ὄντα, τοῦτον ἂν εἰδεῖεν ὅτι φυλάττεσθαι δεῖ. ἀλλ᾽ οὐχ οὕτως ἔχει, ἀλλὰ τοῦ φάσκοντος ἀκοῦσαί τι ἢ ἰδεῖν ἄξιον ἐπιμελείας παντὸς βασιλεὺς ἀκούει. οὕτω δὴ πολλὰ μὲν βασιλέως ὦτα, πολλοὶ δ᾽ ὀφθαλμοὶ νομίζονται· καὶ φοβοῦνται πανταχοῦ λέγειν τὰ μὴ σύμφορα βασιλεῖ, ὥσπερ αὐτοῦ ἀκούοντος, καὶ ποιεῖν ἃ μὴ σύμφορα, ὥσπερ αὐτοῦ παρόντος. οὔκουν ὅπως μνησθῆναι ἄν τις ἐτόλμησε πρός τινα περὶ Κύρου φλαῦρόν τι, ἀλλ᾽ ὡς ἐν ὀφθαλμοῖς πᾶσι καὶ ὠσὶ βασιλέως τοῖς ἀεὶ παροῦσιν οὕτως ἕκαστος διέκειτο. τὸ δὲ οὕτω διακεῖσθαι τοὺς ἀνθρώπους πρὸς αὐτὸν ἐγὼ μὲν οὐκ οἶδα ὅ τι ἄν τις αἰτιάσαιτο μᾶλλον ἢ ὅτι μεγάλα ἤθελεν ἀντὶ μικρῶν εὐεργετεῖν.

Moreover, we have discovered that he acquired the so-called "king's eyes" and "king's ears" in no other way than by bestowing presents and honours; for by rewarding liberally those who reported to him whatever it was to his interest to hear, he prompted many men to make it their business to use their eyes and ears to spy out what they could report to the king to his advantage. As a natural result of this, many "eyes" and many "ears" were ascribed to the king. But if any one thinks that the king selected one man to be his "eye," he is wrong; for one only would see and one would hear but little; and it would have amounted to ordering all the rest to pay no attention, if one only had been appointed to see and hear. Besides, if people knew that a certain man was the "eye," they would know that they must beware of him. But such is not the case; for the king listens to anybody who may claim to have heard or seen anything worthy of attention. And thus the saying comes about, "The king has many ears and many eyes"; and people are everywhere afraid to say anything to the discredit of the king, just as if he himself were listening; or to do anything to harm him, just as if he were present. Not only, therefore, would no one have ventured to say anything derogatory of Cyrus to anyone else, but everyone conducted himself at all times just as if those who were within hearing were so many eyes and ears of the king. I do not know what better reason anyone could assign for this attitude toward him on the part of people generally than that it was his policy to do large favours in return for small ones.

The full significance of this passage has never been recognized. As long ago as the mid-eighteenth century, Thomas Stanley concluded that Xenophon hereby testified that the Persian king had many "Eyes" and "Ears."¹ This was also the understanding of Eduard Meyer, although he thought Xenophon's testimony incorrect.² And it is a view shared by more recent commentators.³

But is this the point which Xenophon intended to make? Is he claiming that, rather than one official called the King's Eye, there were actually many officials so designated? I do not think so. A careful reading of the text reveals that Xenophon is making three points.

First, those who think that there is one officially appointed King's Eye are mistaken. This is explicitly stated: εἰ δέ τις οἴεται ἕνα αἱρετὸν εἶναι ὀφθαλμὸν βασιλεῖ, οὐκ ὀρθῶς οἴεται—"But if any one thinks that the king selected one man to be his 'eye,' he is wrong."

Second, those who think that there are many King's Eyes and Ears are also mistaken. He refers to the *so-called* (*kaloumenous*) King's Eyes and Ears: τοὺς βασιλέως καλουμένους ὀφθαλμοὺς καὶ τὰ βασιλέως ὦτα. And he twice says that there *were* or *are believed to be* (*enomisthēsan* and *nomizontai*) many King's Eyes and King's Ears: ἐκ τούτου δὴ καὶ πολλοὶ ἐνομίσθησαν βασιλέως ὀφθαλμοὶ καὶ πολλὰ ὦτα and οὕτω δὴ πολλὰ μὲν βασιλέως ὦτα, πολλοὶ δ' ὀφθαλμοὶ νομίζονται. The clear implication is that this too is a mistaken conception.

Third, in fact the king has many eyes and ears in a metaphorical sense; that is, people are watching and listening for him, because he is always ready to reward generously anyone who brings him useful information: τοῦ φάσκοντος ἀκοῦσαί τι ἢ ἰδεῖν ἄξιον ἐπιμελείας παντὸς βασιλεὺς ἀκούει—"for the king listens to anybody who may claim to have heard or seen anything worthy of attention." This statement implies that there is no officially appointed post of King's Eye or King's Ear.

Xenophon is undertaking to correct a pair of misconceptions. The first point may be directed primarily against the Greeks, who seem to have believed that there was one official named the King's

Eye. No extant Greek source of the classical period makes the claim that there were many officials named the King's Eyes and the King's Ears. The second point may be a reaction to a conviction widespread among the inhabitants of the Persian Empire, who were held in check by their fear that the king controlled an extensive network of informants. The third point conveys the true state of affairs. Because the king is always ready to reward useful information, many people voluntarily report to him, that is, they serve as de facto eyes and ears. It is this fact which has spawned the legend of the king's ubiquitous intelligence service, the King's Eyes and Ears, and has contributed to the security of the monarch.

There are several potential challenges to this interpretation. According to a number of scholars, Xenophon's claim that (by their reading) the king had many Eyes and Ears is a deduction only, based on commonsense reasoning about the limited effectiveness of a single publicly known agent, and therefore has no value as historical testimony.[4] Yet at the beginning of the passage Xenophon claims to have learned (*katemathomen*) how the king acquired his sources of intelligence. He is confident about his information and can assert firmly that popular conceptions concerning the Eyes and the Ears are wrong. He adds the arguments from probability to strengthen his contention. In this passage Xenophon is putting on the line his reputation as an expert on Persian affairs. Whether he turns out to be right or wrong in this matter, he explicitly claims to know the truth, and his assertion must be treated as historical testimony.

A second objection might be that Xenophon may be writing only of the Persia of his hero, Cyrus the Great. Most people doubt the historicity of this Persia and this Cyrus, viewing the *Cyropaedia* as a historical romance or a utopian fantasy. Thus the veracity of Xenophon's claims in this passage is linked to the large and untidy question of the genre and purpose of the *Cyropaedia*. However, this passage serves the same function as the *eti kai nun* passages in the *Cyropaedia*, in which Xenophon draws a connection between the practices which he attributes to Cyrus in the past and the practices of the Persian Empire of his own day. In such passages he is manifestly proferring factual information about the Persian Empire. This passage belongs to that group, because Xenophon speaks repeatedly in the present tense.

Other testimony survives from the Greek classical period on the subject of the King's Eye.⁵ An evaluation of this testimony will establish not only what were the commonly held Greek conceptions of this curiously named Persian office but also where Xenophon stands in relation to these other Greek sources.

In a scene in the *Persae* (lines 978–85), a play produced by Aeschylus in the year 472, the chorus of Persian elders interrogates an anguished Xerxes about the fate of the Persian nobles who had accompanied the king on his disastrous expedition against Greece. Although these lines pose some textual problems,⁶ the essential meaning is clear: "Didst thou leave behind also thine own all-faithful Eye over the Persians, who counted them by tens of thousands, the son of Batanochos Alpistos . . . son of Sesamas, son of Megabates?"⁷ In this passage Aeschylus seems to regard the Eye as a single high official, presumably a member of the nobility if one is to judge by the chorus' concern for him and his lineage. His function in this case appears to be that of a muster officer or chief of staff.⁸

Herodotus (1.114) relates an anecdote about the childhood of Cyrus the Great in which he displayed early signs of his future greatness. While playing with other children in the rustic village in which he grew up, he was chosen to be king in a boys' game. Cyrus immediately organized his "court," assigning some of his playmates to be builders, others to constitute his bodyguard, one to be message-bearer, and one to be the King's Eye. Although this incident is said to have occurred before this same Cyrus established the Persian Empire, the clear implication is that this was traditional Iranian court practice. Herodotus seems to conceive of the King's Eye as a single official. But, aside from the fact that the Eye is mentioned among other servants and officials whose place is at court, the rank or importance of the post is left unclear and its function unspecified.

In the *Acharnians* (lines 91–125), presented in Athens in 425, the comic poet Aristophanes depicts the return of an Athenian embassy from the Persian court, accompanied by one Pseudartabas, who is addressed as the King's Eye. This pompous and ridiculous figure has come with a message from the king. Here the King's Eye is presented as a single functionary of high rank and status, as is apparent from his trappings, and on this occasion he is serving as a royal emissary. Of course it is probable that Aristophanes chose to parody this official because of the visual possibilities provided by his title. An apparent stage direction preserved by a scholiast claims that the King's Eye should be equipped with a single large eye on his mask.[9]

There is one other reference to the King's Eye which may predate Xenophon's *Cyropaedia*. Plutarch, in his *Life of Artaxerxes* (12.1–3), says that at the battle of Cunaxa one Artasyras, the King's Eye, was the first to inform Artaxerxes of the death of his rebellious brother, Cyrus. For his account of events at Cunaxa Plutarch relies heavily on the *Persica* of Ctesias. Thus Ctesias is a plausible source for the reference to the King's Eye Artasyras. Ctesias, a Greek doctor who served Artaxerxes II, claimed to have been present at the battle of Cunaxa. Although the Byzantine epitome and the extant fragments of his *Persica*, taken as a whole, hardly inspire confidence,[10] still Ctesias had spent years at the Persian court and ought to have known if there was an office of the King's Eye. The natural meaning of Plutarch's words is that there was one Eye. Moreover, this Artasyras was probably a man of some distinction if he was the father of the famous satrap Orontes.[11] The passage is important in any case, for it is the sole reference to a historical appearance of the King's Eye in the classical era.[12]

On the other hand, it is not at all certain that Ctesias was Plutarch's source for this item. In the passage directly preceding this, Plutarch cites Ctesias as his source for the death of Cyrus (11.11). But Plutarch did use other sources for Persian history. In the *Life of Artaxerxes*, besides Ctesias and Xenophon, he also cites Dinon and Heraclides, both of whom composed *Persica*.[13] It would not be out of character for him to insert from memory an item derived from another (possibly later and less reliable) source.

Apparently many Greeks in the fifth and fourth centuries believed that there was a single royal official called the King's Eye. It must be admitted that the references in Aeschylus, Herodotus, Aristophanes, and Plutarch do not categorically exclude the possibility of there being more than one official called the King's Eye, but the natural interpretation of these passages is that it was a single post of considerable importance.[14] Xenophon implicitly confirms that this was a commonly held notion, for in *Cyropaedia* 8.2.10–12 he draws on his special knowledge of Persia to correct this misapprehension. Thus Xenophon stands against the entire extant classical Greek tradition in his claim that neither was there a single King's Eye, nor were there many officials with that title.

The King's Eye / 107

Xenophon also mentions the King's Eye in *Cyropaedia* 8.6.16. He has been discussing Cyrus' arrangements for governing the provinces and proceeds to describe a practice which is reported to have been initiated by Cyrus but at any rate continues in force in his own day. Every year an official, accompanied by a military contingent, is sent on a circuit of the provinces (*ephodeuei*). His mission is to help satraps in need of assistance, to chasten those who are behaving insolently, and to rectify any neglectfulness in matters of collection of tribute, protection of the inhabitants, cultivation of the land, and so on. When the official cannot himself rectify a problem, he forwards a report to the king. Xenophon then says:

καὶ οἱ πολλάκις λεγόμενοι ὅτι βασιλέως υἱὸς καταβαίνει, βασιλέως ἀδελφός, βασιλέως ὀφθαλμός, καὶ ἐνίοτε οὐκ ἐκφαινόμενοι, οὗτοι τῶν ἐφόδων εἰσίν· ἀποτρέπεται γὰρ ἕκαστος αὐτῶν ὁπόθεν ἂν βασιλεὺς κελεύῃ.

And those of whom the report often goes out that "the king's son is coming," or "the king's brother," or "the king's eye," these belong to the circuit commissioners; though sometimes they do not put in an appearance at all, for each of them turns back wherever he may be, when the king commands.

In this passage Xenophon is saying that there are circuit commissioners (*ephodoi*) who are sent out annually to inspect the government of the provinces. He does not say that such officials are called the King's Eye, although some commentators seem to have taken it that way.[15] Rather he says that they are preceded by reports of the advent of a royal dignitary, variously rumored to be the king's son, brother, or Eye. One should not take him to mean that the *ephodoi* are in fact the king's sons or brothers.[16] That is merely the report which sweeps the excited province (*hoi pollakis legomenoi*). By the same token, one ought not to assume that the *ephodos* is the King's Eye, for this is but another variant of the popular rumor. This passage does not authorize the conclusion that the *ephodoi* are identical with the King's Eye, nor that the King's Eye as a post even exists.[17] In other words, there is no essential contradiction between this passage and *Cyropaedia* 8.2.10–12. What both passages make clear is that the King's Eye is the subject of various rumors and misconceptions, even within the Persian Empire.

Perhaps Xenophon's position is not as solitary as may first appear. Even though his contention is in open conflict with the testimony of the other Greek sources from the classical era, it is not contradicted by the sources which ought to count for the most—Greek historians writing about Persia; there is, for all practical purposes, no explicit testimony for the existence of the King's Eye in any major *historical* source for Achaemenid Persia. The one exception, Herodotus' charming story of the boy Cyrus playing at being king, is set in the distant past and derives from a folktale motif. The Eye is mentioned nowhere else in Herodotus' lengthy work, neither in his description of Persian customs and administrative institutions nor in his account of the Persian Wars. It is widely accepted that Herodotus' narrative becomes more historically reliable as it approaches his own time. Yet the sole reference to the King's Eye is set in a very remote chronological context. As for Ctesias' *Persica*, it is preserved in only a highly fragmentary and compressed state, so that it is impossible to be certain about its contents. It was granted earlier that Plutarch's reference to the King's Eye in his *Life of Artaxerxes* could have been taken from Ctesias, although this is by no means a necessary conclusion. It may be more significant that there is no reference to an office of the King's Eye in either the Byzantine epitome or the extant fragments of Ctesias.[18] Herodotus, Ctesias, and Xenophon were the authorities on Persia in the Greek classical period, yet none of them provides unequivocal support for the existence of a King's Eye, and one of them, Xenophon explicitly denies it.

The passages considered so far were written by men for whom the Achaemenid Empire was a living reality.[19] Separate consideration must be given to another set of testimonies written after the fall of Achaemenid Persia.[20] Certainly it is always possible that a post-Achaemenid writer derived his information from an earlier source contemporary with the Achaemenid kingdom, especially in the case of the lexicographers and scholiasts, who frequently went directly to primary sources for their information. But as a rule one cannot be sure of the source and thus cannot properly judge its validity. In addition, it is important to determine whether a late writer is talking about the Achaemenid era or his own day; for even though the Parthian and Sassanian kingdoms, which succeeded the Achaemenid Empire in the Near East, may have derived many practices from their great predecessor (particularly the Sassanians, who in some sense consciously endeavored to revive the Achaemenid state), there were unquestionably developments and changes which affected the nature of even such borrowed institutions. Consequently, one cannot assume that a description of a Parthian or Sassanian institution is an accurate reflection of the situation in Achaemenid times.[21]

Only a few of the later writers persist in what had been the usual Greek notion in the classical period—that there was but one King's Eye.[22]

Dio Chrysostom, an orator and philosopher of the later first and early second centuries A.D., states that the Persian king had *one* functionary called the King's Eye (3.118). He goes on to say that the King's Eye was not a man of standing, but rather some inconsequential person. Thus the king revealed his ignorance of the fact that a good ruler will have friends to be his eyes, that is, to keep an eye on affairs for him. Dio is speaking specifically of the Persian king and uses the past tense. As a contemporary of the Parthian kingdom he presumably refers back to the Achaemenid period.

The late antique lexicographer Hesychius (s.v. βασιλέως ὀφθαλμός) also implies the existence of a single official when he speaks of an overseer (*episkopos*) called the King's Eye, who was sent out by the king to inspect affairs. This reference is of uncertain value, since Hesychius does not specify Persia or the Achaemenid monarchs. He speaks of *basileōs* without the article, which may be taken either as indefinite, "a king," or as the common classical way of referring to the Achaemenid king of Persia.

Aelius Aristides, an orator in the second century A.D., makes a most interesting observation in his sixteenth oration (pp. 424–25 Dindorf). He claims that the Persian king possessed something unusual in the *so-called* King's Eye and King's Ears. Perhaps it offered some utility, but for the most part it appears to have been a deception, so that the king might seem to see and hear twice as much as other men; in this way he protected the kingdom. The entire passage is reminiscent of Xenophon in both thought and expression.[23] While Aristides does not exactly deny the existence of the Eye, he notes that it was to the king's advantage to encourage belief in the omniscience provided him by his Eyes and Ears.

The majority of postclassical writers speak of Eyes (and Ears) in the plural. But only Philostratus, Themistius, and Pollux clearly regard this as an official title.

Philostratus (*Life of Apollonius of Tyana* 1.21), writing in the early third century A.D., speaks of a satrap assigned to a Parthian border fort who was a certain King's Eye (*basileōs tis, oimai, ophthalmos*). The presence of the indefinite adjective *tis* suggests that Philostratus did not regard "King's Eye" as a title reserved for one man (it may also carry overtones of contempt toward this minor functionary). And since this person is said to be a eunuch, is also called satrap, and is put in charge of a fortress, it is not at all clear what the writer assumes the term "King's Eye" to mean. Moreover, Philostratus is narrating an event in the career of Apollonius of Tyana, a peripatetic holy man who lived in the first century A.D. Thus he is providing testimony for the situation in the Parthian, not the Achaemenid, period, and it is probably of little historical value in any case.[24]

Themistius (*Orations* 21.255D), writing in the fourth century A.D., describes the anger of the citizens of a town against a devotee of philosophy. Raising a hue and cry, they summon the King's Eyes, presumably so that the latter can arrest the undesirable character. Themistius seems to be describing the situation in his own day, and the context suggests that he is speaking of the Eastern Roman Empire. In this instance the King's Eyes seem to be some sort of local police.

Pollux, a rhetorician of the second century A.D., is passing in review phrases which employ the Greek word *ōta*, "ears" (2.84). He claims that some people, who reported what they heard and saw, were called King's Eyes and Ears. There is no specification of time, nor does he say that the Persian king is meant. Thus one is forced to conclude that none of these references contributes to a better understanding of Achaemenid institutions, since Philostratus and Themistius manifestly refer to a later period, while Pollux is ambiguous.

The note of the scholiast to Aristophanes *Acharnians* 91–94, which is virtually identical with the definition found in the Suda (s.v. ὀφθαλμὸς βασιλέως), presents a somewhat different situation. It says that the term "King's Eye" indicates one who is influential with the king (or "at court"—*para basilei*); for this is what they called the satraps, through whose agency the king was able to oversee everything.[25] Likewise the spies/eavesdroppers (*ōtakoustai*), through whom the king got reports on everything which happened within his domain, were called King's Ears. In this context the designations King's Eye and King's Ear do not appear to be official titles, but rather are names used of the satraps and spies. If anything, the first part of the note suggests that "King's Eye" is an honorific title for those who have influence with the king. Again, there is no designation of time nor any specific reference to Persia, though the mention of satraps presumably implies this.

Lucian and Heliodorus use "eyes" and "ears" in a purely metaphorical sense; the usage refers, not to the title of an official, but to the means by which the king extends his own limited sense of sight and hearing in order to collect information.[26]

Lucian (*De mercede conductis* 29) is speaking of the indignities which must be borne by one who seeks employment in a rich household. He warns the candidate to beware of the jealous disposition of a master with attractive sons or a young wife: "For the King has many eyes and ears. You must therefore keep your head down, as at a Persian dinner, for fear that a eunuch may see that you looked at one of the concubines and report you to the master!"[27] Aside from the fact that Lucian is speaking of his own time (second century A.D.), surely the reference to eyes and ears in this context is metaphorical, that is, a graphic way of describing the vigilance of the servants rather than a specific title. The expression he uses—"The King has many eyes and ears"—seems already to have been a proverbial expression in Xenophon's day (*Cyropaedia* 8.2.11–12). The allusion to "Persian dinners" indicates Lucian's awareness that the expression originated in a Persian context.

Lucian uses the aphorism again in *Adversus indoctum* 23. Here he is reproaching a lout who hopes to win the king's favor by accumulating many books. This fellow does not realize that the king will also know of his dissipated life-style. Lucian asks: "Don't you know that the King has many eyes and ears?" One can easily imagine how the currency of such an expression from the classical period onward might have encouraged popular belief in the existence of a widespread intelligence network with agents who were designated as King's Eyes and King's Ears.

Most scholars place Heliodorus in the third century A.D., but the dramatic date of his novel *Aethiopica*, is sometime in the Achaemenid era, since Persian dominance of Egypt is assumed.[28] At *Aethiopica* 8.17 the Greek traveling party is offering to the Ethiopians the Persian king's eunuch Bagoas, and the author pauses to explain why eunuchs are valuable to the king. In Persian royal palaces the class of eunuchs serves as the eyes and ears (*ophthalmoi kai akoai to eunouchōn genos*), for their loyalties are undividedly reserved for the king. Again, this usage of eyes and ears is metaphorical and there is no suggestion that these were official court titles.

Of the ten alleged postclassical references to the King's Eye or King's Ear, only five can be considered as providing some sort of testimony for the existence and nature of such posts in the Achaemenid period: those of Dio Chrysostom, Hesychius, Pollux, the scholiast to Aristophanes/Suda, and Aelius Aristides. The other five references must be rejected, either because they refer to a later period than that of the Achaemenid kings (Philostratus and Themistius), or because they use eyes and ears as a general metaphor for vigilance and not as the title of an official post (Lucian and Heliodorus).

Although it is possible that the orators Dio and Aelius Aristides, the lexicographers Hesychius and Pollux, and the Aristophanes scholiast are basing themselves on earlier sources contemporary with the Achaemenid Empire, the information which they give is largely in conflict with the testimony of extant classical sources. Moreover, there is no agreement among them as to the number, social standing, or function of the King's Eye.

The accompanying table summarizes the explicit or implied testimony of the Greek classical and postclassical sources (listed chronologically) regarding the number, social standing, and function of the King's Eye(s). With a few exceptions, the contemporary sources provide a different picture from that of later sources. All sources from the Achaemenid period attest or imply the existence of a single King's Eye. Aeschylus, Aristophanes, and Plutarch's source regard the King's Eye as a high personage. Herodotus is a less secure case, since he mentions the King's Eye along with builders, bodyguards, and palace attendants. Herodotus and Plutarch's source do not specify the function of the King's Eye but Aeschylus mentions him in connection with the enumeration of troops; in Aristophanes he arrives in Athens as an ambassador from the king.

The postclassical testimonies present a far wider array of views. Only three claim, like their predecessors, that there was only one King's Eye; the majority refer to Eyes as well as Ears. Conceptions also vary as to the rank or importance of the King's Eye(s). Philostratus and the scholiast on Aristophanes regard him as a satrap, and thus as a high-ranking government official. Lucian and Heliodorus picture him as a court eunuch. Dio stresses that he is a man of low social standing, and the same can be inferred from the

Source	Number	Rank	Function
CLASSICAL			
Aeschylus *Persae* 978–85	1	a Persian noble	enumerates troops
Herodotus 1.114	1	rank uncertain	function not specified —listed among palace attendants
Aristophanes *Acharnians* 91–125	1	bedecked and bejeweled dignitary	royal ambassador
Source of Plutarch *Artaxerxes* 12.1–3	1	a Persian noble	function not specified
POSTCLASSICAL			
Dio Chrysostom 3.118	1	an inconsequential person	function uncertain —some kind of surveillance of royal domain
Hesychius s.v., βασιλέως ὀφθαλμός	1	rank uncertain	overseer/observer
Philostratus *Life of Apollonius of Tyana* 1.21	multiple	rank uncertain— designated as both eunuch and satrap	in charge of a border fortress
Themistius *Orations* 21.255D	multiple	local officials—thus presumably of low rank	local police or judicial officers
Pollux 2.84	multiple	rank uncertain— because of function probably of low rank	informants/spies
Scholiast to Aristophanes *Acharnians* 91–94/ Suda s.v. ὀφθαλμὸς βασιλέως	multiple	high rank—satraps (and others?) influential with kings	superintend administration of royal domain
Heliodorus *Aethiopica* 8.17	multiple	low rank—eunuchs	(metaphorical usage) loyally watch out for king's interests
Lucian *De mercede conductis* 29	multiple	low rank—household servants/ court eunuchs	(metaphorical usage) spy on other servants
Lucian *Adversus indoctum* 23	multiple	because of function probably of low rank	(metaphorical usage) report information to the king
Aelius Aristides *Orations* 16, (Dindorf) pp. 424–25	1	rank uncertain	sees and hears for the king (i.e., gathers information)

description of these agents' functions in Pollux and Themistius. Thus conceptions of rank run the social gamut. Discrepancies regarding the function of the King's Eye(s) are less jarring. Pollux, Lucian, and Heliodorus essentially present them as spies or informers who report to the king. In referring to these functionaries Hesychius and the scholiast use the verbs *ephoraō* and *episkopeō*, which can be translated either as "observe," in which case they are analogous to royal spies, or as "oversee/supervise," which would connote higher responsibilities. In Themistius they appear to be some sort of local police or judicial officers.

Spies, supervisors, provincial marshals—none of these resembles Aeschylus' chief of staff or Aristophanes' royal emissary. All things considered, the variety of conceptions is stunning, and one should not be blamed for entertaining the suspicion that the Greeks, beset by a diverse array of rumors about the mysterious and intriguing King's Eye(s), did not really know what he or they were.

This plethora of contradictory reports in the Greek sources almost forces an arbitrary selection of materials in any effort to create a consistent portrait of the office of the King's Eye.[29] Progress toward the resolution of this problem must involve a more rigorous analysis and more consistent treatment of the Greek evidence than has been the case in the past. My own view is that nothing of value can be extracted from the amorphous evidence of the later Greek sources. This is not to say that they may not contain valid information, only that at this point it is impossible to determine how much of the testimony about the situation in the Parthian or Sassanian kingdoms can safely be applied to the earlier, Achaemenid period. Furthermore, there does not yet exist a reasonable set of criteria for evaluating and reconciling the often contradictory claims of the later Greek sources.

Two potentially complementary alternatives remain as sources of evidence for the office of the King's Eye: testimony of Greek writers contemporary with the Achaemenid Empire—Aeschylus, Herodotus, Aristophanes, Xenophon, and possibly Plutarch's source—and materials from within the Persian Empire. Of the classical Greek sources, only Xenophon insists that there was neither one nor many officials designated as the King's Eye; the other sources all seem to think there was one high-ranking official with that title. As for Persian sources, no mention of the King's Eye has yet

The King's Eye / 115

been found in any document from the Achaemenid, Arsacid, or Sassanian periods. Extant Oriental sources (in Old Persian, Aramaic, Akkadian, and Elamite) for the Achaemenid period are scarce to begin with, so that the absence of any reference to an office is not decisive proof against its existence. But it is troubling.

The case for the King's Ears is slightly different. Although the Ears are not mentioned by any Greek author before Xenophon (*Cyropaedia* 8.2.10–12), his language implies that the people of his time believed that there were such functionaries. Of course Xenophon's point is that no such royal officials existed, but the King's Ears are mentioned repeatedly in the later Greek sources.[30]

Some Orientalists believe they have found mention of the King's Ears in a fifth-century Aramaic papyrus from Elephantine, in Egypt.[31] The papyrus refers to officials called *gwšky'*, a masculine plural noun, which can be derived from a posited Persian word **gaušaka*. This word, from an Iranian root meaning "to hear," can be translated literally as "listener."[32]

Scholars were quick to proclaim that at last they had found Persian confirmation for the King's Ears, although they disagreed as to the function of these officials.[33] However, Lommel and Pagliaro point out that there is no formal linguistic correspondence between **gaušaka* = "listener" and the Greek *basileōs ōta* = "King's Ears." The elements for such a Greek derivation via popular etymology are lacking. These scholars have raised a serious problem. Indeed, **gaušaka* could more literally be rendered into Greek as *akoustēs*, *ōtakoustēs*, *katēkoos*, or the like. One still has to account for the striking image contained in the Greek designation "the King's Ears." Lommel and Pagliaro would explain this inexact Greek translation of **gaušaka* as an extension of the already familiar concept of the King's Eye. But given that so far there is no trace of the King's Eye in the Persian sources, such a hypothesis begs the question. The existing evidence simply does not permit a claim that the **gaušaka* of Elephantine is the King's Ear.

Troubled by the absence of the King's Eye from surviving Persian records, Iranologists have made valiant efforts to discover the hiding place of this official. In the 1930s, in a monograph titled *Das Auge des Königs*, Schaeder noted that Manichaean documents, some going back to the sect's founder Mani himself, employ a title *ispasaγ* to indicate the second highest level of officials in the Manichaean church, equivalent to the *episkopos* of the Christian church.

Schaeder argued that *ispasay* is derived from a hypothetical Old Persian **spaθaka* (= "observer/overseer/watcher"),[34] and that Mani employed the term for the second level of his church hierarchy because the word had earlier been used to represent a high office. Hypothesizing that a **spaθaka* must have existed in the fifth- and fourth-century Achaemenid Empire, he went on to equate it with the "King's Eye" of Greek literature.[35]

Schaeder himself identifies the fatal weakness of this hypothesis when he says that it would be most conspicuous if the Persian equivalent of a title ocurring in the Greek sources as "the King's Eye" were to leave no trace. But the fact of the matter is that, if Schaeder is correct about there having been a **spaθaka*, then the term has left no trace in the Achaemenid records. Nor is the word extant in Middle Persian or Middle Parthian texts. In short, Schaeder is faced with a lacuna in the evidence which spans the better part of a millennium. His rationale for asserting that the Manichaean title can be traced to an Achaemenid precursor is as follows. He begins by looking for the Achaemenid equivalent of the King's Eye. Since he cannot find it, he hunts about in the later Iranian literature and comes across Manichaean *ispasay*. His intuition leads him to believe that Mani has taken over a term from earlier times, and upon reconstructing an earlier form **spaθaka*, he discovers with great satisfaction that this would correspond nicely to the Greek King's Eye. The reasoning is entirely circular. There is no trace of the hypothetical **spaθaka* in Achaemenid or Parthian documents and no good grounds for claiming that there was such an office. I offer the tentative suggestion that *ispasay*, derived from a root meaning to see, is more or less a semantic equivalent of Greek *episkopos*, and that Mani derived his title from the terminology of the Christian church.

Schaeder's theory eventually fell into disfavor with Iranologists. In its place, the provocative thesis of Pagliaro has gained considerable acceptance.[36] Pagliaro, who follows the fifth-century Greek sources in thinking that the King's Eye was an official of high standing, insists that the absence of all mention of such an office in the Achaemenid documents is not an insurmountable obstacle. However, one ought to be able to find traces in the Parthian or Sassanian records, especially the latter, since the Sassanian kings consciously strove to revive the glories of the Achaemenid Empire. The absence of all trace of a King's Eye in the Middle Iranian and Old Persian sources casts doubt on the credibility of the Greek tradition. This line of reasoning leads Pagliaro to search for the King's Eye in a new direction. An office well documented for the Sassanian period is that of the *bitaxš*, who was evidently a high officeholder at the court of the early Sassanian kings. In one document *bitaxš* is rendered as Greek *epitropos* ("guardian/governor") and as Aramaic *rb trbṣ* ("master/chief of the court"). This evidence suggests that he was some sort of prefect at the royal court. A case can be made for the existence of the office of the *bitaxš* during the earlier Parthian era, for in Sassanian documents the *bitaxš* is sometimes rendered into Greek as *bidix*, an obvious transliteration of the Middle Persian title, and at other times as *pitiaxēs* or *pityaxēs*. The latter looks like a transliteration of an earlier Parthian form which Pagliaro would reconstruct as **patyaxš*, a term which could mean "supervisor" or "overseer."[37] Pagliaro considers it strange that this important office of the Sassanian, and quite possibly the Parthian, period has no clear predecessor in the Achaemenid administrative hierarchy. The King's Eye of the Greek sources would be suitable if only one could account for the difference in name.

Pagliaro then endeavors to show that the hypothetical **patyaxš* and the Greek King's Eye are in fact one and the same and that the striking Greek title is due to a false etymology. Actually the first part is Iranian *pati*, a preposition cognate with dialectical Greek *poti* and meaning "on/upon, near/at, against," while the second element—*axš*—has a root meaning of "to see." But *pati* has been mistaken for a homonymous *pati* = "master/lord," and this has conditioned the treatment of *axš* as "eye." *Patyaxš* = "overseer" has been taken erroneously as "eye of the master," that is, the King's Eye. Finally, Pagliaro observes that the creator of such a false etymology must necessarily have had some facility in both Persian and Greek, and since the false etymology rests on less familiar linguistic data—*axš* is an obscure word, whereas the usual Old Persian and Avestan term for "eye" is *čaša/čašman*—it is in some sense a learned false etymology rather than the popular variety. One possible source would be scribes in the Persian administration who were responsible for the communication of the Persian government with Greeks. They would have had a natural proclivity for making linguistic and etymological observations. By a similarly ingenious argument Pagliaro tries to show that the name of the famous royal Persian bodyguard, designated "the Immortals" (*athanatoi*) by the Greeks, is based on another false etymology. The Persian name for these troops, *anušiya* = "follower," was confused with the Persian word *anaoša* = "immortal." Pagliaro's thesis is preferable to that of Schaeder in several respects. In the first place, the very cleverness of his solution is seductive. Then there is the fact that his alleged Sassanian descendant of the Achaemenid King's Eye, the *bitaxš*, is a political office rather than a level in a religious hierarchy like Schaeder's *ispasaγ*. Finally, if Pagliaro is right in his claim that the Greek designation of Immortals for the king's guard is based on a false etymology, his case for regarding the King's Eye as similarly derived appears even more plausible.[38]

But however superficially attractive Pagliaro's elaborate hypothesis may be, it is open to the same basic criticisms as Schaeder's theory. His posited **patyaxš* is not found in any extant Achaemenid or Parthian sources.[39] And it is not enough to say that a Sassanian institution must derive from Parthian and Achaemenid forebears. Hinz has attacked Pagliaro's reconstruction of Old Persian **patyaxš* from Middle Persian *bitaxš*, claiming instead that the Old Persian source of the Middle Persian official title was *dvitiyaxša*, "second-in-command/vice-king."[40] Moreover, it is hardly likely that scribes in Persian service, who were responsible for bridging the language barrier between their Persian masters and other peoples within and beyond the empire, could make mistakes with words such as *pati* and *anušiya*. Yet, according to Pagliaro, the error involves these common words with which the scribes would have had to deal on a regular basis, not the more obscure *axš*.

Hinz has put forward another candidate for the Persian equivalent of the King's Eye.[41] The Elamite tablets from the Persian ceremonial capital of Persepolis refer to an official called *ti-ti-kaš* or *ti-ti-ya-kaš-be*. These terms can be interpreted as transcriptions of a hypothetical Old Persian **ditaka* or **didiyaka*, in which Hinz detects the root found in Modern Persian *dide*, meaning "eye." They may also correspond to a title ^{lu}*di-dak-ku*, which is found in a cuneiform document from Mesopotamian Nippur dated to the year 417.

This theory must be given serious consideration because it is the only one which claims to find a contemporary reference to the Achaemenid King's Eye. It hinges entirely on the strength of the etymological argument about the derivation and meaning of the Elamite words. While forms of the verb *di–* = "to see" are found in the Old

Persian inscriptions, no noun formed from this root and having the meaning "eye" has been discovered. However, because the extant corpus of Old Persian is quite small, this absence need not be decisive. Moreover, the *lu*-*di-dak-ku* found in the Mesopotamian cuneiform document has been taken by Eilers to mean "fort commander," with the title derived from *didā*, an attested Old Persian word meaning "stronghold/fortress."[42] One could argue that the *ditaka or *didiyaka of the Elamite tablets is similarly derived.

As to the function of these officials at Persepolis, they were involved in the distribution of rations to groups of workers.[43] The *lu*-*di-dak-ku* of the Nippur tablet is called "foreman of the army scribes." He is mentioned third in a list of officials and receives the rations of a middle-level official. Hinz regards these agents as "overseers," but in terms of their activities they are so far removed from the Greek conception of the King's Eye that he is forced to postulate a chief *didiyaka who is the King's Eye of the Greek tradition. Needless to say, there is no authorization for this assumption in the Persian documents.

The awkward but inescapable fact remains that there is no mention of anything which seems to mean "the King's Eye" in the Persian documents for any period. Greek historians tend to assume that there was an Eye, without, perhaps, being fully aware of or giving sufficiently serious consideration to the fact that he is absent from the Oriental records. Schaeder, Pagliaro, and other Orientalists, who are aware of the problems with the Oriental evidence but do not recognize the insecure and internally contradictory character of many of the Greek references to the office, are driven to speculate that the Greeks mistakenly rendered a Persian term. No modern investigator has, to my knowledge, ever seriously advocated that there was no such office and that the Greeks were simply mistaken. Presumably the cumulative force of the Greek testimonies, contradictory though they may be, has seemed too great to ignore. But it should be kept in mind that the Persian king and his fabulous court, situated at a vast remove from the Greek world, exerted a continuing attraction on the imagination of the Greeks, and all manner of stories and rumors will have been in circulation.[44] It is not inconceivable that the King's Eye is the product of some such fancy. After all, at least one Greek author, Xenophon, said that there was no such thing.

How, then, does one account for the widespread belief in the existence of the Eye? There is one more aspect of the Persian tradition which must be considered. Eyes and ears play an intriguing role in the mythological conception of certain gods in the Indo-Iranian pantheon. The Indian gods Varuna and Mitra are said to have their "watchers" or "spies" (*spás*) who wander over the earth and survey the affairs of men. Varuna's watchers "come hither from heaven, with a thousand eyes do they watch over the earth" (*Atharvaveda* 4.6.14). The god himself sees all that is between heaven and earth (4.16.5). In the *Rigveda* the sun is frequently called the "Eye" of Varuna and Mitra (for example, 4.13.2; 10.35.8).

More pertinent still is the Iranian conception of Mithra, who corresponds to the Vedic Mitra. One of the finest *yashts* or hymns in the Avesta, the sacred text of the Zoroastrian religion, is dedicated to Mithra (Yasht 10). Here the god is besought as "the lord of wide pastures, who has a *thousand ears, ten thousand eyes*"; as being endowed "with a *thousand ears*, well-shapen, with *ten thousand eyes*, high, with full knowledge, strong, sleepless, and ever awake"; and as the one "to whom Ahura Mazda gave a *thousand senses* and *ten thousand eyes* to see . . . [with which] he watches the man who injures Mithra, the man who lies unto Mithra."[45] Elsewhere, Mithra is described as

> he, of the *ten thousand spies*, the powerful, all-seeing, undeceivable Mithra. . . .
>
> Whose eight friends sit as *spies* for Mithra, on all the heights, at all the watching-places, observing the man who lies unto Mithra. . . .
>
> Helping and guarding, guarding behind and guarding in front, Mithra, the lord of wide pastures, proves an undeceivable *spy* and *watcher* for the man to whom he comes to help with all the strength of his soul, he of the *ten thousand spies*, the powerful, all-knowing, undeceivable god.[46]

According to these passages, Mithra has thousands of eyes, ears, and other senses, has innumerable spies, and is himself a spy. He watches over the affairs of men, knows all, and cannot be deceived. It ought to be significant that he has the same number of spies and eyes. "The Eyes of Mithra" are his spies or watchers.

Mithra means "compact" in Persian, and Mithra is the god who protects such solemn agreements, punishing those who lie or who break their oaths. He is also associated with the sun,[47] and in Greek and other mythologies the sun is said to see all as it traverses the heavens daily.⁴⁸ Repeatedly in this hymn Mithra is depicted as residing in heaven and watching over all the affairs of men: "Who goes over the earth, all her breadth over . . . touches both ends of this wide, round, earth, whose ends lie afar, and surveys everything that is between the earth and the heavens"; and: "Whom Ahura Mazda has established to maintain and look over all this moving world . . . who, never sleeping, wakefully guards the creation of Mazda; who, never sleeping, wakefully maintains the creation of Mazda."⁴⁹

This last passage calls to mind the claim of the Persian king Darius, in his inscription at Naqsh-i Rustam: "Ahuramazda, when he saw this earth in commotion, thereafter bestowed it upon me, made me king. . . . By the favor of Ahuramazda I put it down in its place. . . ."⁵⁰

Sometimes in the hymn Mithra is portrayed as a king or leader:

> a chief in the assemblies. . . .
>
> Unto him nobody must lie, neither the master of a house, nor the lord of a borough, nor the lord of a town, nor the lord of a province. . . .
>
> Whom the lord of the country invokes for help, with hands uplifted [likewise for the lords of town, borough, and house] . . . Whom the poor man, who follows the good law, when wronged and deprived of his rights, invokes for help, with hands uplifted.⁵¹

Compare the claims of Darius in his monumental inscription on the rock face at Behistun:

> Within these countries, the man who was loyal, him I rewarded well, (him) who was evil, him I punished well; by the favor of Ahuramazda these countries showed respect toward my law. . . .⁵²

Or again at Naqsh-i Rustam:

> By the favor of Ahuramazda I am of such a sort that I am a friend to right, I am not a friend to wrong. It is not my desire that the weak man should have wrong done to him by the mighty; nor is that my desire, that the mighty man should have wrong done to him by the weak.⁵³

It should now be apparent that an analogy can be made between the god Mithra, who surveys all the earth from his vantage in the heavens and punishes the followers of the Lie, and the Persian king, who must maintain surveillance over his earthly empire and punish evildoers. If this conjecture has any validity, one might then be led to expect some earthly counterpart in the Achaemenid kingdom to Mithra's heavenly retinue of one thousand ears, ten thousand eyes, and ten thousand spies. This connection has already been made by Zaehner:

> He [Mithra] is, then, the god of the whole Iranian nation . . . he is the divine image of the Achaemenian king of kings. . . . Like his human counterpart on earth he has a thousand ears and ten thousand eyes through which he knows all things and thanks to which he cannot be deceived. . . . Mithra, as king, protects his subjects and brings them to justice, but just as in India it was the function of the king . . . not only to protect his own subjects but also to wage aggressive war against his neighbors, so does Mithra wage war on the *mithrodruj*, the violator of the treaty, who does not acknowledge the god's supremacy.[54]

There is disagreement among Iranian scholars as to whether the mythological conception of Mithra is influenced by the practice of the Iranian kings, or whether the kings were influenced in their choice of names for their agents by the mythological tradition.[55] The fact that the motif of the god's eyes is found in both Indian and Iranian mythology suggests that it goes far back in time to the period before these two related peoples went their separate ways. Yet it is hard to believe that the leaders of migratory Indo-European tribes had developed a political institution which continued to prove useful to the rulers of the vast Persian Empire more than a thousand years later. It is therefore more likely that the mythological motif was primary and was later transferred to the earthly political sphere.

What matters most for the purposes of this discussion is that the mythological motif of numerous eyes, ears, and spies serving Mithra is extremely strong. Given that Iranian civilization possessed this notion of ever-vigilant gods served by myriads of watchful eyes and spies, and the evidence which suggests that the Persian king strove to represent and imitate the god Mithra in his earthly domain,[56] one cannot help but feel that it must be more than coincidence when the Greeks refer to an official of the Persian king as "the King's Eye."

At this point it is expedient to summarize the findings of this survey, isolate the relevant factors, and try to formulate a satisfactory solution to the puzzle of the King's Eye. The final solution must encompass several factors. In the first place, there is the contradictory testimony of the Greek sources, beginning in the classical era with the notion of the King's Eye as a single high dignitary, and tending to develop, in the postclassical period, into a conception of multiple agents of lower standing serving as a royal intelligence network. Xenophon stands against the entire Greek tradition with his assertion that there was no such official as the King's Eye. The second concern must be the absence of all mention of the King's Eye in sources from within the Persian Empire. In the third place, there almost certainly has to be a connection between the Greek conception of the King's Eye(s) and the Iranian mythological tradition of the god who is assisted in his surveillance of the affairs of mankind by numerous eyes or spies. The best explanation of the Persian office of the King's Eye ought to be the one which accounts in the most satisfactory way for the state of the ancient evidence.

Four possibilities are available: (1) there was one King's Eye; (2) there were many King's Eyes; (3) there was one or more Persian officials whose name was mistranslated by the Greeks as "the King's Eye"; (4) there was no such office as that of the King's Eye.

Perhaps there was a single King's Eye, as the classical Greek sources (except Xenophon) believed. If so, he would probably have been a high-ranking official with close connections to the king. But several difficulties immediately present themselves. In the first place, there would be no obvious relationship between the real office of the King's Eye and the mythological tradition of numerous eyes who were spies or watchers. Next, it would be necessary to explain why there is no mention of such an important office in the Persian sources. And one would have to account for Xenophon's being completely mistaken when he says that there is no such office as the King's Eye.

If there were many King's Eyes, they might be conceived of either as spies, that is, a royal intelligence service, or as inspectors or overseers of some sort. Both notions were prevalent in the empire of Xenophon's day, and both notions occur in the later Greek tradition. In fact there is no wide gap between the two conceptions. Certainly royal inspectors, as they passed through the provinces, would have had their eyes and ears open for useful information which they could report to the king.[57] Such a state of affairs would allow for a clear relationship between myth and reality. Whichever way the influence goes—whether from the temporal bureaucracy to the mythological sphere or, as is more likely, the other way around—the Persian king has his vigilant Eyes, just as does the god Mithra in heaven.

Yet here again the argument falters over the complete absence of these agents from the Persian records, although one might try to get around this obstacle by claiming that an intelligence network would inevitably seek to avoid publicity. An additional stumbling block is posed by the consistent notion of Greek writers of the fifth and fourth centuries that there was just one Eye. Admittedly, one could argue that the Greeks, who had to deal with only one Eye at a time in any given situation, mistakenly assumed that there was but one such official. This error might have been further compounded by the absence of the definite article in Old Persian,[58] such that one could not distinguish between *the* King's Eye and *a* King's Eye. Nevertheless, counterarguments of this sort do not account for Xenophon's firm insistence that there is no such thing as a King's Eye.

With regard to the third possibility, Oriental scholars have displayed considerable ingenuity in their attempts to discover a Persian official title which might have been mistakenly translated by the Greeks as "the King's Eye." But there is no documentary evidence for a *spaθaka* or a *patyaxš* in the Achaemenid period (nor, for that matter, in the Parthian era), and those who are tempted to apply designations from the Sassanian era to the Achaemenid period half a millennium earlier are acting on little more than an intuition that the later Persians may have revived an old office and title. The presumption that the Greeks derived the notion of a King's Eye from a mere mistranslation or false etymology is rendered highly unlikely by the fact that there existed a well-developed Iranian mythological motif in which the god Mithra, who ruled and watched over the world as the Persian king dominated his earthly empire, had his eyes and spies. It would surely be a startling coincidence if this Oriental mythological motif just happened to be paralleled by an accidental mistranslation of a Persian term. Moreover, there is some evidence that the Greeks, from as early as the time of Hesiod (seventh century), were aware of the motif of the gods' "watchers."[59] If, as seems likely, the motif of the god's eyes/spies was known both within and beyond the boundaries of the Persian Empire,[60] then it must have played some role (as yet undetermined) in the development of the concept of the King's Eye, and unsubstantiated theories of false etymologies can be rejected.

There remains the last possibility, the one never seriously considered—namely, that there was no such thing as the King's Eye. It should now be acknowledged that Xenophon's credibility as an expert on Persian affairs rests, in part, with his claim to this effect. The nonexistence of the King's Eye would account most convincingly for the absence of all mention of such an official in the Persian records. In other words, Xenophon is confirmed (admittedly by an argument from silence) by the extant Persian evidence.

In this case, the role of the mythological tradition becomes especially significant. It is reasonable to assume that the Iranian mythological motif of the god Mithra's multitude of eyes, ears, and spies was well known and contributed to the growth of the myth of the King's Eyes. The Persian kings might well have encouraged such a notion, and both Xenophon (*Cyropaedia* 8.2.12) and Aelius Aristides (*Orations* 16, pp. 424–25 Dindorf) note the utility to the throne of the wide diffusion of such a rumor. Compare the words used of Mithra in Yasht 10 with Xenophon's account of the widespread belief in the omniscience of the Persian king. Thanks to his numerous eyes, ears, and spies, Mithra is said to be "with full knowledge, strong, sleepless and ever awake . . . the powerful, all-seeing, undeceivable Mithra."[61] Likewise the inhabitants of the Persian Empire believe that "the king has many ears and many eyes; and people are everywhere afraid to say anything to the discredit of the king, just as if he himself were listening; or to do anything to harm him, just as if he were present. . . . everyone conducted himself at all times just as if those who were within hearing were so many eyes and ears of the king" (*Cyr.* 8.2.12).

It is easy to see how the myth could have contributed to a state of affairs in which "many 'eyes' and many 'ears' were ascribed to the king." On this reconstruction the Greeks eventually fell prey to the story. Not only were they in occasional contact with some of the peoples resident in the Persian Empire during the classical period, but in the subsequent Hellenistic age Greeks were settled throughout the lands of the Near East which had once been subject to the Achaemenid kings. In this way it is possible to account for the variety of conceptions of the King's Eye in the later Greek tradition; in the absence of hard evidence, rumors and anecdotes about these mysterious figures will have proliferated.

The only real obstacle to this theory is the earlier notion of the Greeks of the classical period that there was but one King's Eye. This belief is not so easily accounted for by the influence of the Mithraic myth. Here I offer a suggestion, though it must be admitted that the state of the evidence does not permit absolute proof.

It is not known how the story of the King's Eye first got to the Greeks, but it is conceivable that something was garbled in transmission. The earliest extant Greek reference to the King's Eye is that of Aeschylus. What were Aeschylus' sources of information on Persia and individual Persians in the *Persae*, and how historically reliable is his testimony?[62]

No one will deny that the Athenian poet has created a dramatically effective picture of the Persian scene. He imparts an Oriental flavor through his use of language and through his inclusion of occasional details about weapons, worship, customs, court protocol, and the like. Philologists concede that the majority of allegedly Persian names are in fact of Iranian derivation. But the historical reliability of his account is less certain. The account of the naval battle of Salamis may be correct in its essentials. There is no difficulty in locating Aeschylus' source for the battle, since he was probably present and certainly had access to information from other Athenian participants and eyewitnesses. But it is important also to determine whether Aeschylus had a reliable source for his Persian data. Although it can be granted that the bulk of his names are plausibly Iranian, if one accepts the veracity of Herodotus' account it must be concluded that few of the Persian leaders mentioned by Aeschylus are likely to be historical figures. He does not even mention some of the best-known Persian commanders, such as Mardonius, Achaemenes, and Ariabignes. The list of ancestral Median kings cited by the ghost of Darius is vague and faulty, as is the account of the turmoil following the death of Cambyses.

Broadhead properly points out that the poet's purposes were dramatic rather than historical, and that, although he had to adhere to the essential historical line in those instances in which his audience knew the facts (as in his narrative of the battle of Salamis), he could afford to treat the material more freely in instances in which his Greek audience was less well informed. Clearly this was the case with the material about the Persians—their names, ranks, home lives, national history, and so forth. Aeschylus wanted to emphasize the tragic nature of the situation for the Persians by heaping up the names of noble warriors fallen in battle. The poet and audience were satisfied if the names sounded Persian. As to where he may have obtained so many seemingly authentic Persian names, perhaps he had contact with Persian prisoners of war or with Greeks who had fought on the Persian side. But there is nothing to suggest that he had much reliable information about individual Persians. He does not display great familiarity with the internal workings of the Persian military and administrative hierarchy, nor with the offices at court. In fact, the King's Eye is the only official whom he identifies by specific title. Elsewhere he speaks vaguely of military commanders, companions of the king, and so on. It seems clear that Aeschylus did not have reliable information about the King's Eye or any other Persian office. Somewhere he heard something about an "Eye"[63] and inserted it in his catalogue of fallen Persians precisely because of its exotic Oriental flavor. Why the Eye should have been involved in counting the troops by tens of thousands is a mystery and may just be a conflation with the tradition, found in Herodotus, that this is how Xerxes calculated the size of his huge army.

As for the rest of the fifth-century testimony, Herodotus, writing several decades after Aeschylus, does not specify the function of the King's Eye, and Aristophanes, who presumably brings this officer onstage because of the comic possibilities which he offers, puts him into the unlikely position of an emissary to Athens.[64] The point is that neither seems to know the function of the King's Eye. Either or both may have got the idea from Aeschylus without having any additional source for their testimony.

Thus the early Greeks may have heard little more than vague reports about the King's Eye. Eventually the rumor—based upon the mythological conception of the god Mithra and widespread within the Persian Empire—of a farflung intelligence network of royal eyes or spies, spread to the Greek world and competed with the earlier notion of a single, high-ranking dignitary called the King's Eye. Both notions surface from time to time in the later Greek tradition.

To this point, the case for the nonexistence of the King's Eye has been based for the most part on a critical evaluation of the references in the ancient literary tradition. But it is also possible to take another line of approach, based on the known history of the Achaemenid Empire. Because most of the sources for Achaemenid history are Greek, far more is known about events in the western provinces of the Persian Empire, where the Persians came into contact with the Greek world, than about developments in other parts of the empire. None of the testimony regarding the history of Persian rule in western Asia Minor throughout two centuries of Achaemenid occupation suggests the existence, at any period, of an extensive and efficient intelligence network.

Thucydides (8.5–109) and Xenophon (*Hellenica* 1.1.1–2.1.15) present a detailed picture of Persian involvement in Greek affairs during the latter stages of the Peloponnesian War. From 412 on, Tissaphernes and Pharnabazus, the two Persian satraps in western Asia Minor, were negotiating independently with the Peloponnesians concerning a military alliance against Athens. There is no indication that the king himself was well informed about the progress of events or was involved in any meaningful way until 407, at which time the Spartans, alienated by the duplicity of Tissaphernes and his shabby treatment of their side, dispatched an embassy to the king. Thereafter the king was more directly involved and took prompt and effective action, sending down his younger son, Cyrus, with a substantial sum of money for his Greek allies.[65]

In 401 Artaxerxes II first heard about the incipient rebellion of his brother from Tissaphernes, who had hastened to court to relay this information (*Anabasis* 1.2.4–5). In 397 Pharnabazus journeyed to Susa to convey details of Spartan incursions into Persian territory in western Asia Minor. This conflict had been in progress for some time, beginning as an essentially private quarrel between Tissaphernes and the Spartans, and Tissaphernes had evidently chosen not to bring it to the attention of the central administration. Only after the Spartans had carried out several invasions of Pharnabazus' satrapy did the latter rush off to make a detailed report to the king. (This need not mean that the central government had no knowledge of events in the west, but at best they had only limited awareness of the causes, course, and scale of the altercation with Sparta.) From that point on, the king took decisive action, authorizing the creation of a fleet and the appointment of the Athenian Conon as admiral, and within a short time he engineered the execution of Tissaphernes, whom he presumably held responsible for the imbroglio.[66]

All these cases reveal the same pattern. There is no evidence that the king was well informed about events in the west, as one would expect if he had been able to call upon the resources of the kind of widespread intelligence network which is often presumed to have existed. Instead, he acted only when someone came to him with information (the Spartan embassy, Tissaphernes, Pharnabazus). Similar examples could be cited from later periods. Weiskopf has recently shown that the various satrapal rebellions of the mid-fourth century were due in large part to the absence of good information available to the king, who was therefore susceptible to rumors and to the (often false) accusations leveled against one another by rival provincial officials competing for influence and prestige.[67] It might be possible to speculate that there had been a well-organized intelligence network in the early empire which had subsequently broken down. However, Chester Starr has sagely cautioned against inferring from the more limited information available for earlier periods that the king had formerly exercised firmer control over his aristocratic deputies.[68] The fact that Oroetes, Pissuthnes, and Amorges (just to name those about whom something is known) had all managed to cause trouble in western Asia Minor indicates that in earlier periods, too, the king had not always been particularly well informed about events in distant provinces.

In sum, the known facts of Persian history provide no support to a belief in the existence of a comprehensive network of agents relaying information to the Great King. Nor is there evidence for the existence of anything resembling a King's Eye or an imperial intelligence network in the Near Eastern empires which succeeded the Achaemenids.[69] The lack of evidence for intelligence networks in subsequent empires may serve as a further argument against the existence of such an institution in the Achaemenid period, since these later imperial powers readily borrowed various administrative techniques and institutions from their Persian predecessors. On the other hand (and of equal significance), one occasionally detects in these later empires the existence of a syndrome of spy-paranoia such as has been posited here for the Achaemenid Empire.

It is ironic that the study of the history and institutions of Achaemenid Persia must involve so much reliance on Greek literary sources. The picture which emerges from the Greek sources is not only liable to the distortion that inevitably occurs when a civilization is seen through the eyes of outsiders who do not fully understand it, but in this case the centuries-long rivalry and hostility between Persia and the Greek city-states were bound to reduce the possibilities for observation and understanding and thereby to increase the distortion. Certainly, in the absence of substantial written material from within the Persian Empire, it is necessary to squeeze as much information as possible out of the Greek texts, but in doing so it is also necessary to maintain an awareness of the attendant problems and to exercise caution. Clearly, the King's Eye is a case in which scholars have not been sufficiently critical in their use of the Greek evidence.

Although it is not possible to reconcile all the contradictory testimony, the conclusion that there was no King's Eye in the Achaemenid Empire seems best to account for the available evidence from both the Greek and Persian sides. If this conclusion is accurate, several important consequences follow. In the first place, Xenophon is shown to be correct as against the rest of the Greek tradition, and the *Cyropaedia* has once again proved to be a valuable source for information on the institutions of the Achaemenid Empire. A lesson can be drawn about the dangers of relying indiscriminately on Greek sources for the history and institutions of Achaemenid Persia, especially when those sources are not even in agreement with one another. Finally, the example of the Greeks' long-standing interest in and confusion about the King's Eye provides a clear demonstration of both their fascination with the fabulous Great King of Persia and his mysterious, faraway court and their susceptibility to the stories, myths, and rumors which circulated within the empire.[70] There is nothing surprising in these tendencies, given the Greeks' earlier enthusiasm for a figure such as the Lydian king Croesus. Herodotus, Xenophon, and Plato all exhibited a fascination with the legends surrounding the early Persian kings.[71]

Armayor has argued that there was a stereotypical Greek tradition about the Persians, a tradition which ultimately derived from Homer's depiction of "Orientals" and which had been further developed and propagated by Hecataeus of Miletus and by Herodotus.[72] Such stereotyping would be in accordance with a characteristically Greek pattern of mind, well illustrated by Momigliano, whereby the Greeks became attached to certain preconceived notions about barbarian peoples and cultures and were reluctant to give them up.[73] Armayor carries his assertions to an untenable extreme.[74] But there is probably some truth to his contention that the Greeks had already by the fifth century begun to develop a stereo-

Appendix A / 131

typical conception of the Persian court and king, and it is easy to see how the King's Eye would have been incorporated into this fantastic world.

APPENDIX A

Testimonia from Greek Sources

ACHAEMENID ERA

Aeschylus *Persae* 978–85

Χο. ἦ καὶ Περσᾶν τὸν ἄωτον,
τὸν σὸν πιστὸν πάντ᾽ ὀφθαλμόν,
μυρία μυρία πεμπαστάν,
Βατανώχου παῖδ᾽ Ἄλπιστον
⟨   ⟩
τοῦ Σησάμα τοῦ Μεγαβάτα
Πάρθον τε μέγαν τ᾽ Οἰβάρην
ἔλιπες ἔλιπες; ὢ ὢ ⟨ὢ⟩ δάιων.

Herodotus 1.114

Καὶ ὅτε δὴ ἦν δεκαέτης ὁ παῖς, πρῆγμα ἐς αὐτὸν τοιόνδε γενόμενον ἐξέφηνέ μιν. ἔπαιζε ἐν τῇ κώμῃ ταύτῃ ἐν τῇ ἦσαν καὶ αἱ βουκολίαι αὗται, ἔπαιζε δὲ μετ᾽ ἄλλων ἡλίκων ἐν ὁδῷ. καὶ οἱ παῖδες παίζοντες εἵλοντο ἑωυτῶν βασιλέα εἶναι τοῦτον δὴ τὸν τοῦ βουκόλου ἐπίκλησιν παῖδα. ὁ δὲ αὐτῶν διέταξε τοὺς μὲν οἰκίας οἰκοδομέειν, τοὺς δὲ δορυφόρους εἶναι, τὸν δέ κού τινα αὐτῶν ὀφθαλμὸν βασιλέος εἶναι, τῷ δέ τινι τὰς ἀγγελίας ἐσφέρειν ἐδίδου γέρας, ὡς ἑκάστῳ ἔργον προστάσσων.

Aristophanes *Acharnians* 91–125

Πρ. καὶ νῦν ἄγοντες ἥκομεν Ψευδαρτάβαν,
     τὸν βασιλέως ὀφθαλμόν.   Δι.   ἐκκόψειέ γε
     κόραξ πατάξας, τόν τε σὸν τοῦ πρέσβεως.
Κη. ὁ βασιλέως ὀφθαλμός.   Δι.   ὦναξ Ἡράκλεις.
     πρὸς τῶν θεῶν ἄνθρωπε ναύφαρκτον βλέπεις;
     ἢ περὶ ἄκραν κάμπτων νεώσοικον σκοπεῖς;
     ἄσκωμ᾽ ἔχεις που περὶ τὸν ὀφθαλμὸν κάτω.
Πρ. ἄγε δὴ σὺ βασιλεὺς ἅττα σ᾽ ἀπέπεμψεν φράσον
     λέξοντ᾽ Ἀθηναίοισιν ὦ Ψευδαρτάβα.

ΨΕΥΔΑΡΤΑΒΑΣ
ἰαρταμὰν ἐξάρξαν ἀπισσόνα σάτρα.
Πρ. ξυνήκαθ᾽ ὃ λέγει;   Δι.   μὰ τὸν Ἀπόλλω 'γὼ μὲν οὔ.
Πρ. πέμψειν βασιλέα φησὶν ὑμῖν χρυσίον.
λέγε δὴ σὺ μεῖζον καὶ σαφῶς τὸ χρυσίον.
Ψε. οὐ λῆψι χρῦσο χαυνόπρωκτ᾽ Ἰαοναῦ.
Δι. οἴμοι κακοδαίμων ὡς σαφῶς.   Πρ.   τί δ᾽ αὖ λέγει;
Δι. ὅ τι; χαυνοπρώκτους τοὺς Ἰάονας λέγει,
εἰ προσδοκῶσι χρυσίον ἐκ τῶν βαρβάρων.
Πρ. οὔκ, ἀλλ᾽ ἀχάνας ὅδε γε χρυσίου λέγει.
Δι. ποίας ἀχάνας; σὺ μὲν ἀλαζὼν εἶ μέγας.
ἀλλ᾽ ἄπιθ᾽· ἐγὼ δὲ βασανιῶ τοῦτον μόνος.
ἄγε δὴ σὺ φράσον ἐμοὶ σαφῶς πρὸς τουτονί,
ἵνα μή σε βάψω βάμμα Σαρδιανικόν.
βασιλεὺς ὁ μέγας ἡμῖν ἀποπέμψει χρυσίον;
(ἀνανεύει.)
ἄλλως ἄρ᾽ ἐξαπατώμεθ᾽ ὑπὸ τῶν πρέσβεων;
(ἐπινεύει.)
Ἑλληνικόν γ᾽ ἐπένευσαν ἄνδρες οὑτοιί,
κοὐκ ἔσθ᾽ ὅπως οὐκ εἰσὶν ἐνθένδ᾽ αὐτόθεν.
καὶ τοῖν μὲν εὐνούχοιν τὸν ἕτερον τουτονὶ
ἐγᾦδ᾽ ὅς ἐστι, Κλεισθένης ὁ Σιβυρτίου.
ὦ θερμόβουλον πρωκτὸν ἐξυρημένε,
τοιόνδε γ᾽ ὦ πίθηκε τὸν πώγων᾽ ἔχων
εὐνοῦχος ἡμῖν ἦλθες ἐσκευασμένος;
ὁδὶ δὲ τίς ποτ᾽ ἐστίν; οὐ δήπου Στράτων;
Κη. σίγα, κάθιζε.
τὸν βασιλέως ὀφθαλμὸν ἡ βουλὴ καλεῖ
ἐς τὸ πρυτανεῖον.   Δι.   ταῦτα δῆτ᾽ οὐχ ἀγχόνη;

Plutarch *Artaxerxes* 12.1–3

Ἤδη δ᾽ αὐτοῦ τεθνηκότος, Ἀρτασύρας ὁ βασιλέως ὀφθαλμὸς ἔτυχεν ἵππῳ παρεξελαύνων. γνωρίσας οὖν τοὺς εὐνούχους ὀλοφυρομένους, ἠρώτησε τὸν πιστότατον αὐτῶν· "τίνα τοῦτον ὦ Παρίσκα κλαίεις παρακαθήμενος;" ὁ δ᾽ εἶπεν· "οὐχ ὁρᾷς ὦ Ἀρτασύρα Κῦρον τεθνηκότα;" θαυμάσας οὖν ὁ Ἀρτασύρας τῷ μὲν εὐνούχῳ θαρρεῖν παρεκελεύσατο καὶ φυλάττειν τὸν νεκρόν, αὐτὸς δὲ συντείνας πρὸς τὸν Ἀρτοξέρξην. ἀπεγνωκότα μὲν ἤδη τὰ πράγματα, κακῶς δὲ καὶ τὸ σῶμα διακείμενον ὑπό τε δίψης καὶ τοῦ τραύματος, χαίρων φράζει, ὡς αὐτὸς ἴδοι τεθνηκότα Κῦρον. ὁ δὲ πρῶτον μὲν εὐθὺς ὥρμησεν αὐτὸς ἰέναι, καὶ τὸν Ἀρτασύραν ἄγειν ἐκέλευσεν ἐπὶ τὸν τόπον· ἐπεὶ δὲ πολὺς ἦν λόγος τῶν Ἑλλήνων καὶ φόβος, ὡς διωκόντων καὶ πάντα νικώντων

Appendix A / 133

καὶ κρατούντων, ἔδοξε πλείονας πέμψαι τοὺς κατοψομένους, καὶ τριάκοντα λαμπάδας ἔχοντες ἐπέμφθησαν.

Xenophon *Cyropaedia* 8.6.16

Κατενοήσαμεν δὲ καὶ τοῦτο ὅτι Κύρου κατάρξαντος, ὥς φασι, καὶ νῦν ἔτι διαμένει· ἐφοδεύει γὰρ ἀνὴρ κατ᾽ ἐνιαυτὸν ἀεὶ στράτευμα ἔχων, ὡς ἢν μέν τις τῶν σατραπῶν ἐπικουρίας δέηται, ἐπικουρῇ, ἢν δέ τις ὑβρίζῃ, σωφρονίζῃ, ἢν δέ τις ἢ δασμῶν φορᾶς ἀμελῇ ἢ τῶν ἐνοίκων φυλακῆς ἢ ὅπως ἡ χώρα ἐνεργὸς ᾖ ἢ ἄλλο τι τῶν τεταγμένων παραλίπῃ, ταῦτα πάντα κατευτρεπίζῃ· ἢν δὲ μὴ δύνηται, βασιλεῖ ἀπαγγέλλῃ· ὁ δὲ ἀκούων βουλεύεται περὶ τοῦ ἀτακτοῦντος. καὶ οἱ πολλάκις λεγόμενοι ὅτι βασιλέως υἱὸς καταβαίνει, βασιλέως ἀδελφός, βασιλέως ὀφθαλμός, καὶ ἐνίοτε οὐκ ἐκφαινόμενοι, οὗτοι τῶν ἐφόδων εἰσίν· ἀποτρέπεται γὰρ ἕκαστος αὐτῶν ὁπόθεν ἂν βασιλεὺς κελεύῃ.

POST-ACHAEMENID SOURCES

Dio Chrysostom 3.118

ὁ μὲν Πέρσης ἕνα τινὰ ἔσχεν, ὀφθαλμὸν βασιλέως λεγόμενον· τοῦτον οὐ σπουδαῖον ἄνθρωπον, ἀλλ᾽ ἐκ τῶν ἐπιτυχόντων· ἀγνοῶν ὅτι τοῦ ἀγαθοῦ βασιλέως οἱ φίλοι πάντες εἰσὶν ὀφθαλμοί.

Hesychius s.v. *βασιλέως ὀφθαλμός*

ἐπέμπετό τις ὑπὸ βασιλέως ἐπίσκοπος, ὃς ἐφεωρᾶτο τὰ πράγματα, ὃν τοῦ βασιλέως ὀφθαλμὸν ἐκάλουν.

Philostratus *Life of Apollonius of Tyana* 1.21

σατράπης δὲ τῇ φρουρᾷ ταύτῃ ἐτέτακτο, βασιλέως τις, οἶμαι, ὀφθαλμός.

Themistius *Orations* 21.255D

ὀξέως τε ἐπύθοντο, καὶ ἐπαράμενοι πᾶσαν τὴν πόλιν ἐπικαλοῦνται τοὺς βασιλέως ὀφθαλμούς, εἰ ἀναπνεῖ ἔτι καὶ τὸν ἥλιον ἀφορᾷ ὁ μιαιφόνος.

Pollux 2.84

ἐκαλοῦντο δέ τινες ὦτα καὶ ὀφθαλμοὶ βασιλέως, οἱ τὰ λεγόμενα διαγγέλλοντες καὶ τὰ ὁρώμενα·

Scholiast to Aristophanes *Acharnians* 91–94 =
Suda s.v. *ὀφθαλμὸς βασιλέως*

ἀντὶ τοῦ μέγα δυνάμενος παρὰ βασιλεῖ· οὕτως δὲ ἐκάλουν τοὺς σατράπας, δι᾽ ὧν πάντα [Suda: πάντας] ὁ βασιλεὺς ἐπισκοπεῖ· ὡς βασι-

134 / The King's Eye

λέως ὦτα τοὺς ὠτακουστάς, δι' ὧν ἀκούει τὰ πραττόμενα ἑκάστῳ πανταχοῦ.

Lucian *De mercede conductis* 29

ἢν μὲν γὰρ καὶ ζηλότυπός τις ᾖ καὶ παῖδες εὔμορφοι ὦσιν ἢ νέα γυνὴ καὶ σὺ μὴ παντελῶς πόρρω Ἀφροδίτης καὶ Χαρίτων ᾖς, οὐκ ἐν εἰρήνῃ τὸ πρᾶγμα οὐδὲ ὁ κίνδυνος εὐκαταφρόνητος. ὦτα γὰρ καὶ ὀφθαλμοὶ βασιλέως πολλοί, οὐ μόνον τἀληθῆ ὁρῶντες, ἀλλ' ἀεί τι καὶ προσεπιμετροῦντες, ὡς μὴ νυστάζειν δοκοῖεν. δεῖ οὖν ὥσπερ ἐν τοῖς Περσικοῖς δείπνοις κάτω νεύοντα κατακεῖσθαι, δεδιότα μή τις εὐνοῦχός σε ἴδῃ προσβλέψαντα μιᾷ τῶν παλλακίδων, ἐπεὶ ἄλλος γε εὐνοῦχος ἐντεταμένον πάλαι τὸ τόξον ἔχων ἃ μὴ θέμις ὁρῶντα ἕτοιμος κολάσαι, διαπείρας τῷ οἰστῷ μεταξὺ πίνοντος τὴν γνάθον.

Heliodorus *Aethiopica* 8.17

Περσῶν γὰρ βασιλείοις αὐλαῖς ὀφθαλμοὶ καὶ ἀκοαὶ τὸ εὐνούχων γένος, οὐ παίδων, οὐ συγγενείας τὸ πίστον τῆς εὐνοίας μετασπώσης, ἀλλὰ μόνου τοῦ πιστεύσαντος ἀναρτώσης.

Lucian *Adversus indoctum* 23

οὐκ οἶσθα ὡς ὦτα καὶ ὀφθαλμοὶ πολλοὶ βασιλέως;

Aelius Aristides *Orations* 16, pp. 424–25 Dindorf

ὁ μὲν γὰρ τῶν Περσῶν βασιλεὺς ἐδόκει τι διάφορον κεκτῆσθαι τὸν καλούμενον βασιλέως ὀφθαλμὸν καὶ βασιλέως ὦτα· καὶ τοῦτο ἴσως μὲν ἦν τινα καὶ χρείαν παρέχον, τὸ δὲ πλεῖστον ἐμοὶ δοκεῖν ἀλαζόνευμα, ἵνα δὴ διπλᾶ τῶν ἄλλων ἀνθρώπων ὁρᾶν καὶ ἀκούειν δοκοίη. οἱ δὲ τοῦτο δὴ κάλλιστον καὶ σοφώτατον εὗρον πρὸς ὑπερβολήν· ἀμφότεροι γὰρ ἀλλήλοις ὦτα καὶ ὀφθαλμοὶ κατέστησαν, καὶ τὴν παρὰ τῆς φύσεως χρείαν ἐδιπλασίασαν, καὶ τὴν φυλακὴν τῆς ἀρχῆς οὐκ ἀλλότριαν, ἀλλ' οἴκοθεν ὡς ἀληθῶς ἐποιήσαντο, κοινώσαντες ἅπαντα.

APPENDIX B.
Intelligence Networks in the Ancient World

The preceding chapter has evaluated Greek and Persian evidence for the existence in Achaemenid Persia of one or more officials called the King's Eye. This appendix examines the issue from a different perspective, by considering whether any institution resembling the King's Eye existed in other ancient empires, both those which succeeded the Achaemenid kings as the ruling power in the Near East—the Macedonian dynasty of the Seleucids, the Parthians, Sassanian Persians, and the Roman Empire—and the Mauryan Empire in neighboring India.

THE SELEUCID KINGDOM

The Seleucid kingdom replaced the Achaemenid Empire in western Asia. Alexander the Great had taken over certain elements of Persian ceremonial and bureaucracy because they were well adapted to circumstances in the Near East and were reassuringly familiar to the conquered peoples, and the Seleucid rulers continued in this vein. Ruling over so many diverse peoples and political structures, they confronted essentially the same problems as the Persians had before them and thus should often have been willing to employ solutions developed by their predecessors. Although one cannot always be sure of the nature and extent of the fusion of Greco-Macedonian and Persian elements in Seleucid institutions, and although scholars differ in their estimates, there were no precedents in Greek history for such an empire before Alexander.

Consequently, it is tempting to look for a Seleucid institution parallel to the Persian King's Eye(s), to provide possible corroboration for the existence of such an office under the Persians. The problem is that rather little is known about Seleucid administrative institutions. Given the dearth of documents available from the period, the lack of attestation for a Seleucid institution is not particularly strong evidence. Nevertheless the fact remains that there is no trace in those records of an official or officials called the King's Eye. The name might conceivably have been changed because, to the Greeks, it had strong overtones of Oriental despotism; yet I can find no mention of a Seleucid spy or intelligence service under any name. One would expect the existence of a network of royal inspectors or overseers, but the degree to which royal agents were officially constituted and centrally organized is unclear. The king had a different juridical relationship to different parts of the empire—to free cities, colonies, temple estates, royal land, and so on. The satraps were his delegates and would have reported back to him, as would the commanders of military troops and garrisons, city governors, local partisans of the king, and other officials. It is not known whether there was also a system of inspectors or intelligence agents.

In sum, no trace remains of anything like a King's Eye in the Seleucid Empire. This circumstance may be an accidental consequence of the scarcity of evidence or may stem from a conscious refusal on the part of the Seleucids to employ Persian institutions. However, the simplest and most economical explanation is that no such office existed in the Seleucid kingdom and that there was no Persian precedent for it.

ARSACID PARTHIA

Very little information, either documentary or literary, is available for the Parthian kingdom, which recovered the Iranian heartland from the Seleucids. The Parthians were influenced by both Hellenistic and native Iranian practices. However, the hallmark of their era was decentralization, a feudal structure in which the central government had only limited control over vassal kingdoms, distant satrapies, and the estates of the high nobility. One would not expect an elaborate network of royal spies or agents, and I have yet to find any evidence for this.

SASSANIAN PERSIA

The Sassanians established a much greater degree of centralized control over their empire than had their Parthian predecessors. Moreover, they regarded themselves as successors of the Achaemenid kings. Thus one might expect them to revive Achaemenid institutions such as the King's Eye. Yet no such post is attested. Orientalists are disturbed by the absence of all mention of a King's Eye in the Oriental sources for any period, including this one, and have developed elaborate theories to account for the state of the evidence. Yet these theories, predicated on unattested offices and alleged false etymologies, are all ultimately unsatisfactory. Here again the available evidence provides no corroboration, not even well-attested analogies, for the Achaemenid King's Eye.

THE ROMAN EMPIRE

Far more and better information survives about the administration of western Asia in the Roman era. Moreover, it is commonly acknowledged that the Romans took over much of the institutional machinery of the Hellenistic kingdoms.

There is much talk of the *frumentarii* as a secret service in the later Roman Empire, but it is impossible to establish a connection between this institution and Hellenistic and Persian practice. Sinnigen traces the evolution of the *frumentarii* into a secret service in the late first or early second century A.D., centuries after Rome's initial assumption of control in the Near East.[75] According to his reconstruction, this was an indigenous Roman development at a time of increasing centralization and growing bureaucracy, evolving out of the corps of army supply sergeants. Even Sinnigen admits that the *frumentarii* had other duties involving imperial communications and taxes. Indeed, the evidence for their espionage activities comes from sources of questionable credibility—the fantastic *Historia Augusta* and church fathers with a persecution complex. Jones has expressed doubts about whether the late imperial successors of the *frumentarii*—the *agentes in rebus*—were really an espionage service, as has often been claimed.[76]

Thus there appears to be no direct connection between the alleged Roman secret service and Hellenistic or Persian institutions. At best, the Roman example may show how such a service could develop in a centralized state. Given that the Achaemenid Empire had been, in many respects, an essentially decentralized state, the analogy is not compelling. At worst, Roman traditions about a spy service may provide a parallel for other occurrences of spy-paranoia in antiquity, such as that which seems to have circulated around the shadowy figure of the Persian King's Eye.

MAURYA INDIA

The one ancient state for which there is much talk about spies and the distinct possibility of an intelligence network analogous to that alleged for Achaemenid Persia is ancient India. This case involves, not a successor state to the Persian Empire, but rather a civilization which was cognate and in contact with Persia.[77] Indian myth, like its Iranian counterpart, spoke of gods with numerous eyes/spies, and at a later time there were Indian officials with the title "the five senses of government."

The major source of evidence for the common belief that Indian kings controlled an extensive network of spies is a treatise entitled *Arthashastra*. This composition was attributed to Kautilya, the Brahman vizier of Chandragupta, who founded the Maurya Empire toward the end of the fourth century. The *Arthashastra*, regarded as the finest product of an old Indian literary genre concerned with the art of government, speaks of multitudes of spies serving in many guises, eavesdropping on government ministers, foreign foes, merchants, peasants, and even other spies and utilized for a variety of functions, including internal and external security, the dissemination of government propaganda, and ascertaining public opinion.

However, there is a serious question whether this account represents the historical situation in Maurya India. For one thing, controversy continues over the date of composition of the *Arthashastra*. Indian scholars tend to accept the authorship of Kautilya and use the work to reconstruct the political institutions of Maurya India. They postulate a highly centralized, regimented, spy-ridden society. But there are several problems with this interpretation.

First, European scholars tend to date the work centuries later, some as late as the fourth century A.D. They note that the attribution of works of literature to great men of earlier times was as common in India as in Greece. There are anachronisms that cannot stem from the early Maurya period. For instance, the work portrays the situation of small kingdoms competing among themselves rather than that of the large Maurya Empire. A recent statistical study of the language of the *Arthashastra* virtually proves that it is a compilation with multiple layers, dating from the time of Kautilya to the mid-third century A.D.[78] It follows that the *Arthashastra* cannot be a true reflection of political institutions in any one historical period.[79]

Second, the *Arthashastra* does not claim to be a description of the contemporary political system, but rather a speculative work on how the state ought to be organized in order to prosper.[80] Therefore it is, in certain respects, akin to Plato's *Republic*, Xenophon's *Cyropaedia*, and Aristotle's *Politics*. It would probably be as serious an error to reconstruct the Maurya state from the description in the *Arthashastra* as to reconstruct the government of Athens in the fourth century on the basis of the information contained in the *Republic*. The spy network of the *Arthashastra* might be as nonexistent as the Guardians.

Third, whereas a significant quantity of inscriptional evidence is available for the reign of Ashoka (mid-third century), there is no trace of the elaborate spy network or other prominent features of the polity described in the *Arthashastra*.[81] The king and his ministers themselves tour the country and make inspection, thus assuming the function of the spies of the *Arthashastra*.

Another element of the tradition concerning spies in ancient India is the *Indica* of Megasthenes, the Seleucid ambassador to the court of Chandragupta. The original work is lost, but substantial fragments can be found in Arrian (*Indica*), Strabo, and Diodorus Siculus. Megasthenes claimed that Indian society was divided into seven castes, including a caste of "overseers" (*episkopoi* in Arrian, *ephoroi* in Strabo), who report back to the king on events in the kingdom. At first sight this appears to be a confirmation of the spy system outlined in the *Arthashastra*, and the date of Megasthenes' work is secure.

Comparison of Megasthenes' *Indica* and the *Arthashastra* shows some agreement and some disagreement.[82] However, it should be noted that Megasthenes is wrong about the seven castes, confusing some real castes with various vocations that did not form caste-groups. And the terms used by Arrian and Strabo seem more appropriate to royal overseers or inspectors than to undercover spies. As to the reliability of Megasthenes, the consensus seems to be that, although he is superior to the fanciful, rumor-mongering Ctesias, who earlier wrote an *Indica*, Megasthenes is not a highly critical or discerning researcher.[83] He makes glaring errors about things which he should have been able to find out; for example, he is wrong about the seven castes; wrong in denying the existence of slavery, stealing, or lying in ancient India; wrong in denying that India had been invaded before Alexander; and wrong in claiming that the Indians had no writing and no skill in metallurgy. Since Megasthenes presumably had to rely on translators, much may have been garbled or lost in transmission, and the translators may not have been very competent. Moreover, Megasthenes visited only a part of India, and it is uncertain how much time he spent there.

He accepts fantastic stories of strange peoples, gold-digging ants, visits by Heracles and Dionysus, and the like from earlier Greek writers. Here one sees the manifestation of a tendency in Greek civilization to maintain belief in a myth or stereotype about a foreign people even in the face of evidence to the contrary. There is no reason to doubt that Megasthenes had heard stories about spies in India. But what could he have done to verify the existence of a deliberately *secret* network? He will have been susceptible to popular rumor in India as well as to Greek tradition. Greeks who had been brought up on stories of Persian "Eyes" were predisposed to believe this sort of thing.

In sum, the existence of an elaborate spy network in ancient India remains no more than a possibility. What is perhaps more significant is the way in which the idea of spy networks appeals to the popular imagination, creating paranoia, rumors, even the fantastic elaborations of the *Arthashastra* (which, in all its incredible complexity, could never really have existed). This is the context in which to view Greek and Near Eastern notions about the ubiquitous Persian King's Eye. Apparently spy-paranoia was prevalent in a number of ancient Asian civilizations.[84] Not that spies may not have existed, but it is a subject prone to tendentious exaggeration. Governments may even encourage these rumors. Xenophon and Aelius Aristides both suggest that the Persian king encouraged the notion that his Eyes and Ears were everywhere, seeing that it terrified the populace into submission and acquiescence. Sharma has demonstrated that the author of the *Arthashastra* saw the possibilities for using religious superstition to terrorize the populace and thus increase the king's control.[85] Rumors of an elaborate spy network would accomplish the same end.

6

Xenophon, Plato, and Persia

The previous chapters have been devoted, in large measure, to an exploration of the role of Persia and of the attitudes expressed toward Persia in the writings of Xenophon. As it turns out, there is no simple answer to the question: "How did Xenophon feel about the Persians and their empire?" Apparent attitudes, whether expressed openly or only indirectly implied, vary from one context to another. Clearly it is not simply a case of Xenophon's cherishing a deep-seated hatred for the barbarians, as has commonly been claimed. If this were the case, how would one account for a passage such as *Oeconomicus* 4, or the treatment of the younger Cyrus in the *Anabasis*, or an entire work such as the *Cyropaedia*?

In fact Xenophon exhibits a surprisingly wide spectrum of attitudes at different times and in different places. In the technical and philosophical treatises, where references to Persia are incidental and Xenophon has no special case to make, there is no trace of hostility or scorn for Persia, and at times, especially in the *Oeconomicus*, he envinces considerable respect and admiration.

There are passages in the *Anabasis* and *Agesilaus* which contain seemingly negative judgments on the Persians, and those who believe that Xenophon despised the Persians point to these instances as proof of their contentions. But one must take into consideration the context of these passages and see how they fit into the larger pattern of the work. A good example of the benefits to be gained from this approach is provided by that critical scene in the *Anabasis*, following the seizure of the Greek generals, in which Xenophon and other speakers publicly accuse the king and Tissaphernes of treachery, denying that one can ever expect trustworthiness from their kind. This episode must be seen in its historical and literary context.

The speakers are arguing for a particular policy—active resistance and no negotiations—and therefore stress the untrustworthiness of the barbarian. Thus there are obvious practical reasons, rooted in the immediate set of circumstances, which account for the position adopted by the speakers. There is no justification for taking this as Xenophon's final word on the subject. Indeed, when this scene is viewed in the context of the entire work, one cannot possibly maintain that Xenophon's purpose is to expose the inherent faithlessness and untrustworthiness of all Persians. The distinguishing feature of the younger Cyrus, for whom Xenophon has great admiration, is his *pistis*, his trustworthiness. By way of contrast, the Greek mercenaries on the return march are deceived, betrayed, and lied to time and again by fellow Greeks. Finally, in the climactic speech of the work, Xenophon persuades a barbarian prince of the value of trust in human affairs.

In the historical narrative of the *Agesilaus*, Xenophon's apparent attitude toward Agesilaus' Persian opponents is essentially neutral whereas Agesilaus is showered with praise. This treatment is only natural in an encomiastic work. One memorable passage in the part of the work which deals with Agesilaus' virtues involves a series of contrasts between the luxury, greed, and despotism of the Persian king and the moderation, fairness, and justice of Agesilaus. In this patently rhetorical passage, Xenophon has made the Persian king a foil for the virtues of Agesilaus; his primary aim is exaltation of Agesilaus rather than denigration of the king. What is truly astonishing about the *Agesilaus* is the prominence of Persia throughout its pages, and this is the key to the hidden apologetic purpose of the work. By concentrating on Agesilaus's campaigns against the Persians, Xenophon hopes to divert the reader's attention from that period of several decades during which the Spartan king was engaged in repressive activity against Greek states. Likewise, he seeks to forestall accusations of medism by depicting Agesilaus as a lifelong panhellenic champion. Certainly the fact that Xenophon could bring himself to play upon anti-Persian sentiments in this way says something about him as well as about the mood in contemporary Greece. But it does not constitute proof of Xenophon's own antipathy toward Persia. Panhellenism is not elsewhere a significant component of Xenophon's thought.

The *Cyropaedia* is the shining positive statement of Xenophon's admiration for Persia. While there can be no denying that much of its didactic content has been inspired by Greek thought, the choice of a Persian king as the spokesman for these values must imply a measure of respect for Persia on Xenophon's part. Of vital significance is the fact that, as regards those issues which constitute the main concerns of the *Cyropaedia*—education, military science, administration of an empire—Xenophon has been influenced by Persian ideas and values, many of which he may have encountered while in the company of the younger Cyrus and his Persian entourage. It has also been argued that the epilogue, with its expression of bristling hatred for Persia, was either a late and tendentious addition to the text or, more probably, was not written by Xenophon at all. Even if it be regarded as an integral part of the work, it cannot wholly negate the significance of the rest. For the *Cyropaedia* embodies a synthesis of Greek and Persian thought.

In closing, it is legitimate to ask whether the position on Persia which has been attributed to Xenophon in these pages is, after all, so extraordinary for his place and time. In this instance Plato can provide a point of comparison, for like Xenophon he was an Athenian, a member of the aristocracy, a disciple of Socrates, and a prolific writer. Admittedly, the subject of Plato's view of the barbarians is a large and complicated one, meriting an independent investigation, and obviously these few pages cannot do it justice. Nevertheless, even a cursory analysis of Plato's references to Persia will be profitable.

Vourveris has already addressed the problem of Plato's attitude toward the barbarians in general and toward the Persians in particular in his monograph Πλάτων καὶ βάρβαροι.[1] Vourveris' main thesis is as follows. Plato leaves no doubt that in his view the Greeks stand far above the barbarians. He was, like his contemporary Isocrates, one of the great publicists of the panhellenic concept. Spurred by patriotism and ethnic consciousness, he opposed the fatal divisions in the Greek world at a time when it was threatened by the barbarian East. His Hellenic patriotism and his detestation for the barbarian are especially conspicuous in the *Menexenus*. In passages in which he equates Greeks and barbarians, the barbarian practice is the subject of impartial scientific investigation. Nor should one be misled by occasional criticism of the Greeks and praise for barbarian ways. Plato's cosmopolitanism and liberal temper have been exaggerated by modern scholars. In fact he was a typical product of his time, and as such he recognized that the Greeks, with their capacity for reason, were superior to the barbarians.

Vourveris' facile notion that Plato was implacably hostile to the barbarians and a dogmatic panhellenist will not survive a careful and unbiased examination of the pertinent Platonic passages.[2] The fact is (and Vourveris' equivocations betray his awareness of this) that the works of Plato, like those of Xenophon, explicitly or implicitly express a range of attitudes, and sometimes these sentiments are in apparent conflict.

The fundamental flaw in Vourveris' approach is that he accepts one set of statements as representing Plato's true beliefs while rationalizing away all passages which reflect a different point of view. Thus he accepts the antibarbarian message of *Menexenus* (239B–246A) and *Laws* 3.692–701 but rejects the favorable sentiments of passages such as *Alcibiades* 1.120–23. The speech in the *Alcibiades*, with its praise for the education of Persian princes, is summarily dismissed as a pedagogical myth behind which stands the practice of the Academy. Therefore, one need not worry about the awkward fact that this passage flagrantly contradicts other passages in *Laws* 3, where the decline of Persia is said to be due to the faulty education of Persian princes. However, selective rationalization is a double-edged sword, and it would be easy enough to deploy arguments of a similar sort against Vourveris' interpretation. One can as well claim that the *Menexenus* speech is a parody of Athenian public funeral oratory and that Plato is exaggerating Athenian patriotism and hostility to the barbarians for satirical purposes. Moreover, in *Laws* 3 Plato has clearly created an overly schematic picture of Persia and Athens in order to make a philosophical point. This is not to deny that the *Alcibiades* passage may be equally contrived, with historical accuracy sacrificed to Plato's philosophical ends. The point is that, as in the case of the Xenophontic corpus, one must give an impartial hearing to all the references to Persia. Furthermore, one must always be aware of the context of a reference and of the point Plato seeks to make.[3]

According to Vourveris, Plato believed that there was a great gulf between Greeks and barbarians and that the difference was the Greek capacity for reason. But where is the evidence to substantiate the claim that Plato thought the barbarians incapable of reason?[4] As for his recognizing profound differences between his own people and the rest of mankind, although Plato sometimes does describe the world in terms of Greeks and barbarians, he is only using a common Greek figure of speech. In point of fact, he knows such a simple dichotomy to be untrue. In one passage he acknowledges that it is logically false to divide the world into Greeks and barbarians, insofar as barbarians differ from one another in race, culture, and language.[5] In another passage he states that all people, even Greeks, are of mixed ancestry.[6] Plato makes no essential distinction between Greeks and barbarians as to their needs, rights, natural reactions, capacity for good and evil, standing in the divine plan of the universe, and so on. Great lawgivers and men of achievement have appeared among both Greeks and barbarians.[7] Socrates urges his disciples to search for wisdom about the immortality of the soul among barbarians as well as among Greeks.[8] Barbarian souls are given the same judgment in the afterlife as Greek souls and are equally capable of both virtue and vice.[9]

At times Plato does contend that all Greeks are related by blood, that they should not enslave nor war upon each other, and that they must stand strong and united against the barbarian threat.[10] But in many other passages Plato shows his awareness of the falseness of the Greek/barbarian dichotomy and recognizes the essential similarities which prevail among the different races of mankind. In light of these contradictory passages, it is safest to assume that Plato's primary concern in preaching Greek unity is to end the internecine warfare which plagued the Greek homeland in the fourth century. The warning to stand united against the barbarian threat is revealed as a device to attain humanitarian ends rather than as a harangue prompted by hatred or scorn for the barbarians.

If Plato does not share the common Greek view that the Persian king, thanks to his fabulous wealth and power, is the happiest of men,[11] this attitude is a logical consequence of his antimaterialist philosophical outlook and would apply with equal force to rich and powerful Greeks. For Plato, the king is a symbol of materialism and greed, but this need not imply any special contempt for barbarians as a whole. If he deplores the sad condition of Persia's subjects, he also deplores the sad condition of much of the Greek world. Cyrus and Darius are praised as great and wise men.[12] The Persian program for the education of princes is exemplary.[13] The early Persian Empire was praiseworthy, and its decline is treated as parallel to, and no worse than, that of the Athenian democracy.[14] If the Persian Empire has declined, it is not because of any innate inferiority of its people but rather because of the faulty education of the kings and an improper system of government. The Persian king, like other despots, has been corrupted by power. Therefore, if Persian soldiers fight poorly, it is because they have no incentive for risking their lives on behalf of a despot.[15]

The most perplexing passage is in the *Menexenus* (239A–246A), but even here, although Persia is clearly the enemy of Athens, there is no lack of respect for the Persians. The speaker goes so far as to concede that the Persians understandably oppose Athens, since they are acting in their own defense. At one point the speaker seems to say that it is natural for Athenians, as pure-blooded Greeks, to hate barbarians. Yet Plato elsewhere rejects the notion of undiluted racial strains, and this contradiction serves only to increase one's doubts about whether the speaker in this dialogue represents Plato's views, or whether he is even meant to be taken seriously.[16]

In sum, Vourveris is wrong to deny that Plato showed enlightenment in dealing with the barbarian world.[17] It is apparent even from this brief survey that in many passages Plato takes a quite rational and dispassionate view of barbarians and is relatively free from typical Greek prejudices. There is occasional hostility, but not scorn, and much of the blame is laid to the Persian king rather than to his people. For that matter, the root of evil is despotism itself, which is wicked and corrupting in a Greek or barbarian setting. In Plato's judgment, the Persian Empire had once been good, and the Persian people were capable of political virtue and perfectibility.

It should be obvious that, with regard to Persia, Plato and Xenophon held certain sentiments in common, and that the references to Persia in particular and to barbarians in general in Plato's works represent much the same sort of problem as the references in Xenophon. Both express a range of attitudes that are not always easily reconcilable. Neither is averse to giving an overly schematic or distorted view of Persian history, culture, or institutions in order to make a philosophical point. Both have a tendency to idealize the Persia of old at the expense of contemporary Persia. Most significant of all is the fact that Plato is an example—contemporary with Xenophon—of a Greek who has a rational, reasonable, sometimes even quite favorable, attitude toward the Persians.

Xenophon can now be seen to hold a prominent place in a continuous tradition of Greek thought about Persia and the barbarian world. In the previous century Aeschylus and Herodotus had shown considerable respect and sympathy for the Persian foe, and the free-thinking Sophists, recognizing the essential falseness of the Greek/barbarian dichotomy, had insisted on the predominance of geographic and cultural factors over racial traits in the formation of a national character.[18] The ancient sources make it clear that Alexander the Great, who conquered the Persian Empire in the decade between 334 and 324, displayed respect for the culture of the Persians, adopting elements of Persian dress and court ceremonial, and that he had a sound appreciation of the ability of the Persians and other Iranians, employing them in his administration, army, and court. Alexander also married several high-ranking Iranian women and arranged for the leading Macedonians in his entourage to do the same. It is well known that Alexander encountered considerable resistance from his Macedonian officers and troops over his Orientalizing ways and his use of Iranians in the army and at court.[19] His seemingly enlightened attitudes contrast sharply with the open scorn for the barbarians expressed by Isocrates and by Alexander's tutor, Aristotle.[20]

The issue of Alexander's attitude toward the Persians and other barbarians and his plans for them in his vast, heterogeneous empire has generated much scholarly controversy. Some have claimed that Alexander was a solitary genius and a visionary in terms of his racial and cultural policies.[21] Others have sought to minimize the ideological significance of these policies, regarding them as spontaneous, pragmatic responses to a series of crises which demanded immediate, temporary solutions.[22] This is not the place to enter into a full-scale discussion of this topic. It should be said, however, that the whole matter of Alexander's treatment of the Persians has become so highly charged at least in part because his conduct is not easily reconciled with conventional notions about fourth-century Greek attitudes toward the Persians. The preceding chapters have revealed that there flourished in the earlier part of the fourth century an entirely different conception of the Persians from that of Isocrates and Aristotle. Alexander, who was almost certainly familiar with Xenophon,[23] may have been influenced by this intellectual tradition.[24]

In any case, it should now be clear that Greek attitudes toward the Persians were rather more complex than has generally been conceded. This recognition of the full range of Greek conceptions about the Persians in the classical period can lead to a better understanding of the portentous encounter of Greeks and barbarians in the Hellenistic era which was ushered in by the conquests of Alexander.

Notes

Introduction

1. All dates cited in the text and notes are B.C. unless otherwise specified.
2. For the life of Xenophon, Edouard Delebecque, *Essai sur la vie de Xénophon* (Paris, 1957), is comprehensive, if often highly speculative. Cf. Hans R. Breitenbach, *Xenophon von Athen* (Stuttgart, 1966), reprinted from Pauly's *Realencyclopädie der classischen Altertumswissenschaft*, vol. IX A2, cols. 1571–78; George Cawkwell, Introduction to Rex Warner, trans., *Xenophon: A History of My Times* (Harmondsworth, 1978), 8–15.
3. Contemporary Greek interest in Persia can be inferred from the appearance of works in a wide range of genres, including the quasi-historical *Persica* of Ctesias, the poetic *Persae* of Timotheus, and Antisthenes' philosophical dialogue *Cyrus*.

Xenophon's conception of himself as an expert on Persia may perhaps be inferred from his concern to use the proper terms in matters which relate to Persia. Oswyn Murray, "'Ο Ἀρχαῖος Δασμός," *Historia* 15 (1966): 142–56, has shown that Xenophon rejects the traditional term *phoros*, used by fifth-century historians to indicate tribute paid to Persia by her subjects, and employs instead *dasmos*. This Greek term is semantically parallel to the Persian term *baji*, which is attested in inscriptions and would have been used by the Persian administrative bureaucracy. Xenophon is also the first extant author to call a Persian provincial governor *satrapes*, a Greek approximation of the Persian *khshathrapavan*, whereas Herodotus and Thucydides had used *hyparchos*. See Rüdiger Schmitt, "Der Titel 'Satrap,'" in *Studies in Greek, Italic, and Indo-European Linguistics*, ed. Anna M. Davies and Wolfgang Meid (Innsbruck, 1976), 379. Xenophon is the only Greek author to employ the term *karanos*, presumably a Persian designation for the extraordinary position which the younger Cyrus held in Anatolia from 407 (*Hellenica* 1.4.3). And he is the first Greek writer to use the term *paradeisos*, derived from Old Persian *paradayadā* or a cognate Iranian word, for a pleasure park. See chap. 1, n. 11. This list of terms is illustrative rather than exhaustive. Cf. Emile Benveniste, "Relations lexicales entre la Perse et la Grèce ancienne," in *La Persia e il mondo greco-romano* (Rome, 1966), 484.

4. For the later popularity and influence of Xenophon's works, see Karl Münscher, *Xenophon in der griechisch-römischen Literatur*, Philologus Supplementband 13 (Leipzig, 1920), who maintains that the *Cyropaedia* was one of the most widely read books in antiquity (p. 45).

5. For Greek attitudes toward barbarians in the late fifth and first half of the fourth century, see Julius Jüthner, *Hellenen und Barbaren* (Leipzig, 1923), 13–28; Olivier Reverdin, "Crise spirituelle et évasion," in *Grecs et barbares*, Entretiens Hardt 8 (Geneva, 1961), 85–107.

6. See M. B. Sakellariou, "Panhellenism: From Concept to Policy," in *Philip of Macedon*, ed. Miltiades B. Hatzopoulos and Louisa D. Loukopoulos (Athens, 1980), 129–34.

7. From the translation of George Norlin, *Isocrates*, vol. 1 (Cambridge, Mass., 1928).

8. In an important monograph Raoul Lonis, *Les usages de la guerre entre grecs et barbares: Des guerres médiques au milieu du IVe siècle avant J.-C.* (Paris, 1969), has made a strong case that the ordinary Greek soldier made no significant distinction between Greeks and barbarians when it came to the conduct of warfare.

9. Charles H. Kahn, "Plato's Funeral Oration: The Motive of the *Menexenus*," *Classical Philology* 58 (1963): 220–34, regards that most enigmatic of Platonic works, the *Menexenus*, as directed to a similar purpose.

10. Delebecque, *Essai*, 199. This attitude is still widespread; see, for example, Peter J. Rahn, "The Date of Xenophon's Exile," in *Classical Contributions: Studies in Honor of Malcolm Francis McGregor*, ed. Gordon S. Shrimpton and David J. McCargar (Locust Valley, N.Y., 1981), 107 n. 30: "That he [Xenophon] hated Persia is obvious in all his works. . . ."

11. William E. Higgins, *Xenophon the Athenian* (Albany, N.Y., 1977), xii–xiii, bluntly condemns those who work in such methodological circles.

12. Joan M. Todd, "Persian *Paedia* and Greek *Historia*: An Interpretation of the *Cyropaedia* of Xenophon, Book One" (Ph.D. diss., University of Pittsburgh, 1968), 2–8, surveys the opinions of classical scholars as to the reliability of the historical information provided by Xenophon.

Chapter 1

1. Two passages in the *Symposium* (3.13 and 4.11) employ what was evidently a common Greek figure of speech in which the Persian king's vast wealth or power is held to be worth less than some simple virtue or possession, in these cases a devoted son and physical beauty.

Four passages from the *Memorabilia* incorporate statements of fact about the Persian Empire—the Persians' supremacy in Asia (2.1.10); the Persians' accumulation of more wealth and power than the world had ever seen (3.5.11); the presence in the empire of wild hill peoples such as the Mysians and Pisidians in Asia Minor, who had remained outside Persian control and launched occasional raids into the settled plains from their mountain strongholds (3.5.25–27). For a comprehensive discussion of this last phenomenon, see Pierre Briant, "'Brigandage,' dissidence, et conquête en Asie achéménide et hellénistique," *Centre de Recherches d'Histoire*

Ancienne 21 = Annales littéraires de l'Université de Besançon, no. 188 (1976): 163–279; and the king's habit of compelling individuals who were endowed with special wisdom or skills to leave their homes and serve him at court (4.2.33). See Gerold Walser, "Griechen am Hofe des Grosskönigs," in *Festgabe Hans von Greyerz*, ed. Ernst Walder (Bern, 1967), 189–202. *Hipparchicus* 1.17 and *On Horsemanship* 6.12 refer to "the Persian method" of mounting a horse (*ton Persikon tropon*), a technical term for being given a boost up onto the horse. This terminology probably results from the fact that Persian cavalrymen bore heavier armor and equipment than their Greek counterparts and that Persian horses were larger than those ridden by the Greeks. As a result, the Persian knight needed a boost, whereas his Greek counterpart was expected to leap onto his mount unassisted, the boost being reserved for the old, the sick, or the inexperienced. On the equipment of Greek and Persian cavalrymen, see John K. Anderson, *Ancient Greek Horsemanship* (Berkeley, 1961), especially 142–50. *On Horsemanship* 8.6 states that the Persians competed in downhill races without bringing harm to their horses. In *On Horsemanship* 12.11–12 Xenophon prescribes a set of offensive weapons for Greek cavalrymen—a saber for cutting and two cornel-wood javelins—which may be derived from Persian armament. Xenophon had personal experience of the efficacy of Persian cavalry, both on the Anabasis and during his service with the Spartans in Asia Minor. Paul A. Rahe, "The Military Situation in Western Asia on the Eve of Cunaxa," *American Journal of Philology* 101 (1980): 79–96, believes that Xenophon learned from the younger Cyrus about the coordinated use of cavalry and heavy infantry on the plains of Asia and was able to lend his expertise to Agesilaus when the latter created a cavalry force to use against the Persian satraps in western Asia Minor in the mid-390s. See also Anderson, *Ancient Greek Horsemanship*, 151.

In *Oeconomicus* 12.20 Ischomachus, the experienced and successful manager of a country estate, tells Socrates that, in order to make servants good, one must supervise their work and deliver befitting rewards and punishment. He recounts the story in which an expert on horses, asked by the Persian king how most quickly to fatten a horse, recommended the "eye of the master" (*despotou ophthalmos*). Ischomachus adds that, in other matters also, the eye of the master has great effect. This piece of folk wisdom appears elsewhere in Greek literature ([Aristotle] *Oeconomica* 1345a, [Plutarch] *Moralia* 9D), but always in a Persian milieu, as if the Persian connection was significant.

Most references to Persia and Persians in these passages seem quite incidental and provide little scope for inferences about Xenophon's attitudes. *Oeconomicus* 12.20 does imply that wisdom and good sense are to be found among the barbarians, and the picture of the Persian king expressing admirable concern for, and taking personal part in, the management of his affairs has affinities with the two passages from the *Oeconomicus* discussed in the text.

2. Translation of E. C. Marchant, *Xenophon: Memorabilia and Oeconomicus* (Cambridge, Mass., 1918), 477.

3. *Epistles* 7.332A–B, *Laws* 3.695C–D, *Phaedrus* 258B. The Greek tra-

dition of Darius as a lawgiver may have a basis in fact. Darius, who was in many respects a second founder of the Persian Empire, may have sought to codify the laws of the various peoples resident in the empire and perhaps even to introduce a unified legal code for the entire realm, in the tradition of great imperial figures in the ancient Near East dating back to Hammurabi and beyond. See Muhammad A. Dandamayev, "Politische und wirtschaftliche Geschichte," in *Beiträge zur Achämenidengeschichte*, ed. Gerold Walser, Historia Einzelschrift 18 (Wiesbaden, 1972), 25–27; Richard N. Frye, "The Institutions," ibid., 91–93.

4. Roland G. Kent, *Old Persian: Grammar, Texts, Lexicon*, 2d ed. (New Haven, 1953), DB 1.20–22 (pp. 117, 119). Cf. DB 4.65–67 (pp. 129, 132), DNb 16–21 (pp. 138, 140).

5. It should be noted that this diatribe delivered by Socrates expresses Xenophon's views rather than those of his revered mentor. Aside from the a priori likelihood that this chapter reflects Xenophon's own interest in and knowledge of Persia, it is certain on chronological grounds that Xenophon could not have heard Socrates discourse on the death of the younger Cyrus, since Xenophon was absent from Athens between the time of Cyrus' death in battle and the execution of Socrates.

6. Leo Strauss, *Xenophon's Socratic Discourse* (Ithaca, N.Y., 1970), 113.

7. One of the most striking features of *Oeconomicus* 4 is the fact that many of its assertions about Persian provincial administration have parallels in the *Cyropaedia*. These parallels are reserved for discussion in chapter 4.

8. Pierre Briant, "Forces productives, dépendance rurale, et idéologie religieuse dans l'empire achéménide," *Centre de Recherches d'Histoire Ancienne* 32 = *Annales littéraires de l'Université de Besançon* 237 (1980): 15–68. Briant deals with these matters more briefly in "Appareils d'état et développement des forces productives au Moyen-Orient ancien: Le cas de l'empire achéménide," *La Pensée* 217–218 (1981): 9–23.

9. According to Robert C. Zaehner, *The Teachings of the Magi: A Compendium of Zoroastrian Beliefs* (London and New York, 1956), 19, Zoroastrianism made a positive virtue of agriculture. Those who are fighting on the side of Good in the great Cosmic War of Good and Evil were urged to make the earth strong and fruitful so that it might resist the onslaught of death and disease, the minions of Evil. See also Mary Boyce, *A History of Zoroastrianism*, vol. 1: *The Early Period* (Leiden, 1975), 205–6.

10. Briant's argumentation here is not circular, for it is not based primarily on Xenophon and other Greek sources but on Persian royal monuments, the Iranian corpus of sacred writings known as the Avesta, and a study of what he refers to as the Asiatic or tributary mode of production throughout antiquity. For the role of agriculture in the Persian royal ethos, see also Wolfgang Fauth, "Der königliche Gärtner und Jäger in Paradeisos. Beobachtungen zur Rolle des Herrschers in der vorderasiatischen Hortikultur," *Persica* 8 (1979): 1–53.

11. One concrete example of the way in which Xenophon was influ-

enced by Persian practices which he learned about on the Anabasis is the hunting park which he built on his estate at Scillus after his return to Greece. His description of this park in the *Anabasis* (5.3.7–13) is reminiscent of the Persian paradises described elsewhere: the younger Cyrus' parks at Sardis (*Oeconomicus* 4.20–25) and Celaenae (*Anabasis* 1.2.7); Pharnabazus' park at Dascylium (*Hellenica* 4.1.15–16); a Persian park in Mesopotamia (*Anabasis* 2.4.14); a satrap's park in Syria (*Anabasis* 1.4.10); Astyages' paradise (*Cyropaedia* 1.3.14, 1.4.5); the elder Cyrus' injunction to his companions to keep parks (*Cyropaedia* 8.6.12). Xenophon is also the first Greek writer to use the Persian term *paradeisos*. The studies of Pierre Grimal, *Les jardins romains, à la fin de la république et aux deux premiers siècles de l'empire: Essai sur le naturalisme romain* (Paris, 1943), and Elizabeth B. Moynihan, *Paradise as a Garden: In Persia and Mughal India* (New York, 1979), on the history of the private park or pleasure garden suggest that there were no such facilities in mainland Greece before Xenophon built his park at Scillus, and that through his writings Xenophon popularized the notion and influenced its development in Hellenistic and Roman times.

Both Fauth, "Der königliche Gärtner," passim, and Briant, "Forces productives," 33–37, discuss the role of the paradise in the royal ideology and associated propaganda of the Achaemenid kings. The paradise, a conspicuous haven of peace and prosperity, symbolizes the power of the king (and his delegates in the provinces) to bring security and productivity to the lands and peoples of the empire.

12. David M. Lewis, *Sparta and Persia* (Leiden, 1977), 148–52.

13. Translation of R. D. Hicks, *Diogenes Laertius* (Cambridge, Mass., 1959), 181.

14. For Oriental influences at Ephesus, see Plutarch *Lysander* 3.3 and Lewis, *Sparta and Persia*, 116 and n. 60. On the priest Megabyzus see ibid., 108 n. 1. On Anahita, whose cult became especially prominent in the reign of Artaxerxes II, and her identification with the Greek Artemis, see Mary Boyce, *A History of Zoroastrianism*, vol. 2: *Under the Achaemenians* (Leiden, 1982), 201–4, 216–21.

Chapter 2

1. Breitenbach, *Xenophon*, col. 1646; Hartmut Erbse, "Xenophons Anabasis," *Gymnasium* 73 (1966): 485–505. But Rahn, "The Date of Xenophon's Exile," 103–19, makes a very persuasive case that Xenophon was not exiled until 394 or 393, and then for his close connections to Sparta.

2. Breitenbach, *Xenophon*, col. 1646.

3. Higgins, *Xenophon*, 93–94. Higgins does not deny that apologetic aims may play a role in the work, only that to view the *Anabasis* solely in terms of a *Tendenz* is too narrow an approach. He rightly points out that commentators have been seeking explanations outside the work which ought to be found in the work itself.

4. Josef Morr, "Xenophon und der Gedanke eines all-griechischen Eroberungszuges gegen Persien," *Wiener Studien* 45 (1926/27): 186–201;

Jean Luccioni, *Les idées politiques et sociales de Xénophon* (n.p., 1947), 38–44.

5. Delebecque, *Essai*, 199–206. Delebecque is talking about *Anabasis* 1.1–5.3.6. He thinks the *Anabasis* as we have it was composed in two parts, with what he calls the "Parabasis" (from 5.3.7 on) being written at a later time for different reasons and thus reflecting a change of attitude. All of Delebecque's attempts to date Xenophon's works, by relating the attitudes which he perceives in them to contemporary events, are highly subjective. One result of the analysis of the *Anabasis* in this chapter is a demonstration that the motif of trust and deceit is prominent throughout the work. The persistence of the motif implies that the *Anabasis* has a unified intellectual conception and was therefore probably composed at one time.

6. Fernand Robert, "Les intentions de Xénophon dans l'Anabase," *Information littéraire* 2 (1950): 55–59.

7. Against Morr and Luccioni, it can be countered that the lesson of the *Anabasis* is not the ease with which the Ten Thousand managed to escape from the heart of a tottering Persian Empire, but rather the great dangers and difficulties, both external and internal (such as the extreme internal dissension and near disintegration of the Greek army on several occasions in the later books), which an invading Greek army, especially a panhellenic army, would have had to face. Donald W. Engels, *Alexander the Great and the Logistics of the Macedonian Army* (Berkeley, 1978), 121, maintains that "the terrain of the Persian Empire was in a real sense the Persian king's most formidable weapon." It created immense logistical problems both for Alexander, who succeeded in conquering Persia, and for those who tried and failed (such as Crassus, Antony, and Julian). Moreover, anyone conquering the Persian Empire would necessarily inherit the weaknesses of that empire which emerge from Xenophon's account—its unwieldy size, which impeded communications and defense, and the presence within its boundaries of savage independent tribes—as the experiences of Alexander and his successors attest. And although the superiority of Greek hoplites is not to be doubted, a careful reading of Xenophon's account will show that the battle of Cunaxa was essentially a draw and that some of the barbarian troops acquitted themselves admirably, both then and in later attacks on the retreating Greek army.

Isocrates minimized the difficulties and exaggerated the successes of the Ten Thousand in order to prove that Persia was ripe for conquest (*Panegyricus* 146–49; *Philippus* 90–91, 97); see Georges Mathieu, *Les idées politiques d'Isocrate* (Paris, 1925), 62–63. It could also be argued that Isocrates feared that others would infer from Xenophon's account how difficult the task had been unless he tampered with the details. Whatever the motives, his misinterpretation influenced the conception of later historians, both ancient (e.g., Polybius 3.6) and modern. For a further refutation of this interpretation of the *Anabasis*, see George L. Cawkwell, Introduction to Rex Warner, trans., *Xenophon: The Persian Expedition* (New York, 1972), 26–29.

Robert's approach is open to the same dangers inherent in Delebecque's methodology pointed out in n. 5 above. The *Anabasis*, with its rich and varied content, must surely be more than the resumé of an old war-horse.

8. G. B. Nussbaum, *The Ten Thousand: A Study in Social Organization and Action in Xenophon's Anabasis* (Leiden, 1967), 1–13, 147–56.

9. Higgins, *Xenophon*, 82–98. Higgins' chapter on the *Anabasis* is one of the best in his book. He proceeds from the salutary premise that Xenophon is intelligent and has something to say. His interpretations are sometimes tenuous, sometimes convincing, but always provocative, and in general they increase the reader's enjoyment and understanding of Xenophon's works.

10. Leonard Wencis, "*Hypopsia* and the Structure of Xenophon's *Anabasis*," *Classical Journal* 73 (1977): 44–49.

11. In fact Herodotus, influenced by the techniques of poetry and drama, had already taken this approach to the writing of history; see Charles W. Fornara, *Herodotus: An Interpretative Essay* (Oxford, 1971), 59–74. It is reasonable to assume that Xenophon was familiar with the work of Herodotus, who earlier had also traveled widely in the Persian Empire and likewise claimed expertise on Persian affairs. The *Cyropaedia* furnishes strong indications of Xenophon's familiarity with his account. See chap. 4 and nn. 17 and 18 there.

12. However, as recent research has shown, this seeming objectivity is a pose. Thucydides has selected events and shaped speeches in such a way that they lead the reader to a particular conclusion. See now W. Robert Connor, *Thucydides* (Princeton, 1984), 3–19.

13. Jacob Burckhardt, *Griechische Kulturgeschichte*, vol. 3 (Berlin and Leipzig, 1931), 422: "Dabei ist das Werk schmucklos, ohne alle gesuchte Beredsamkeit; die Wirkung wird völlig dem Geschehenen überlassen." Hippolyte Taine, "Xénophon: l'Anabase," in *Essais de critique et d'histoire*, 10th ed. (Paris, 1904), 152: "Xénophon ne parle pas de lui-même; point de réflexions generales; rien que des faits, exposés avec autant de naïveté que de concision." Nussbaum, *Ten Thousand*, 1–2, also notes the influence of Thucydides in the objectivity which lets events unfold and explain themselves.

14. Werner Jaeger, *Paideia: The Ideals of Greek Culture*, vol. 3 (Oxford, 1943), 159.

15. Dionysius of Halicarnassus *Letter to Pompeius Geminus* 4.777; Dio Chrysostom 18.14–17; Eunapius *Vitae Sophistarum* 453 (Boissonade). I am indebted for all these references to J. Joel Farber, "Xenophon's Theory of Kingship" (Ph.D. diss., Yale University, 1959), ix–xiv. For a detailed account of the reaction to Xenophon in antiquity, see Münscher, *Xenophon in der griechisch-römischen Literatur*.

16. See W. R. Connor, "A Post-Modernist Thucydides," *Classical Journal* 72 (1977): 289–98, who summarizes these and other trends in recent Thucydidean scholarship, some of which might usefully be applied to the analysis of Xenophon's *Anabasis*.

17. See chapter 4 for a discussion of the links between the *Anabasis* and the *Cyropaedia*.

18. Wencis, "*Hypopsia*," passim.
19. Higgins, *Xenophon*, 84.
20. This notion was so pervasive that Eduard Meyer, *Geschichte des Altertums*, vol. IV.1, 3d ed. (Stuttgart, 1939), 35 n. 1, felt constrained to defend the essential truthfulness of the Persian people, both ancient and modern, against the conviction of nineteenth-century scholars that they were born liars.
21. On the role of the Lie in Zoroastrianism, see Abraham V. W. Jackson, *Zoroastrian Studies* (New York, 1928), 28–31, 67, 99–103; James H. Moulton, *Early Zoroastrianism* (London, 1913), 131–37; Robert C. Zaehner, *The Dawn and Twilight of Zoroastrianism* (London, 1961), 34–37.

There has long been a dispute among Iranologists as to whether the Achaemenid kings and their Persian subjects were indeed devotees of the demanding ethical and religious system first formulated by the prophet Zarathustra. Recent scholars have tended to accept the proposition that they were. Darius' Behistun inscription, though political in purpose, is surprisingly expressive of his personal religious feelings and reflects a Zoroastrian ethical outlook. He is a convinced dualist and equates rebellion against himself with the working of *drauga* (Lie/Deceit). An inscription by Xerxes claims that he destroyed the sanctuaries of the *daevas* (demons) and replaced them with the rites of Ahura Mazda. Zaehner, *Dawn and Twilight*, 154–61, sensibly notes that, whether or not Darius and his successors were formally disciples of Zoroaster, in its essentials their religion was closely akin to his teachings. The most recent work on the operations of cult, as known from the Elamite tablets at Persepolis dated to the reign of Darius, shows clearly the primacy of a religion based on Zoroastrian principles. See Heidemarie Koch, *Die religiösen Verhältnisse der Dareioszeit* (Wiesbaden, 1977), 171–84. And now the second volume of Boyce's *History of Zoroastrianism*, destined to be the definitive book on the subject for some time to come, maintains that the Persian kings were unequivocally Zoroastrians throughout the entire existence of the empire. Boyce cites the occurrence, in the Achaemenid clan, of names with Zoroastrian connotations from at least the early sixth century and hypothesizes that Cyrus the Great was able to enlist widespread support for his rebellion against his Median overlord, including that of Median nobles, because Cyrus championed the increasingly popular Zoroastrian religion against the Old Iranian faith of the Median king Astyages (pp. 41–43).

22. This is different from the Greek conviction that it is permissible to deceive enemies. In *Agesilaus* 1.17 Xenophon declares that, in time of war, deceiving an enemy becomes a righteous and just act: ὅσιόν τε καὶ δίκαιον. Similar words are put into the mouth of Socrates (*Memorabilia* 4.2.15). See the discussion later in this chapter for more on the Greek attitude toward lies and deception.
23. Translation from Ilya Gershevitch, *The Avestan Hymn to Mithra* (Cambridge, 1959), 75 (Yasht 10.2). For the date of composition of the hymn see ibid., 13–22.
24. Ibid., 26ff.

25. Kent, *Old Persian*, A²Sa, A²Sd, A²Hb (pp. 154–55).
26. Ctesias apud Athenaeus *Deipnosophistae* 10.45.
27. Norman O. Brown, *Hermes the Thief* (New York, 1947).
28. Kenneth J. Dover, *Aristophanes' Clouds* (Oxford, 1968), 263 at line 1458.
29. For Greek attitudes toward lying (in ancient and modern times), see the interesting discussion of P. Walcot, "Odysseus and the Art of Lying," *Ancient Society* 8 (1977): 1–19. See also Lionel Pearson, *Popular Ethics in Ancient Greece* (Stanford, 1962), index s.v. "deceit," "oaths," "treachery and betrayal"; Kenneth J. Dover, *Greek Popular Morality in the Time of Plato and Aristotle* (Berkeley, 1974), 249–51.
30. Albin Lesky, *A History of Greek Literature*, trans. James Willis and Cornelis de Heer (New York, 1966), 620: "He admittedly based his *Hellenica* on one leading idea which is prominent in the inserted preface 5.4,1; the rise of Sparta to be the ruler of Greece was necessarily followed by the decline of her power; in the spirit of ancient Greek piety, this was related to the wrath of the gods, for the Spartans had broken the oath that they would leave the autonomy of the Greek states unimpaired." Higgins, *Xenophon*, 104, stresses the insidious role of deception throughout the *Hellenica*. Xenophon's highest praise is reserved for the citizens of Phlius, who maintain their *pistis* (loyalty) to Sparta through thick and thin (*Hellenica* 7.2). For *pistis* in the *Agesilaus*, see chapter 3.
31. Henry Wood, The *Histories of Herodotus* (The Hague, 1972), 21–33.
32. Although Nussbaum's quadripartite division has influenced my discussion here, our schemes are not identical. His is predicated on the changing purposes of the Greek mercenaries; mine is based on stages in the development of the motif of trust and deceit.
33. Some historians believe that Cyrus actually plotted against his brother and that Tissaphernes is therefore reporting the truth. Whatever the facts, what matters in this consideration of the *Anabasis* as a document of ideas is that Xenophon claims that Tissaphernes *slandered* Cyrus. This statement sets the tone for what follows.
34. Xenophon *Hellenica* 3.4.5–6, 11.
35. For the historical Tissaphernes, see now Thomas Petit, *Tissapherne: Les mésaventures d'une ambition*, Mémoires de l'Université de Liège (Liège, 1978–79). Cf. [?] Nicolai, *Die Politik des Tissaphernes* (Bernburg, 1863).
36. Arnold W. Gomme, *A Historical Commentary on Thucydides*, vol. 1 (Oxford, 1945), 153; Lionel Pearson, "Prophasis and Aitia," *Transactions of the American Philological Association* 83 (1952): 205–23 and "Prophasis: A Clarification," *Transactions of the American Philological Association* 103 (1972): 381–94; Hunter R. Rawlings III, *A Semantic Study of Prophasis to 400 B.C.*, Hermes Einzelschrift 33 (Wiesbaden, 1975), 56–57.
37. *Anabasis* 1.9.7–8. The translation here, as elsewhere in this chapter, is from Carleton L. Brownson, *Xenophon: Anabasis* (London and New York, 1921). The Greek text is as follows: πρῶτον μὲν ἐπέδειξεν αὐτὸν ὅτι περὶ πλείστου ποιοῖτο, εἴ τῳ σπείσαιτο καὶ εἴ τῳ συνθοῖτο καὶ εἴ τῳ

ὑπόσχοιτό τι, μηδαμῶς ψεύδεσθαι. καὶ γὰρ οὖν ἐπίστευον μὲν αὐτῷ αἱ πόλεις ἐπιτρεπόμεναι, ἐπίστευον δ᾽ οἱ ἄνδρες· καὶ εἴ τις πολέμιος ἐγένετο, σπεισαμένου Κύρου ἐπίστευε μηδὲν ἂν παρὰ τὰς σπονδὰς παθεῖν.

38. Cyrus had taken over many of Tissaphernes' prerogatives when he was dispatched to Asia Minor, and Tissaphernes' hostility toward him, even his slander of Cyrus before Artaxerxes (if it was that), may have been motivated by bitterness over his demotion in favor of the young prince.

39. Other details in the encomium of Cyrus indicate that Xenophon knew something about Persian values and customs or, at the least, that he was a shrewd and discerning observer of the conduct of Cyrus and the other Persians in his camp. Cyrus' harsh punishment of malefactors in his province (1.9.13), though it has disturbed modern commentators, receives no criticism from Xenophon and is in complete accord with the Zoroastrian dualist view of the universe, in which the war between Good and Evil is waged without respite or mercy.

Elsewhere in the encomium (1.9.20–21) Xenophon refers to the fact that Cyrus regarded his friends as partners or co-workers—*synergoi*—and, anxious to have as many partners as possible, endeavored vigorously to promote his friends' interests. This distinctive choice of words calls to mind the fact that Darius, in the Behistun inscription, stresses the favor which he shows to those who "co-operate" with him (Kent, *Old Persian*, DB 4.65–67). The Old Persian word *hamataxšata* is semantically equivalent to the Greek *synergos*. Xenophon may here be demonstrating his familiarity with the etiquette of a Persian court by rendering into Greek an honorific title or, at the least, an authentic Persian way of referring to royal intimates.

Xenophon also refers to the fact that Cyrus was technically a slave (*doulos*) of the Persian king (1.9.29). Indeed, this is how the Persian king referred to his subjects, even members of the nobility and governing hierarchy of the empire. At Behistun Darius speaks repeatedly of *manā bandakā*, "my slave," in reference to high-ranking subordinates.

See now Boyce, *History of Zoroastrianism*, II, 211–16, who feels that in the *Anabasis* and *Cyropaedia* Xenophon displays an awareness of many authentic aspects of Zoroastrian practice.

40. Perhaps Xenophon also stresses Cyrus' trustworthiness for another reason. He may mean to defend his own conduct in following Cyrus by demonstrating that it was only natural to trust Cyrus, a man who inspired confidence in all with whom he came in contact.

Other commentators have been bothered by the apparent discrepancy between Cyrus' actions and Xenophon's praise of his *pistis*. Ivo Bruns, *Das literarische Porträt der Griechen* (1896; reprint, Hildesheim, 1961), 137–44, thinks that Xenophon was dazzled by Cyrus, who belonged to an alien and marvelous world, and as a result failed to perceive the wickedness of Cyrus' attempt on his brother's throne. Higgins, *Xenophon*, 83–84, who maintains that Xenophon's irony often goes undetected, argues that modern readers have missed Xenophon's signs indicating that Cyrus was authoritarian, cruel, unjust in seeking what belonged to others, materialistic, headstrong, and full of deceit.

I believe that Bruns is overly naive, Higgins excessively subtle. Xenophon knew what Cyrus was up to but made allowances for it, presumably because he regarded Cyrus' cause as just (and he would have heard only Cyrus' side of the story). Professor A. E. Raubitschek has drawn my attention to a similar ambivalence toward deceit in the plays of Sophocles, where deceit is tolerable under certain circumstances.

It might be possible to argue that Cyrus misleads the Greeks without quite lying to them. If one looks closely at the wording of the two passages in which he proclaims, as the purpose of the campaign, his desire to punish the Pisidians and the Syrian satrap Abrocomas (1.2.1, 1.3.20–21), it can be maintained that these are half-truths rather than lies—that he has told the truth so far as it goes, but omitted to mention his main purpose. Such deception through a clever choice of words might have been tolerated by the Greeks, who insisted on adherence to the letter, rather than to the spirit, of an agreement (see Brown, *Hermes the Thief*, 8–9).

To those who might protest that Cyrus, as a Zoroastrian, was forbidden to engage in such duplicity, I would only suggest that Zoroastrian society presumably tolerated less flagrant violations of its ideal standards in the same way that Christian society does. See Boyce, *History of Zoroastrianism*, II, 54–57, for a discussion of the Persian kings' willingness to go against Zoroastrian precepts on burial for reasons of state.

41. There is no compelling reason why Xenophon, who was technically only a guest of his Boeotian friend Proxenus, should have been present at the command conferences; at 3.1.4 he is quite explicit about the fact that he was "neither general nor captain nor private" (οὔτε στρατηγὸς οὔτε λοχαγὸς οὔτε στρατιώτης). However, Professor J. K. Anderson has pointed out to me that Xenophon must have done something to gain the confidence of the Greek officers who chose him as their leader after the murder of the generals, and that, furthermore, Xenophon's description of his own actions just before the charge at Cunaxa, when he advanced to receive last-minute orders from Cyrus (1.8.15–17), implies that he held some position of responsibility, perhaps as aide-de-camp or chief of staff for Proxenus, who was one of the commanders of Cyrus' Greek mercenaries. In that case he could have been present at the meetings of the Greek generals with Tissaphernes.

42. In accordance with the practice of Herodotus and Thucydides, ancient historians customarily took liberties with the speeches they inserted in their narratives. Such speeches often serve an editorial purpose, crystallizing the issues, providing commentary on events, and characterizing the protagonists.

43. Delebecque, *Essai*, 32–33, who thinks that *Hellenica* 1 and 2 were written before Xenophon left Athens to join Cyrus in 401, points out that Xenophon does not seem to manifest the same hostility toward Tissaphernes in these early writings.

44. Consider, in addition to his positive portrayal of the younger Cyrus, the brief neutral description of Tiribazus, a Persian official whom the Ten Thousand encounter while traversing western Armenia (*Anabasis* 4.4.4–6), and the quite favorable image of the satrap Pharnabazus which runs through the *Hellenica*.

160 / Notes

45. Irony is a sustained and palpable feature of this section of the *Anabasis*. Higgins, *Xenophon*, 12–15, discusses Xenophon's often overlooked penchant for irony.

46. ὁ ἐμὸς ἔρως τούτου αἴτιος τὸ τοῖς Ἕλλησιν ἐμὲ πιστὸν γενέσθαι, καὶ ᾧ Κῦρος ἀνέβη ξενικῷ διὰ μισθοδοσίας πιστεύων τούτῳ ἐμὲ καταβῆναι δι' εὐεργεσίαν ἰσχυρόν. ὅσα δ' ἐμοὶ χρήσιμοι ὑμεῖς ἐστι τὰ μὲν καὶ σὺ εἶπας, τὸ δὲ μέγιστον ἐγὼ οἶδα· τὴν μὲν γὰρ ἐπὶ τῇ κεφαλῇ τιάραν βασιλεῖ μόνῳ ἔξεστιν ὀρθὴν ἔχειν, τὴν δ' ἐπὶ τῇ καρδίᾳ ἴσως ἂν ὑμῶν παρόντων καὶ ἕτερος εὐπετῶς ἔχοι.

47. As with Greek tragedy, every contemporary reader must have known the bare essentials of the story and been able to appreciate the irony of this scene.

48. Ctesias, who was, like Xenophon, a participant in some of these events, gives quite a different picture of Clearchus (Felix Jacoby, ed., *Die Fragmente der griechischen Historiker*, vol. III.C.1 [Leiden, 1958], no. 688 F27. Cf. Plutarch *Artaxerxes* 18). He reports that Tissaphernes was able to entrap the Greek generals through the agency of Menon. Clearchus foresaw the plot and put up resistance, but he was forced into compliance by the others. Ctesias, acting on behalf of the Persian queen mother, Parysatis, provided some comfort and assistance to the imprisoned Clearchus. When the Greeks were executed (except for Menon, who was presumably spared in reward for his complicity), a miracle occurred which showed the gods' favor toward Clearchus, for a great wind heaped up a burial mound over his body and a shady grove soon sprang up above it.

Ctesias' version differs from Xenophon's account in several essential respects. According to Ctesias, Menon is an active partner of Tissaphernes and is spared because of his collusion, whereas Xenophon makes him as much a dupe as Clearchus and insists that he suffered a terrible death. More important, in Ctesias' version it is Clearchus who foresees Tissaphernes' treachery and tries to oppose it, whereas Xenophon has Clearchus completely taken in by Tissaphernes and forcing the others to go along against their better judgment.

Cawkwell, Introduction to *Persian Expedition*, 24–26, seems to accept much of Ctesias' version and argues that Menon and Proxenus accused Clearchus of conspiring against Tissaphernes. Tissaphernes' preexisting suspicions were thus confirmed, and he understandably summoned Clearchus for trial. This is a clever scenario. But Ctesias' source is Clearchus, who is then in a Persian prison and is likely to give a self-serving version. Xenophon's treatment, in which both Clearchus and Menon are outwitted by Tissaphernes, is subtler and less open to suspicion of bias.

Whatever the truth of the matter, the existence of a discrepant version of these events accentuates the particular slant which Xenophon gave to his portrait of Clearchus.

49. *Cyropaedia* 8.8.2–3: οἶδα γὰρ ὅτι πρότερον μὲν βασιλεὺς καὶ οἱ ὑπ' αὐτῷ καὶ τοῖς τὰ ἔσχατα πεποιηκόσιν εἴτε ὅρκους ὀμόσειαν, ἠμπέδουν, εἴτε δεξιὰς δοῖεν, ἐβεβαίουν. εἰ δὲ μὴ τοιοῦτοι ἦσαν καὶ τοιαύτην δόξαν εἶχον οὐδ' ἂν εἰς αὐτοῖς ἐπίστευσεν, ὥσπερ οὐδὲ νῦν πιστεύει οὐδὲ εἰς ἔτι, ἐπεὶ ἔγνωσται ἡ ἀσέβεια αὐτῶν. οὕτως οὐδὲ τότε ἐπίστευσαν ἂν

Notes / 161

οἱ τῶν σὺν Κύρῳ ἀναβάντων στρατηγοί· νῦν δὲ δὴ τῇ πρόσθεν αὐτῶν δόξῃ πιστεύσαντες ἐνεχείρισαν ἑαυτούς, καὶ ἀναχθέντες πρὸς βασιλέα ἀπετμήθησαν τὰς κεφαλάς. For the question whether Xenophon wrote the epilogue to the *Cyropaedia*, see chapter 4.

50. Herodotus provides several stories which demonstrate the Persians' absolute commitment to the fulfillment of oaths and promises; examples are 4.201 (the siege of Barca) and 9.104 (Xerxes and Artaynte). It is also worth noting that, in that famous passage of Aristophanes' *Acharnians* (lines 98–114) in which a Persian dignitary—the King's Eye—is presented to the Athenian assembly by a group of Athenian envoys who have just returned from the Great King's court, the Persian speaks the truth (to the extent that one can make Greek out of his barbarian gibberish), but his words are willfully misrepresented by the Athenian envoys.

The Jews were also struck by the steadfastness of the Persian king once he had given his sanction to an edict. The Old Testament contains several references to "the law of the Medes and the Persians which cannot be revoked" (Daniel 6:8, 6:12, 6:15; Esther 1:19, 8:8); and in the Book of Daniel, Darius is bound to honor his own edict and cast Daniel into the lions' den even though it goes against his own wishes.

Leo Raditsa, "Iranians in Asia Minor," in *The Cambridge History of Iran*, vol. III.1: *The Seleucid, Parthian, and Sassanian Periods*, ed. Ehsan Yarshater (Cambridge, 1983), 109, describes the reputation, during the Hellenistic period, of a temple at Zela in Pontus which had been consecrated by Artaxerxes II: ". . . men came from everywhere to make oaths on matters of crucial importance in the sanctuary of the Persian gods at Zela (Strabo xii.3.37). That the Persian gods guaranteed men's words says something for the moral authority of the Achaemenians and their gods in Pontus and Cappadocia."

51. He speaks of ἐπιορκία, ἀσεβεία, ἀπιστία, ὁμόσας, ἠδέσθη, πιστά, and the like.

52. H. D. Westlake, "Individuals in Xenophon, *Hellenica*," *Bulletin of the John Rylands Library* 49 (1966–67): 255, notes that "speeches delivered in the early stages of his command [i.e., Xenophon in the *Anabasis*] were designed mainly to bolster the morale of the Greeks."

53. Shortly afterward one Greek captain actually defected with some of his men to the Persian side (3.3.5). This incident suggests that the Greek leadership had to cope with a faction which favored negotiating a settlement with the Persians.

54. In fact Xenophon took measures to provide a makeshift cavalry contingent for the Greeks (3.3.19–20).

55. In *Hellenica* 2.4.43 Xenophon tells how the leaders of the newly restored democracy at Athens killed the generals of the Thirty, who had come for a conference. Presumably oaths and assurances had been given and then ignored. The fact that Xenophon expresses no outrage there makes the righteous indignation of the speeches in the *Anabasis* look like a rhetorical ploy. Certainly Greeks were capable of comparable iniquity.

56. Perhaps one is even entitled to be skeptical about the alleged report

of the prisoner that Tiribazus was planning such an ambuscade, in which case the attack on his camp is a second, unprovoked breach of the truce by the Greeks.

57. 7.6.41 proves that Heraclides is a Greek.

58. In a speech to the assembled Greek troops, Xenophon does claim that Seuthes has played false in the matter of wages and has deceived his Greek allies (7.6.15, 21, 23). But these statements are made without recrimination, since Xenophon's purpose is to excuse himself of misconduct rather than to accuse Seuthes. As we shall see, Xenophon later persuades Seuthes to pay the wages and so much as says that Seuthes was misled by Heraclides (7.7.48). Even at that time Seuthes does not have the cash with which to pay the Greek troops and is forced to substitute cattle, sheep, and slaves (7.7.53). The implication is that he had not withheld moneys due with intent to defraud.

59. All the words translated as "deceive" in this passage are forms of *exapataō*.

60. This impression is confirmed by Xenophon's statement to the same effect in *Agesilaus* 11.4: καὶ τοὺς μὲν ὑπὸ φίλων ἐξαπατωμένους οὐκ ἔψεγε (subject is Agesilaus), τοὺς δὲ ὑπὸ πολεμίων πάμπαν κατεμέμφετο καὶ τὸ μὲν ἀπιστοῦντας ἐξαπατᾶν σοφὸν ἔκρινε, τὸ δὲ πιστεύοντας ἀνόσιον—"If friends proved deceivers he forebore to blame their victims, but he heaped reproaches on those who let an enemy deceive them; and he pronounced deception clever or wicked according as it was practised on the suspicious or the confiding" (Edgar C. Marchant, trans., *Xenophon: Scripta Minora* [Cambridge, Mass., 1925], 129).

61. Wencis, "*Hypopsia*," has already commented on the climactic nature of this speech. His analysis of the *Anabasis* in terms of the motif of *hypopsia*—suspicion—has close connections at certain points with my investigation of the themes of trust and deceit in the same work, and this speech is the dramatic culmination for both lines of enquiry.

62. Although there is no consistent scheme of retribution for lies and deceit in the *Anabasis*, many deceivers are deceived in turn and punished in the end, whereas Xenophon and the Greeks are ultimately saved. Even the archvillain Tissaphernes, though he escapes serious discomfiture in the *Anabasis*, meets a fitting demise in the *Hellenica* (3.4.25). And the greedy and treacherous Greek general Menon is subjected to the most excruciating of deaths (*Anabasis* 2.6.29). Xenophon's insistence on this point is significant, since Ctesias reports that Menon was spared. See n. 48 above.

63. See n. 30 above.

64. Loyalty—of servant to master, of vassal to lord, of family members to one another—is the glue which helps to bind together a society that lacks fully developed juridical and political institutions. In their early days the Greeks had been in such a position, and the importance of loyalty and fidelity for the orderly functioning of society is a central concern in the *Odyssey*. The Persians, for all their vast empire and administrative bureaucracy, still lived according to a code of values which responded to the needs of the tribal and nomadic existence which they had only recently left be-

hind, and accordingly they placed greater emphasis on such social virtues as *pistis*.

Chapter 3

1. There is also a brief preface (1.1–5), which justifies the work and recounts Agesilaus' ancestry and acquisition of the throne, and a transitional passage between the second and third sections (10).
2. *Agesilaus* 1.10–12. This and the other quotations of the *Agesilaus* in this chapter are from the translation of Marchant, *Xenophon: Scripta Minora*.
3. Lonis, *Usages de la guerre*, establishes that Greek soldiers in the fourth century extended the same treatment to Greeks and barbarians in time of war, from which he infers that the average Greek did not regard himself as superior to barbarians.
4. Such as *proskynesis*, here misleadingly translated as "cringe." The Greeks reserved such homage for the gods, but it was a part of court protocol among the Persians and did not, so far as can be told, imply the divinity of the king.
5. See Frank E. Adcock, *The Greek and Macedonian Art of War* (Berkeley, 1957), 7.
6. As is known from *Hellenica* 3.4.25–26.
7. Xenophon claims, in the first line of the *Agesilaus*, that his purpose is to write an *epainos* or laudation.
8. εἴ γε μὴν αὖ καλὸν Ἕλληνα ὄντα φιλέλληνα εἶναι . . . εἰ δ' αὖ καλὸν καὶ μισοπέρσην εἶναι. . . .
9. *Misopersēs* is a hapax legomenon. Cf. Plato *Menexenus* 246, where Athens' hostility to the barbarian is denoted by the term *to misobarbaron*.
10. It is also worth noting that there is in the *Agesilaus* no intimation that the Persian Empire is weak or tottering on the brink of collapse, a fanciful notion advanced by Isocrates and embraced by too many modern historians. See Chester G. Starr, "Greeks and Persians in the Fourth Century B.C.: A Study in Cultural Contacts before Alexander," *Iranica Antiqua* 11 (1975): 69–75.
11. The formal comparison begins at 9.1, but the train of thought actually goes back to 8.6.
12. That the Persian king was, for the Greeks, the supreme symbol of unbounded wealth and power, is clear. A number of Greek sources preserve what must have been a commonplace in which somebody says that he would not trade some simple virtue or possession for all the Persian king's money or empire. This claim occurs in several places in Xenophon (*Symposium* 3.13 and 4.11) and Plato (*Lysis* 211E; *Euthydemus* 274A; *Eryxias* 393D). Plato railed against the shallowness of those who believed the Persian king to be the most fortunate member of the human race, since they took into account only materialistic criteria and ignored such truly valuable commodities as friendship, good health, self-knowledge, and a clear conscience (*Sophist* 230D; *Gorgias* 470E; *Apology* 40D).
13. The Socratics were also prone to idealize Sparta's way of life and

constitution, as in the fragments of Critias, Plato's *Republic* and *Laws*, and Xenophon's *Constitution of the Lacedaemonians*. See François Ollier, *Le mirage spartiate*, vol. 1: *Étude sur l'idéalisation de Sparte dans l'antiquité grecque de l'origine jusqu'aux cyniques* (Paris, 1933), 210–93; E. N. Tigerstedt, *The Legend of Sparta in Classical Antiquity* (Lund, 1965), 241–80.

14. For example, Bruns, *Das literarische Porträt*, 126–37; and Albrecht Dihle, *Studien zur griechischen Biographie* (Göttingen, 1956), 27–29. See appendix B at the end of this chapter for further discussion of the connections between the *Agesilaus* and Isocrates' *Evagoras*.

15. It is generally believed that Artaxerxes II, who occupied the throne for most of Xenophon's adult life, was one of the least impressive of Persian kings. Plutarch *Life of Artaxerxes* 6.3 reports the taunt of the younger Cyrus that his brother the king, because of his faintheartedness and softness, was unable to keep his horse on the hunt or his throne in time of danger. Cyrus is likely to have been the source for Xenophon's conception of Artaxerxes, so Xenophon would have received a hostile and polemic picture. (Of course, this portrayal may only have been propaganda meant to encourage Cyrus' partners in rebellion.) And the author of the epilogue to the *Cyropaedia* lays much of the blame on Artaxerxes for the decline of contemporary Persia (8.8.12). Starr, "Greeks and Persians," who is concerned in large part with the reign of Artaxerxes II, provides a valuable corrective to this ancient prejudice by pointing out that, despite the abuse of Artaxerxes in the Greek sources and his momentary political and military setbacks, "in the end Persian forces won every time" (p. 72). In any case, the terms in which Xenophon criticizes the Persian king do not seem inspired by a distinct individual personality.

16. Xenophon derived his account of Agesilaus' deeds in the *Agesilaus* from his *Hellenica*. For further discussion of this matter see appendix A at the end of this chapter. Klaus Bringmann, "Xenophons Hellenika und Agesilaos," *Gymnasium* 78 (1971): 228–30, provides a convenient summary of matters in the *Hellenica* which have been altered or omitted altogether in the *Agesilaus*.

17. Bruns, *Das literarische Porträt*, 126–37; Friedrich Leo, *Die griechisch-römische Biographie nach ihrer literarischen Form* (Leipzig, 1901), 87–95; Dihle, *Studien*, 27–29; Arnaldo Momigliano, *The Development of Greek Biography* (Cambridge, Mass., 1971), 46–52.

18. Bruns, *Das literarische Porträt*, 136–37.

19. Dihle, *Studien*, 28. John K. Anderson, *Xenophon* (New York, 1974), 167–69, maintains that Xenophon wanted to depict a noble character and that the account is authentic insofar as it displays values to which Agesilaus (and Xenophon) subscribed, however much he may have failed to realize them. Xenophon deliberately suppressed the negative elements of Agesilaus' career, yet even a casual reading of the *Hellenica* proves that he was aware of Agesilaus' failings and occasionally indulged in implicit criticism of Agesilaus and Sparta. Bruns, *Das literarische Porträt*, 131–32, is almost alone in maintaining that the *Agesilaus* is essentially accurate in its portrayal of the personality and character of Agesilaus.

Notes / 165

20. Luccioni, *Idées*, 192–200.
21. Dihle, *Studien*, 28.
22. Delebecque, *Essai*, 462–70.
23. Breitenbach, *Xenophon*, cols. 1702–7.
24. Higgins, *Xenophon*, 76–82.
25. Delebecque, *Essai*, 470, is aware of an apologetic purpose among Xenophon's several aims in the *Agesilaus*.
26. Translation of C. L. Sherman, *Diodorus Siculus: Library of History*, vol. 7 (Cambridge, Mass., 1952).
27. Plutarch cites Xenophon, Theophrastus, Duris, Theopompus, Hieronymus the Philosopher, Dicaearchus, Callisthenes, Dioscorides, records at Lacedaemon, and a letter of Agesilaus to Hidrieus the Carian. See Isaäc Bos, Introduction to *Plutarchus' Leven van Agesilaus* (Groningen, 1947) for a discussion of the sources. G. L. Cawkwell, "Agesilaus and Sparta," *Classical Quarterly*, n.s. 26 (1976): 64 n. 12, suggests that Plutarch relied heavily on Theopompus and thinks it possible that he derived information from Xenophon only indirectly, via the account of Theopompus. But he is mistaken in his belief that Plutarch does not cite Xenophon directly (he does so in 4.1).
28. It is conceivable that Plutarch, who was from Boeotia and who in *De malignitate Herodoti* launches a scathing attack on Herodotus for his alleged hostility and unfairness to Thebes, is also predisposed against Agesilaus as a perennial opponent of Thebes. But the venom and irrational fury of the *De malignitate* are absent in the *Life of Agesilaus*.
29. The actual facts of Agesilaus' career are not at issue here, only Xenophon's literary treatment of that career. For historical studies of the career of Agesilaus, besides the dissertation of E. Zierke, *Agesilaos. Beiträge zum Lebensbild und zur Politik des Spartanerkönigs* (Frankfurt, 1936), see the recent articles by R. E. Smith, "The Opposition to Agesilaus' Foreign Policy, 394–371 B.C.," *Historia* 2 (1954): 274–88; Cawkwell, "Agesilaus and Sparta"; D. G. Rice, "Agesilaus, Agesipolis, and Spartan Politics, 386–379 B.C.," *Historia* 23 (1974): 164–82; Robin Seager, "The King's Peace and the Balance of Power in Greece, 386–362 B.C.," *Athenaeum* 52 (1974): 36–63.
30. For the purposes of this inquiry, it is not necessary to decide whether Xenophon was responding to verbal attacks or to written works critical of Agesilaus. Dietfried Krömer, *Xenophons Agesilaos: Untersuchungen zur Komposition* (Augsburg, 1971), 70–71, notes that there is no evidence for the latter. On the other hand, there must have been some contemporary or near-contemporary written sources for the bias against Agesilaus which surfaces in Diodorus and Plutarch.
31. Krömer, *Xenophons Agesilaos*, 130–31, thinks this story was excluded because it had no political importance. Yet Xenophon includes in the *Agesilaus* other stories of equal unimportance, such as the anecdote about the racing stable of Agesilaus' sister, Cynisca (9.6). Since Xenophon's avowed aim is encomiastic, not historical or even biographical, there is little likelihood that political importance is his criterion for inclusion. He selects stories which best illustrate the character of Agesilaus.

Krömer also thinks that Xenophon's brief coverage of the period after the battle of Coronea is due simply to the fact that "inessential" details from the *Hellenica* narrative have been left out. But one cannot seriously maintain that such major matters as Agesilaus' collaboration with Persia in the King's Peace or his involvement in the affairs of Phoebidas and Sphodrias can be classified as inessential details. Moreover, in his considerably more detailed account of the period before Coronea, Xenophon includes many details that are inessential from the standpoint of historical significance, such as Agesilaus' efforts to help his friends make money from the sale of booty (1.18) or his care for abandoned children (1.21). Of course these anecdotes contribute to a picture of Agesilaus' character, and that is why they are included.

32. Xenophon represents Agesilaus as an envoy sent by the Spartan state to Ariobarzanes, the satrap of Hellespontine Phrygia, who was at that time in revolt against the Persian king (*Ages.* 2.26–27). However, on the basis of a statement in Nepos' *Timotheus* (1.3) and several anecdotes in Polyaenus (2.1.16, 2.1.26, 7.26), historians are inclined to believe that Agesilaus was actually little more than a hired *condottiere* in the service of the Persian rebel. See Karl J. Beloch, *Griechische Geschichte*, vol. III.1, 2d ed. (Berlin and Leipzig, 1922), 193 and n. 3.

33. See J. Hatzfeld, "Agésilas et Artaxerxès II," *Bulletin de correspondance hellénique* 70 (1946): 238–46, for the historical context of this incident.

34. Momigliano, *Greek Biography*, chaps. 2 and 3 passim, while investigating the origins of Greek biography notes that both encomium and apology played a role in the development of the biographical genre. Some of the Sophists wrote rhetorical encomia of mythical figures, such as Gorgias' *Helen*, which were largely apologetic in tone; Xenophon and Plato each produced a version of the *Apology* of Socrates; and Isocrates defended himself in his *Antidosis*. It is significant that both Isocrates and Xenophon made important contributions to the early development of encomium and apology. One should not expect encomium, apology, or biography to have been firmly delineated as genres this early; thus it should occasion no surprise when one type verges into the other.

The recent article by Charles D. Hamilton, "Agesilaus and the Failure of Spartan Hegemony," *The Ancient World* 5 (1982): 67–78, reached me only after this chapter was substantially complete. Hamilton's approach has many points of contact with my own. In particular, he recognizes the apologetic nature of the *Agesilaus*, seeing it as a response to contemporary criticisms of the Spartan king, and emphasizes that Xenophon has deliberately ignored events which were the object of "the most telling potential criticisms, centering on Agesilaus' long record of hostility to Thebes and the failure of his hellenic policies" (p. 70).

35. Delebecque, *Essai*, 464. Hans R. Breitenbach, *Historiographische Anschauungsformen Xenophons* (Diss. Basel, 1950), p. 105–15, discusses panhellenism in Xenophon's works and demonstrates in detail the absence of panhellenic sentiments in the *Hellenica*.

36. Bruns, *Das literarische Porträt*, 126–37.

37. Friedrich Rosenstiel, *De Xenophontis Historiae Graecae parte bis edita* (Berlin, 1882); Gustav Friedrich, "Zu Xenophons Hellenika und Agesilaos," *Jahrbuch für klassische Philologie* 153 (1896): 289–99; Alfons Opitz, *Quaestiones Xenophonteae: De Hellenicorum atque Agesilai necessitudine*, Breslau Philologische Abhandlung 46 (Breslau, 1913); Gaetano De Sanctis, "La genesi delle Elleniche di Senofonte," *Annali della Scuola Normale Superiore di Pisa, Lettere, Storia e Filosofia*, 2d ser. 1 (1932): 15–35. All these studies are summarized and evaluated in William P. Henry, *Greek Historical Writing: A Historiographical Essay Based on Xenophon's Hellenica* (Chicago, 1967), 107–33.

38. Bringmann, "Xenophons Hellenika und Agesilaos," 224–41.

39. De Sanctis, "Genesi," 20.

40. Breitenbach, *Xenophon*, col. 1702, thinks that the influence of the *Evagoras* on Xenophon has been overrated and that Xenophon is more heavily indebted to the older forms of epinikion and epitaph.

41. On this point see especially Bruns, *Das literarische Porträt*, 126–37, and Dihle, *Studien*, 27–29. On Isocrates' *Evagoras* in general see Bruns, *Das literarische Porträt*, 115–26; Leo, *Biographie*, 87–95; Momigliano, *Greek Biography*, 49–50; Johannes Sykutris, "Isokrates' *Evagoras*," *Hermes* 62 (1927): 24–53, reprinted in *Wege der Forschung: Isokrates*, ed. Friedrich Seck (Darmstadt, 1976), 74–105; Jaeger, *Paideia*, 84–86.

42. It was suggested above that the comparison of Agesilaus and the Persian king in the *Agesilaus* may have been inspired by a passage in Isocrates' *Evagoras* in which Evagoras was compared with Cyrus the Great of Persia.

43. See p. 49 and n. 19 above.

44. Isocrates may also be anxious to excuse Conon, another of his patrons. Conon's son, Timotheus, was a pupil of Isocrates, and Isocrates became a staunch defender of Timotheus' policies and actions. See Mathieu, *Idées politiques*, 96–98.

45. Isocrates coyly states that Evagoras lived just so long as to avoid the infirmities of old age (71). One must look to Theopompus frag. 10 and Aristotle *Politics* 1311B for the sordid story of Evagoras' murder by a eunuch.

46. Sykutris, "Isokrates' *Evagoras*." Sykutris' interpretation of this disproportion is somewhat different from mine. He thinks that Isocrates' primary goal is to acquit Evagoras on the charge of tyranny. But he may be overestimating the importance of this accusation, since kingship was the normal form of government on Cyprus, even in the Greek states. What is remarkable in this case is not the lengthy treatment of Evagoras' acquisition of the throne, but rather the negligible coverage of his expansionist activities.

47. The absurd insinuation that Evagoras might have conquered the Persian Empire is reminiscent of Xenophon's improbable claim that Agesilaus could have conquered Persia if he had not been recalled from Asia Minor in 394 (*Agesilaus* 1.36).

48. For the career of Evagoras see the excellent article by E. A. Costa, "Evagoras I and the Persians, ca. 411 to 391 B.C.," *Historia* 23 (1974): 40–56. Valuable observations are also to be found in a chapter devoted to

Evagoras in Michael N. Weiskopf, "Achaemenid Systems of Governing in Anatolia" (Ph.D. diss., University of California at Berkeley, 1982), 144–96.
49. Jaeger, *Paideia*, 86.
50. Costa, "Evagoras I."
51. Münscher, *Xenophon in der griechisch-römischen Literatur*, 3–25, discusses the possible literary influences of Xenophon and Isocrates on each other. He cites Johannes Dahmen, *Quaestiones Xenophonteae et Antistheneae* (Diss. Marburg, 1897), app. I, 52–55, for a list of correspondences between Xenophon and Isocrates in his Cyprian speeches.
A case can be made for direct personal contacts between Xenophon and Isocrates (both of whom came from the Attic deme Erchia). Diogenes Laertius 2.55 preserves the statement of Aristotle to the effect that innumerable encomia and eulogies were written on the occasion of the death of Xenophon's son, Gryllos, who perished in the preliminaries to the battle of Mantinea in 362. Aristotle adds that the motive of these encomiasts and eulogists was, in part, to gratify Xenophon. Diogenes also reproduces the statement of Hermippus that Isocrates wrote one of these encomia of Gryllos. On the basis of these testimonia, Krömer, *Agesilaos*, 145–46, suggests that Gryllos may have been a pupil of Isocrates and that it was Isocrates' encomium which inspired a flood of imitations, perhaps by members of his school. After all, Isocrates had invented the genre of prose encomium of a contemporary. For a political interpretation of these events, see François Ollier, "La renommée posthume de Gryllos, fils de Xénophon," *Bulletin Association Guillaume Budé* (1959): 425–37.

Chapter 4

1. See p. 14 and chap. 2, n. 7, for a summary and critique of the interpretations of the *Anabasis* by Morr, Luccioni, and Robert; pp. 49–50 for Delebecque's approach to the *Agesilaus*.
2. Eduard Schwartz, *Fünf Vorträge über den griechischen Roman*, 2d ed. (Berlin, 1943), 69; Wilhelm Prinz, *De Xenophontis Cyri institutione* (Göttingen, 1911).
3. Erwin Scharr, *Xenophons Staats- und Gesellschaftsideal und seine Zeit* (Halle, 1919), 25–45.
4. There are several noteworthy exceptions to the tendency of classical scholars to minimize or deny the Persian elements in the *Cyropaedia*: Jaeger, *Paideia*, 160–66; Rainer Nickel, *Xenophon* (Darmstadt, 1979), 25; Todd, "Persian *Paedia*." See also Wolfgang Knauth, *Das altiranische Fürstenideal von Xenophon bis Ferdousi* (Wiesbaden, 1975).
5. Higgins, *Xenophon*, 44.
6. Farber, "Xenophon's Theory of Kingship," xix, who remarks upon classicists' and Orientalists' divergent approaches to the work, gives a brief bibliography of Orientalists from an earlier generation who quarried the *Cyropaedia* for data on Persia. Orientalists continue to respect the *Cyropaedia* as a source; see, for example, Boyce, *History of Zoroastrianism*, II, 211–16. Classicists continue to minimize its historical value, most recently J. M. Cook, *The Persian Empire* (New York, 1983), 20–21.

Notes / 169

7. For the *Nachleben* of the *Cyropaedia*, see Münscher, *Xenophon in der griechsich-römischen Literatur*.
8. See J. Joel Farber, "The *Cyropaedia* and Hellenistic Kingship," *American Journal of Philology* 100 (1979): 503–4.
9. Most recently Higgins, *Xenophon*, chap. 3.
10. Here and elsewhere I have used the translation of Walter Miller, *Xenophon: Cyropaedia* (Cambridge, Mass., 1914).
11. The *Cyropaedia* was treated as a historical work by Plato (*Laws* 3.694C–698A—see the appendix at the end of this chapter), Dionysius of Halicarnassus (letter to Pompeius Geminus 4.777), and those Hellenistic historians who modeled their lives of Alexander and other leading figures of the age on the *Cyropaedia*. Cicero's denial that Xenophon intended to write history in the *Cyropaedia* (*Epistulae ad Quintum fratrem* 1.1.23) carries the clear implication that some people felt otherwise. These passages are briefly summarized and analyzed by Farber, "Xenophon's Theory of Kingship," vi–xiv.
12. Farber, in the introduction to "Xenophon's Theory of Kingship," provides a convenient summary of some of the wildly divergent opinions held by ancient and modern commentators on the essential character of the *Cyropaedia*.
13. Historical memoir in the *Anabasis*, prose encomium of a contemporary in the *Agesilaus*, philosophical dialogue in the *Symposium* and *Memorabilia*.
14. For example, Luccioni, *Idées politiques*, 213–14: "une vie romancée," "un roman historique"; Delebecque, *Essai*, 395: "une livre pseudo-historique"; Higgins, *Xenophon*, 44: "history turned to fiction."
15. ὅσα οὖν καὶ ἐπυθόμεθα καὶ ἠσθῆσθαι δοκοῦμεν περὶ αὐτοῦ, ταῦτα πειρασόμεθα διηγήσασθαι.
16. 1.2.1, 1.4.25, 1.4.27, 8.5.28, 8.6.16, 8.6.20.
17. The *Persica* of Ctesias has not survived, but a considerable number of fragments are preserved in other authors and there is an epitome of the latter part of the work by the Byzantine Photius. The story of Cyrus up to and including his conquest of Media is available in the fragments of the history of Nicolaus of Damascus, who is widely believed to have derived his version from Ctesias. Jacoby, *Fragmente*, vol. II.2 (Berlin, 1926), 251, was convinced of this, and Friedrich W. König, *Die Persika des Ktesias von Knidos*, Archiv für Orientforschung 18 (Graz, 1972), includes Nicolaus' narrative in his collection of fragments of Ctesias. Photius then takes up the story of Cyrus' reign, conquests, and death.
For a recent discussion of Ctesias and his methods, see Robert Drews, *The Greek Accounts of Eastern History* (Cambridge, Mass., 1973), 103–16. See below, chap. 5, n. 10, for editions of Ctesias' *Persica*.
18. See p. 83 for Ctesias' account of the death of Cyrus.
19. Xenophon is implicitly critical of Herodotus for failing to understand the meaning of Croesus' association with Delphi. He has Croesus admit to having offended the god by testing the oracle beforehand (cf. Herodotus 1.46–49) and then relentlessly importuning the oracle with

selfish requests. Even so, the oracle answered Croesus with truth, although Croesus failed to understand its meaning. Thus Xenophon vindicates the oracle against the charge, which Herodotus' account might imply, that it had treated Croesus shabbily although he had given it many valuable donations. See E. Lefevre, "Die Frage nach dem βίος εὐδαίμων: Die Begegnung zwischen Kyros und Kroisos bei Xenophon," *Hermes* 99 (1971): 283–96, for a detailed examination of how Xenophon has restructured Herodotus' account of this meeting.

20. In chapter 2 the suggestion was made that in the *Anabasis* Xenophon may have employed literary techniques borrowed from Herodotus. For a more detailed analysis of Xenophon's familiarity with and use of Herodotus, see Karl-August Riemann, *Das herodoteische Geschichtswerk in der Antike* (Munich, 1967), 20–27.

21. The ancient catalogue of Antisthenes' works (Diogenes Laertius 6.15–18) lists a second work titled Κῦρος ἢ περὶ βασιλείας, but there may be some confusion here. For the fragments and a brief commentary see Fernanda Caizzi, *Antisthenis Fragmenta* (Milan, 1966).

22. Olof Gigon, *Sokrates. Sein Bild in Dichtung und Geschichte* (Bern, 1947), 294.

23. For a general account of Antisthenes see William K. C. Guthrie, *A History of Greek Philosophy*, vol. 3 (Cambridge, 1969), 304–11. On Antisthenes' *Cyrus* and Xenophon see Th. Birt, "Zu Antisthenes und Xenophon," *Rheinisches Museum* 51 (1896): 153–57; Dahmen, *Quaestiones Xenophonteae*; F. Susemihl, "Der Idealstaat des Antisthenes und der Dialog Archelaos, Kyros, und Herakles," *Jahrbuch für klassische Philologie* (1887): 207–14; Ragnar Höistad, *Cynic Hero and Cynic King: Studies in the Cynic Conception of Man* (Uppsala, 1948); Heinrich Dittmar, *Aischines von Sphettos. Studien zur Literaturgeschichte der Sokratiker* (Berlin, 1912).

Perhaps Xenophon also used other Greek historical works which have not survived, or whose remains are too fragmentary for a connection to be established. Breitenbach, *Xenophon*, col. 1709, puts forward the names of Dionysius of Miletus, Hellanicus, Xanthus, and Charon of Lampsacus.

24. See Robert Drews, "Sargon, Cyrus, and Mesopotamian Folk History," *Journal of Near Eastern Studies* 33 (1974): 387–93.

25. Delebecque, *Essai*, 395–96, gives a partial list of these passages. Xenophon was aware that this could lead him into anachronism. In 8.6.16 he describes Cyrus' provisions for inspection of the provinces as follows: κατενοήσαμεν δὲ καὶ τοῦτο ὅτι Κύρου κατάρξαντος, ὥς φασι, καὶ νῦν ἔτι διαμένει. . . .—"We have noticed also that this regulation is still in force, whether it was instituted by Cyrus, as they affirm, or not. . . ." In other words, Xenophon is reporting a tradition that Cyrus instituted this practice but recognizes that it is not necessarily legitimate to trace all such current practices back to Cyrus' time.

26. For example, compare *Cyr.* 7.2.2–3 with Herodotus' account of the capture of Sardis (1.84); *Cyr.* 8.7 with Ctesias' account of Cyrus' last moments (frag. 9 in Jacoby, *Fragmente*, IIIC.1, no. 688).

27. Compare *Cyr.* 8.7 with Herodotus' version of the death of Cyrus

(1.214); *Cyr.* 1.2.1 with Ctesias' account of the genealogy of Cyrus, which underlies the account of Nicolaus of Damascus, in Jacoby, *Fragmente*, vol. II.1 (Berlin, 1923), no. 90 F66.

28. Pages 76–78 provide a more detailed comparison of the accounts of Xenophon and Herodotus.

29. Herodotus 1.95, 1.214. According to Pierre Carlier, "L'idée de monarchie impériale dans la *Cyropédie* de Xénophon," *Ktema* 3 (1978): 133, "Pour reconstruire son histoire de Cyrus, Xénophon dispose donc d'une très grande liberté: il peut sur chaque point choisir celle des traditions grecques ou orientales qui lui convient le mieux et même, à l'occasion, substituer à des sources incertaines, insuffisantes et contradictoires sa propre interprétation des événements."
Joan M. Bigwood, "Ctesias of Cnidus" (Ph.D. diss., Harvard University, 1964), 186, notes that Ctesias devoted five books to tales of Cyrus the Great. This gives an indication of the extent of the traditions available to Xenophon, whether in Ctesias or in the Near Eastern tradition.

30. These traditions are authentic in the sense that they were in circulation and were taken over by Xenophon. They were not necessarily all true representations of past events, any more than many of the traditions about early Greek history which surface in Herodotus' or Thucydides' pages. But no one has ever accused Herodotus of inventing the tale of Polycrates' ring.

31. The Persian frame is comprised largely of book 1 and 7.36–8.7, that is, the education of Cyrus in Persia and Media and his creation of an administrative structure for the empire after the conquest of Babylon. The Greek core of the work, 2–7.35, covers the period of military campaigning and includes all manner of speeches, discourses, and dialogues on a wide range of topics. A parallel may be drawn between the Persia of the *Cyropaedia* and the Crete of Plato's *Laws*. Glenn R. Morrow, *Plato's Cretan City: A Historical Interpretation of the Laws* (Princeton, 1960), has observed that Plato is clearly familiar with many aspects of Cretan life, laws, and customs, but that he ultimately employs this Cretan setting as a forum for airing his own views (which are highly influenced by the Athenian experience) on the nature of the ideal state.

32. For example, Higgins, *Xenophon*, 44, quoted on p. 62.

33. Breitenbach, *Xenophon*, col. 1708.

34. Delebecque, *Essai*, 387. This claim makes no sense at all. It is possible that Xenophon had been banished from Athens in the first place for cooperating with Persian Cyrus. And, if Delebecque is right to date the *Cyropaedia* to the late 360s or early 350s, then this is a time when the Persian king and his functionaries in western Asia Minor were stirring up trouble in Athens' overseas empire and pursuing a general policy of keeping the Greek states weak. If anything, Xenophon is taking a chance by praising Persia to a hostile Greek world, and this observation only serves to emphasize the significance of his choice of setting.

35. In Aeschylus' *Persae* (768–72) the ghost of Darius, while describing the previous kings of Asia, emphasizes that Cyrus was blessed with good fortune and the favor of the gods. Moreover, he was *euphrōn*—either "benevolent" or "of sound mind"—and, as a ruler, brought peace.

For Herodotus, Cyrus is not only a great conqueror but also a wise king who respects the sagacity of Solon and heeds the advice of Croesus. In the last pages of the *Histories* he warns his own people that, if they wish to maintain rule of an empire, they must not give in to enervating luxury.

Antisthenes apparently used Cyrus as a barbarian example, parallel to the Hellenic Heracles, of how exertion or toil (*ponos*) is a good thing (apud Diog. Laert. 6.2). The few surviving fragments of his *Cyrus* suggest that it was marked by moralizing apothegms about "doing good" and "unlearning evil."

Plato classifies Cyrus alongside Lycurgus of Sparta as a paradigm of excellence in character and statesmanship and recommends that Dion of Syracuse imitate his example (*Epistles* 4.320D). Elsewhere he maintains that in Cyrus' day Persia was properly governed under a moderate constitution, midway between slavery and freedom, whereby the ruler won the devotion and affection of his subjects by his equitable treatment of them and allowed all to speak freely and offer advice (*Laws* 3.694A–B). See the appendix at the end of this chapter for further consideration of this passage.

Isocrates, in *Evagoras* 37, alludes to the fact that Cyrus, who destroyed the power of the Medes and established the Persian Empire, is the object of more wonder than any other figure of postlegendary times.

The Hebrew tradition also regarded Cyrus with favor: 2 Chronicles 36:23; Ezra 1:1–2; Isaiah 44:28, 45:1. Given the celebrity of Cyrus among other ancient peoples, it is most surprising that he was ultimately forgotten by the Iranians themselves. The only Achaemenid kings mentioned in the *Shahnama* and other Persian literature based on the oral tradition are Darab and Dara; the former is remembered as a contemporary of Philip of Macedon, while the latter, his son, is apparently Darius III, who lost the empire to Alexander.

36. I categorically reject the assertion of Delebecque, *Essai*, 200, that Xenophon was forced to praise Cyrus in the *Anabasis* in order to defend his own choice to follow Cyrus on his march to Cunaxa. Delebecque points to Xenophon's treatment of Cyrus in the first two books of the *Hellenica*, which he thinks were written before 401, as reflecting Xenophon's true opinion of Cyrus, and maintains that his attitude toward Cyrus there is quite negative. I do not detect the hostility which he claims to find there. Furthermore, Delebecque's refusal to grant the possibility that Xenophon may have changed his mind after meeting and traveling with Cyrus must be based on an (unwarranted) assumption that Xenophon could not really respect this Persian prince.

37. At 1.5.15–17 Cyrus intervenes in a quarrel between troops of Clearchus and Menon; they are warned that if they fall out, the barbarian troops will instantly destroy Cyrus and themselves. At 1.6.4–11 the traitor Orontas is tried in a tent surrounded by Greek soldiers and disposed of in secrecy.

38. For the Ctesian passage, see n. 27 above.

Drews, "Sargon," argues that Ctesias had picked up, in the streets of Babylon, a popular account of the origins of Cyrus which is modeled on a traditional "rags to riches" motif seen earlier in the story of Sargon of

Akkad. The popular origin of such a story about Cyrus is plausible, in which case Artaxerxes did not have to invent a negative tradition, only to manipulate it. But I would prefer to see Artaxerxes' counterpropaganda, rather than visits to the taverns in Babylon, as the basis for Ctesias' account. Moreover, as has been pointed out by Drews, *Greek Accounts*, 199 n. 76, Ctesias' description of Cyrus' military career does not appear to have been particularly flattering: "Ctesias presented Cyrus as anything but a world conqueror. Taking over all Upper Asia from Astyages and capturing Lydia by trickery, Cyrus is left with only one real conquest—the Derbicae. . . . And that victory was mostly the result of aid rendered by Cyrus' ally, King Amorges of the Sacae."

39. Kent, *Old Persian*, AmH and AsH (p. 116).
40. Ibid., DB 1.3–6 (pp. 116, 119).
41. The Cyrus Cylinder is translated in James B. Pritchard, ed., *Ancient Near Eastern Texts Relating to the Old Testament*, 2d ed. (Princeton, 1955), 315–16.
42. Roland G. Kent, "The Oldest Old Persian Inscriptions," *Journal of the American Oriental Society* 66 (1946): 206–12. Some Iranologists believe these plaques to be modern forgeries. Oscar White Muscarella, "Excavated and Unexcavated Achaemenian Art," in *Ancient Persia: The Art of an Empire*, ed. Denise Schmandt-Besserat (Malibu, Calif., 1980), 31–32, points out that the provenience of the plaques really is not known. Herzfeld acquired them in Hamadan (Ecbatana) but did not see them excavated.
43. It is noteworthy that in essence the younger Cyrus is calling for a return to the Persian "ancestral constitution," which has gradually been perverted. At this very time the slogan *patrios politeia*—"ancestral constitution"—was being exploited in Greek politics, in Athens at the time of the Thirty (Xenophon *Hellenica* 2.3.2) and in Sparta with the ephors' decree abolishing Lysander's decarchies (*Hellenica* 3.4.2). One wonders whether Cyrus, who had been exposed to the Hellenic world and had close friends among the Greeks, may have been inspired to this propaganda theme by his knowledge of its exploitation in contemporary Greek politics. On the theme of *patrios politeia* see Alexander Fuks, *The Ancestral Constitution* (London, 1953), and Moses I. Finley, "The Ancestral Constitution," in *The Use and Abuse of History* (New York, 1975), 34–59.

There is a curious postscript to this war of propaganda waged between Cyrus and Artaxerxes over the reputation of a long-dead ancestor. Iranian archaeologists have recently been devoting attention to a tomb at Buzpar, in southwest Fars Province, which appears to be a humbler replica of the tomb of Cyrus the Great at Pasargadae. It has been proposed that this may be the tomb of the younger Cyrus, put there by the queen mother Parysatis, who, according to our sources, had always favored the younger son. If this is the case, her choice of a model is significant. Achaemenid kings and members of the royal family had, since the days of Darius, abandoned the freestanding pedestal-type tomb, such as was constructed for Cyrus at Pasargadae, and preferred instead monumental tombs carved out of cliff faces, such as those at Naqsh-i Rustam near Persepolis. If Parysatis, or whoever saw to the burial of the younger Cyrus, is returning to the old model, it should be regarded as a conspicuous continuation of the identification between the younger and elder Cyrus upon which the young prince had tried to capitalize. For the posited tomb of the young Cyrus, see A. Shahbazi, "The Achaemenid Tomb in Buzpar (Gur-i Dukhtar)," *Bastan Chenassi va Honar-e Iran* 9/10 (1972): 56; Boyce, *History of Zoroastrianism*, II, 210. But David Stronach, in a personal communication, has expressed doubts about the identification of the Buzpar tomb as that of the younger Cyrus. He points out that it is too modest for a member of the royal family, that the tomb of Cyrus was visible for anyone to see and copy, and that there were no cliffs available in the remote Buzpar valley. He prefers to see it as the tomb of some local dynast. On the tomb of Cyrus the Great, see p. 84 and below, n. 73.

44. It is legitimate to ask how Xenophon would have communicated with Persians in Cyrus' camp and whether he would have had much personal contact with Cyrus himself. As for the first, a language barrier certainly existed, but it would not have been insurmountable. There is no reason to think that Xenophon knew Persian or any other Near Eastern language. But records of similar situations in antiquity and experience in our own day indicate that people thrown together in a situation like that of the multiethnic army traveling with Cyrus usually manage to communicate. Of course sign language, gestures, and pictures can be used to communicate messages of only the most basic sort. But there were no doubt many non-Greeks who learned some Greek, and perhaps some Greeks learned enough Aramaic, the lingua franca of the Persian Empire, to converse with their Near Eastern counterparts. Thus I see no obstacle to Xenophon's collecting information from barbarian songs and stories, as he tells us he did, even if at second or third hand and in translation. Herodotus, who, so far as is known, spoke no foreign languages, had done so before him. See D. J. Mosley, "Greeks, Barbarians, Language, and Contact," *Ancient Society* 2 (1971): 1–6, for numerous examples of Greeks overcoming the language barrier.

As to whether Xenophon was on familiar terms with Cyrus, it is not easy to say. He had been formally presented to Cyrus by his friend and host Proxenus (*Anabasis* 3.1.8), and it would appear from their chance encounter just before the clash at Cunaxa that Cyrus knew Xenophon by sight (*Anabasis* 1.8.15–17). Cyrus certainly spoke Greek, as is demonstrated by his brief conversation with Xenophon just before the battle and by several incidents on the march to Babylonia (for example, at 1.5.15–17, where Cyrus addresses two quarreling factions of Greek soldiers). But Xenophon was technically a mere observer, and there is no way of knowing whether he had attended the council meetings which Cyrus held with his commanders (see chap. 2, n. 41). Thus there is no direct evidence that Xenophon and Cyrus had spent any significant amount of time together.

On the other hand, there is no reason why they should not have been acquainted. After all, Xenophon had come along on the expedition in order to win the favor and seek the patronage of Cyrus (*Anabasis* 3.1.4–5). Cyrus was always interested in cultivating Greeks who could be useful to him, and Xenophon was a member of that class of Greek aristocrats to which a number of Cyrus' mercenary commanders belonged. Furthermore, it is hard to account for Xenophon's assumption of a leadership role with the Ten Thousand after the death of Cyrus if he had not been a figure of some prominence earlier. Finally, Xenophon's obvious infatuation with Cyrus must have been sparked by some personal contact, even if it is granted that he was young and easily impressed.

Even if it cannot be demonstrated that Xenophon had spent time with Cyrus, he could have been exposed to Cyrus' propaganda through his friend Proxenus and the other Greek commanders, who were in contact with Cyrus, or through other soldiers or civilians in Cyrus' camp. No doubt the camp was always abuzz with stories of Cyrus. What else did Xenophon have to do on the march to Babylonia?

45. See Georges Cousin, *Kyros le jeune en Asie Mineure* (Nancy, 1904), xxxix–xli; Dihle, *Studien*, 24–25. The connection between the two Cyruses is further illuminated by the fact that Xenophon has apparently transferred some of the historical Persians of the *Anabasis* to the *Cyropaedia*. See Breitenbach, *Xenophon*, cols. 1713–14.

46. See pp. 85–86.

47. Xenophon also makes the connection between the two in a problematic passage in the *Oeconomicus* (4.16–19), where he seems to slide almost unconsciously from the elder to the younger Cyrus without making the reader aware of the transition. This has created so much confusion that scholars disagree about whether Xenophon refers to the elder and younger Cyrus in succession, or to the latter throughout. See A. Pelletier, "Les deux Cyrus dans l'Economique de Xénophon," *Revue de Philologie*, 3d ser. 18 (1944): 84–93. Is it possible that the two have become virtually one for Xenophon?

48. For example, Delebecque, *Essai*, 394.

49. See n. 41 above.

50. See n. 27 above.

51. Translation of A. D. Godley, *Herodotus*, vol. 1 (Cambridge, Mass., 1920).

52. Xenophon, like Herodotus before him, consistently refers to Babylonia as Assyria. Modern scholars usually refer to it as the neo-Babylonian or Chaldaean Empire. C. F. Lehmann-Haupt, "Der Sturz des Kroisos und das historische Element in Xenophons Kyropädie," *Wiener Studien* 50 (1932): 152, notes that the satrapy which included Babylonia was called Assyria in Darius' time. Now see Peyton R. Helm, "'Greeks' in the Neo-Assyrian Levant and 'Assyria' in Early Greek Writers" (Ph.D. diss., University of Pennsylvania, 1980), 289–305.

53. The Nabonidus Chronicle is translated in Pritchard, *Ancient Near Eastern Texts*, 306–7. The Greek, biblical, and cuneiform sources for the fall of Babylon are examined in detail and are largely reconciled by Raymond P. Dougherty, *Nabonidus and Belshazzar* (New Haven, 1929), 167–200.

54. Gobryas/Ugbaru of the *Cyropaedia* and the Nabonidus Chronicle is probably to be identified with the Ugbaru who was a general of Nebuchadnezzar and who had held a command in southern Babylonia

some twenty years before; Andrew R. Burn, *Persia and the Greeks* (London and New York, 1962), 55 n. 22. It is less likely that he is to be identified with the Gobryas (Gaubaruva in Old Persian) who was one of the seven conspirators who overthrew the Magi and installed Darius as king some seventeen years after the fall of Babylon. The latter is clearly marked as a Persian (Herodotus 3.70; Darius' Behistun inscription, Kent, *Old Persian*, DB 4.84 [pp. 130, 132]).

55. Some early translators of the Nabonidus Chronicle thought the text contained a reference to the death of the king. This was taken as confirmation of Xenophon's report that Gobryas killed him. But more precise reconstructions of the text have shown that the reference is actually to the deaths—presumably of natural causes—of Gobryas and the queen. See Pritchard, *Ancient Near Eastern Texts*, 306–7; A. K. Grayson, *Assyrian and Babylonian Chronicles* (Locust Valley, N.Y., 1975), 110–11; Lehmann-Haupt, "Sturz des Kroisos," 154–59.

56. See n. 19 above.

57. John K. Anderson, *Military Theory and Practice in the Age of Xenophon* (Berkeley, 1970), 165–91, has suggested that Xenophon modeled his account of the battle of Thymbrara on the battle of Leuctra in 371. Delebecque, *Essai*, 400–404, thinks Xenophon's obvious interest in and knowledge of Egyptian arms and tactics is based on information brought back to Greece in the 360s by veterans who had fought in Egypt with Agesilaus or Chabrias.

58. Photius' epitome of Ctesias omits events before the siege of Sardis. Thus it is not known whether Ctesias told of one battle or two. Likewise, there is no way of identifying Croesus' allies in Ctesias' account. Photius does preserve details of the capture of Sardis, from which it is apparent that Ctesias made no mention of a pyre. He reports several attempts by Cyrus to imprison Croesus, with the latter being released each time by divine intervention, whereupon Cyrus relented and gave him the city of Barene in Media.

59. Chapter 5 of the Book of Daniel also has the city fall during a drunken revel.

60. Burn, *Persia*, 54, thinks that the Greek accounts reflect the fighting at Opis on the northern frontier and that the walls of Babylon are a confusion for the Median Wall, built by Nebuchadnezzar to protect the northern flank and seen by Xenophon and the Ten Thousand on their march to Cunaxa (*Anabasis* 1.7.15).

61. Breitenbach, *Xenophon*, col. 1716.

62. For the date see Beloch, *Greichische Geschichte*, III.2, 123.

63. No such son and successor of Astyages is mentioned elsewhere. Friedrich W. König, *Älteste Geschichte der Meder und Perser* (Leipzig, 1934), 37–44, has argued that Xenophon, perhaps depending on Iranian tradition, tended to conflate stories about Cyrus the Great and his grandfather, also named Cyrus, who lived at the time of Cyaxares, the father of Astyages. This would account for the presence of Cyaxares in the *Cyropaedia*. König uses the same argument to explain Xenophon's description of Cyrus' foes as "Assyrians," since Cyrus I lived in the last days of the

Assyrian Empire. However, this suggestion is unnecessary; Xenophon is only following a Greek convention, seen also in Herodotus, by calling the neo-Babylonian empire "Assyrian." See n. 52 above.

64. One can conceive of such a tradition arising among the Medes themselves as a device to preserve their national pride. This is a common face-saving tactic among conquered peoples. Cf. the Egyptian tradition, preserved in Herodotus, that Cambyses was the son of an Egyptian princess (3.2). Persian legend perpetuated a tradition that Alexander the Great was actually the son of the Persian king by a daughter of Philip of Macedon (this story is found in the *Shahnama* of Ferdowsi, translated in Reuben Levy, *The Epic of the Kings: Shahnama* [Chicago, 1967], 228–30). In our own day the natives of the island of Tanna, part of the New Hebrides, in the southwest Pacific, who live under British colonial administration, believe that Britain's Prince Philip is actually an islander who was taken away to Europe at birth and will one day return to rule them (*San Francisco Chronicle*, June 26, 1980, p. 25).

65. Pointed out by Wilhelm Gemoll, review of *Studi Senofontei* by Luigi Castiglioni, *Philologische Wochenschrift* 43 (1923): 481, and reaffirmed by Farber, "Xenophon's Theory of Kingship," xvi.

66. Herodotus 1.127; for the Nabonidus Chronicle see n. 53 above.

67. καὶ κελεύειν ὡς τάχιστα ἐπιπέμπειν στράτευμα, εἴπερ ἐπιθυμοῦσι Πέρσαι τὴν ἀρχὴν τῆς Ἀσίας αὐτοῖς καὶ τὴν κάρπωσιν γενέσθαι.

68. This principle of excellence as a legitimation of the right to rule is advanced by the Mede Artabazus, who points out that, just as bees willingly obey the queen bee, "so also do men seem to be drawn by something like the same sort of instinct toward you" (5.1.24–25). Cyaxares himself admits that "I was not made king of the Medes because I was more powerful than they all, but rather because they themselves accounted us to be in all things better [*beltionas*] than themselves" (5.5.34).

69. In *Anabasis* 1.9.29 Xenophon emphatically asserts that many of Artaxerxes' supporters defected to Cyrus, whereas no one (except Orontas) betrayed Cyrus.

In his use of propaganda, the younger Cyrus displayed strong affinities with both the Cyrus of the *Cyropaedia* and the historical Cyrus. Farber, "Hellenistic Kingship," examines the way in which Xenophon's Cyrus uses catchwords and manipulates his subjects into obedience. His conduct, which he habitually justifies on moral grounds, often has a pragmatic end—to secure his kingship. Max Mallowan, "Cyrus the Great (558–529 B.C.)," *Iran* 10 (1972): 10–11, notes that the real Cyrus was a master of propaganda, as can be seen from the Cyrus Cylinder, the Babylonian verse chronicle of Nabonidus' fall, and the stories of Cyrus' merciful treatment of conquered kings, all no doubt propagated with Cyrus' encouragement or active participation.

70. τὰ μὲν δὴ κατὰ τὴν Κύρου τελευτὴν τοῦ βίου, πολλῶν λόγων λεγομένων, ὅδε μοι ὁ πιθανώτατος εἴρηται.

71. König, *Persika*, 57, though noting the similarity between the accounts of Xenophon and Ctesias, prefers to attribute this to a common Iranian source rather than to Xenophon's use of Ctesias' text.

72. Bardiya in the Behistun inscription, Marphius in Hellanicus (apud Schol. Aeschylus *Persae* 775), Mardos in Aeschylus *Persae* 774, Smerdis in Herodotus, Mergis or Merdis in Justin.

73. On the tomb of Cyrus the Great, see David Stronach, *Pasargadae: A Report on the Excavations Conducted by the British Institute of Persian Studies from 1961 to 1963* (Oxford, 1978), 24–43.

74. Aristobulus apud Arrian *Anabasis* 6.29, Strabo 15.3.7. Aristobulus ought to have known, for he was commissioned by Alexander to restore the tomb of Cyrus. See Robin Lane Fox, *Alexander the Great* (London and New York, 1973), 408, 542.

75. Arthur E. Christensen, *Les gestes des rois dans les traditions de l'Iran antique* (Paris, 1936), 122–35. For this motif Christensen specifically cites the *Shahnama*'s narrative of the last days of Kay Khusro, Manushtchihr, and Vishtasp. The tradition apparently has persisted. The *San Francisco Chronicle*, August 2, 1980, p. 8, reported that the late Shah of Iran, on his deathbed, left instructions for his burial and the succession, as well as a message to the Iranian people.

Christensen also refers to another common pattern of Iranian epic, in which a founder-figure, after gaining or restoring an empire by successful wars, assumes the role of organizer of the realm and civilizer. He cites the stories of Jamshid and Ardashir-i Pabhaghan. This is, of course, precisely the pattern of Cyrus in the *Cyropaedia*. And, like the ideal Iranian king, Cyrus is both brave and wise.

76. Christensen, *Gestes*, 76, points out that in Iran in the Sassanian period (third to seventh centuries A.D.) there was a popular literary genre called *andarz*, "instruction." One of the types of *andarz* is the address of a father to his son. Of course, this genre might well have had its roots in earlier times.

77. The epilogue (8.8) presents unique problems and is discussed separately later in this chapter.

78. Breitenbach, *Xenophon*, discusses the didactic elements of the *Cyropaedia* under three main headings: "die persönlichen moralischen Qualitäten des Feldherrn," "die militärischen Qualitäten des Herrschers," "staatsmännische Anordnungen und Qualitäten des Königs."

79. "The Persian laws, however, begin at the beginning and take care that from the first their citizens shall not be of such a character as ever to desire anything improper or immoral..." (*Cyr.* 1.2.3). The implied contrast is with sophistic Greek educational practices.

80. Strabo, for his account of Persia in 15.3, borrows heavily from Herodotus, but occasionally he corrects Herodotus. He has firsthand information about the practices of the Magi in Anatolia in his day, but there is no evidence that he has been to Persia. He cites Aeschylus and Polyclitus but does not mention Herodotus, Xenophon, or Ctesias by name. His account shows many correspondences with the *Cyropaedia*, but it is not clear whether he derived this material directly from Xenophon. It appears, then, that Strabo's Persian *logos* is a synthesis of various Greek sources, some lost to us, but probably including Xenophon. As a consequence, it is difficult

to determine whether he can be cited as confirmation of material in the *Cyropaedia*.

81. A discourse on the education of Persian princes in the *Alcibiades* (1.120–23), a work attributed to Plato, states that the young prince is instructed in the cardinal virtues by the four wisest men of the Persians.

82. See pp. 8–11.

83. Higgins, *Xenophon*, 48.

84. One element of the program of education in the *Cyropaedia* is consistent with attested practices of education in the ancient Near East. Mallowan, "Cyrus," 14, alludes to Assyrian reliefs which show that hunting formed part of the training of soldiers in imperial Assyria, and he believes that the Persians took over this practice. But this does not constitute proof that Xenophon derived this concept from Persian sources, for Pierre Vidal-Naquet ("The Black Hunter and the Origin of the Athenian *ephebeia*," in *Myth, Religion, and Society*, ed. R. L. Gordon [Cambridge, 1981], 147–62) has shown that hunting played a part in the training and initiation into manhood of Spartan cadets and Athenian ephebes. Note, finally, that Xenophon, or whoever wrote the *Cynegeticus* or treatise on hunting contained in the Xenophontic corpus, recommends hunting as a preparation for war.

85. Rahe, "Military Situation," 79–96.

86. In this passage Xenophon prescribes the most effective offensive weapons for a cavalryman—a saber for cutting, rather than a thrusting sword; and two cornel-wood javelins, one to throw, the other to save for thrusting, rather than the weak and unwieldy long spear. John K. Anderson, "Notes on Some Points in Xenophon's Περὶ Ἱππικῆς," *Journal of Hellenic Studies* 80 (1960): 7–8, states that ". . . Xenophon in the *Cyropaedia* gives his heroes the arms and tactics that he would like to have seen in the Greece of his own day," but Anderson does not maintain here that these arms are derived from authentic Persian equipment. However, he takes this additional step in *Ancient Greek Horsemanship*, 151, where he suggests that Xenophon's preference for two cornel-wood javelins rather than a Greek lance is to be explained by a cavalry engagement between Agesilaus' horsemen and Persian cavalry in which the Greek force was driven back and defeated. In his account of this battle in the *Hellenica* (3.4.13–14), Xenophon attributes the Persian success to their superior weaponry.

87. These passages are usually marked by some variation of the phrase *eti kai nun*—"and even now/and still today." Delebecque, *Essai*, 395–96, gives a partial list of these passages.

88. The significance of Xenophon's pronouncements about the mysterious King's Eye (8.2.12) will be discussed in the next chapter.

89. Kent, *Old Persian*, DB 1.12–17 (pp. 117, 119).

90. In Ctesias' account of the rise of Cyrus, Cyrus is himself the royal cupbearer at the Median court and, like Nehemiah, is dispatched on a number of state missions (Nicolaus of Damascus in Jacoby, *Fragmente*, II.1, no. 90 F66). Ctesias, who spent time at the Persian court, ought to have been familiar with court protocol and with the influence of various courtiers.

91. See chap. 1, pp. 10–11. It also follows that, as a case is made for the historical accuracy of the *Cyropaedia*, a stronger case is established for *Oeconomicus* 4. This is especially true for those institutions in both the *Oeconomicus* and the *Cyropaedia* which are said in the latter work to be still in existence in Xenophon's own time: the *syllogos* or place of military muster at Thymbrara in Syria, the annual tours of the circuit commissioners, the separation of civil and military commands.

92. Delebecque, *Essai*, 395, maintains that the Greek, and especially the Athenian, reading public was vitally interested in Persia and the Orient, and that Xenophon catered to this interest.

93. Herodotus denied that the Persians had a marketplace and quoted Cyrus' rebuke of the Greeks as "men who have a place set apart in the midst of their city where they perjure and deceive each other" (1.153). Strabo denied that Persians engage in buying or selling (15.3.19). Xenophon, who may be implicitly correcting Herodotus, maintains that merchants are excluded from the so-called Free Square, where the functions of government, education, and military training are carried out, but are relegated to another part of town (1.2.3).

94. Boyce, *History of Zoroastrianism*, II, 211–16. Samuel K. Eddy, *The King Is Dead: Studies in the Near Eastern Resistance to Hellenism*, 334–31 B.C. (Lincoln, Neb., 1961), 53, emphasizes the considerable agreement between Xenophon's description of the grand procession staged by Cyrus at Babylon (*Cyr.* 8.3.1–4) and the depiction, on the relief sculpture at Persepolis, of the New Year's Festival.

95. Animal sacrifice is the norm in the *Cyropaedia*. Some Orientalists, basing their view on Zarathustra's denunciation of cruelty to the ox, believe that animal sacrifice was forbidden by the Zoroastrian religion. Koch, *Verhältnisse*, notes that the government contributed no animals, only bread, fruit, wine, and beer, for the cult operations at Persepolis. On the other hand, Zaehner, *Dawn and Twilight*, 84–88, argues that Zarathustra may have objected only to cruel and excessive sacrifice of living creatures. Middle Persian texts mention animal sacrifice. And Herodotus and Strabo describe it as part of Persian cult (Herodotus 1.132; Strabo 15.3.15).

96. See the judgment of Jaeger, *Paideia*, 162: "In Xenophon Cyrus is . . . presented . . . as the purest and finest type of Persian. . . . Xenophon came to realize that the knightly Persians, hereditary enemies of Greece, had a system of paideia closely akin to the fine old Greek ideal of *kalokagathia*. And indeed the comparison affected his view of the Greek ideal in its turn, so that he blended some traits drawn from the Persian aristocracy with his picture of Greek areté. That is the only way to explain a book like the *Cyropaedia*, which presents to Greek readers the ideal of statesmanlike and kingly virtue embodied in a Persian monarch."

97. Carl Schneider, *Kulturgeschichte des Hellenismus*, vol. 1 (Munich, 1967), 7, has, with some justice, claimed that Xenophon hereby anticipated the coming Hellenistic age, when Greek and Oriental cultures met and sometimes merged.

98. Two interesting recent discussions of this phenomenon are T. P. Wiseman, *Clio's Cosmetics: Three Studies in Greco-Roman Literature*

(Leicester, 1979); and Emilio Gabba, "True History and False History in Classical Antiquity," *Journal of Roman Studies* 71 (1981): 50–62.

99. Robert Graves, Preface to *Claudius the God* (New York, 1935), 5–6: "Some reviewers of *I, Claudius* . . . suggested that in writing it I had merely consulted Tacitus' *Annals* and Suetonius' *Twelve Caesars*, run them together, and expanded the result with my own 'vigorous fancy.' This was not so, nor is it the case here. . . . [Graves then gives a long list of ancient sources consulted.] Few incidents here given are wholly unsupported by historical authority of some sort or other and I hope none are historically incredible." Gore Vidal, Afterword to *Burr* (New York, 1973), 429–30: ". . . the story told is history and not invention."

100. Hubert A. Holden, *The Cyropaedia of Xenophon*, vol. 4 (Cambridge, 1890), 196–97.

101. Gustav Eichler, *De Cyrupaediae capite extremo* (Diss. Leipzig, 1880).

102. For example, Breitenbach, *Xenophon*, cols. 1741–42; Higgins, *Xenophon*, 57 and n. 70. An exception to the recent trend is Marcel Bizos, whose approach and attitude, reflected in the introduction to his Budé edition, *Cyropédie* (Paris, 1971), xxvi–xxxvi, are akin to my own position.

103. Delebecque, *Essai*, 405–8.

104. Ibid., 405–6.

105. A detailed statistical analysis of the verbal and syntactic characteristics of the epilogue might help to resolve the question of authenticity but is beyond the scope of this study. So far, however, statistical studies of Xenophon's compositional style have not provided a successful yardstick for establishing the authenticity or nonauthenticity of disputed works. See Breitenbach, *Xenophon*, cols. 1913–21, for the failure of scholars to reach a consensus on the authenticity of the *Cynegeticus*, despite stylistic studies.

Léopold Gautier, *La langue de Xénophon* (Geneva, 1911), 130 n. 1, claims: "Les raisons linguistiques nous paraissent assez probantes pour lever tous les doutes au sujet de . . . l'épilogue de la Cyropédie." But he does nothing to substantiate this assertion.

106. It might be possible to claim that the epilogue, insofar as it laments the decline of contemporary Persia from the high standards of earlier times, fits with the program of propaganda which, on my reconstruction, the younger Cyrus used to engender support for his cause. I have argued that the *Cyropaedia* was, at least in part, inspired by Cyrus' propaganda, so why could not the same be true of the epilogue? Here again, the problem is the hostile tone of the epilogue and the castigation of the Persian people as a whole. Cyrus was certainly not hostile to his own people, and he laid the blame for Persia's decline squarely at the feet of the king.

107. For this reason it is difficult to accept Higgins's contention (*Xenophon*, 57–58) that the epilogue contains the great message of the work— that when the great man is gone society crumbles, and that it was a noble delusion on Cyrus' part to think that his work would endure, since men, rather than institutions, are what ultimately matter. Higgins's vision of this work is characteristically subtle and provocative. But it probably is not what Xenophon had in mind, for it is belied both by Xenophon's avowed

purpose—to investigate the character of successful rule—and by the very nature of the work, with its extensive concern for institutions. Any view of the *Cyropaedia* which claims that the eight books are all an elaborate house of cards, which is set up only to be destroyed in the epilogue, is unacceptable.

108. οὕτω δ' ἔχει καὶ ταῦτα ὥσπερ καὶ τ'ἄλλα· ὅταν μὲν ὁ ἐπιστάτης βελτίων γένηται, καθαρώτερον τὰ νόμιμα πράττεται· ὅταν δὲ χείρων, φαυλότερον.

109. It is hard to believe that Xenophon, the survivor of the Anabasis, would have made the statement found in 8.8.21: . . . κατὰ γὰρ τὴν χώραν αὐτῶν ῥᾷον οἱ πολέμιοι ἢ οἱ φίλοι ἀναστρέφονται—". . . for enemies may range up and down their land with less hindrance than friends." This is the sort of "lesson" of the Anabasis drawn by Isocrates from his armchair in Athens, but Xenophon drew no such conclusion in the *Anabasis*.

110. Delebecque's argument that the parallels between the two epilogues tend to reinforce the claims to authenticity of each was anticipated by Arnaldo Momigliano, "Per l'unita logica della *Lacedaemonion Politeia*," in *Terzo contributo alla storia degli studi classici e del mondo antico* (Rome, 1966), 341–45; Jaeger, *Paideia*, 326 n. 56.

111. Delebecque, *Essai*, 194–95, 329, and Luccioni, *Idées politiques*, 167–74, think it should properly be the last chapter. Kathleen M. T. Chrimes, the *Res Publica Lacedaemoniorum Ascribed to Xenophon* (Manchester, England, 1948), argues that it was originally the first chapter, in which case there would be no parallel with the *Cyropaedia* (she also denies the attribution of the *Constitution* to Xenophon). Momigliano, "Unita logica," 341–45, and Higgins, *Xenophon*, 66, insist that the chapter has not been misplaced, though for very different reasons.

112. The anonymous author of the epilogue was probably a near-contemporary of Xenophon and Plato. Once the Persian Empire had been conquered by Alexander the Great, the issue of Persia would have been less likely to arouse the emotional reaction found in the epilogue.

113. Translation of George Burges, *The Works of Plato*, vol. 5 (London, 1852), 107.

114. As Diogenes Laertius recognized (3.34), Plato and Xenophon were engaged in a rivalry of sorts, though neither deigns to mention the other by name. The rivalry may stem from a dispute over which disciple was the true preserver of the memory of the martyred Socrates. Each writes a version of the *Apology* or defense of Socrates, each makes Socrates a protagonist in philosophic dialogues, and each uses Socrates as a mouthpiece for his own ideas. Likewise, each writes utopian works on the nature of the ideal state—Plato in the *Republic* and *Laws*, Xenophon in the *Cyropaedia*.

115. Diogenes Laertius 3.34: καὶ ἐν τοῖς Νόμοις Πλάτων πλάσμα φησὶν εἶναι τὴν παιδείαν αὐτοῦ· μὴ γὰρ εἶναι Κῦρον τοιοῦτον.

116. Farber, "Xenophon's Theory of Kingship," vi–viii, thinks Diogenes and many modern commentators have misunderstood the *Laws* passage. "From what follows it is plain that he is criticizing Cyrus not for the education he received but for his failure to raise his own sons properly, a branch

of 'oikonomia.' Plato is here attacking Xenophon on philosophic, not historical, grounds, for Xenophon had admitted [in the epilogue] that Cyrus' sons turned out badly." Aside from the matter of the epilogue, which I do not regard as authentic, there are still several problems with this contention. In the first place, Plato does reject Xenophon's picture of the education of Cyrus, for he depicts him as a rough and untutored peasant: "Probably he spent all his life from boyhood in soldiering. . . . [Cyrus' children] were without training in their father's craft, which was a hard one, fit to turn out shepherds of great strength, able to camp out in the open and to keep watch and, if need be, to go campaigning" (*Laws* 3.694D–695A; here and elsewhere the translation used is that of R. G. Bury, *Plato: Laws* [London and New York, 1926]).

In the second place, Xenophon's Cyrus, who has received the exemplary education described in *Cyropaedia* 1.2 and who is aware of the importance of careful administration in all matters, as is demonstrated throughout the *Cyropaedia*, is hardly one to neglect the proper management of his own household, including the education of his sons. Indeed, one of his earliest decisions after the conquest of Babylon is to model his court there after the system practiced in Persia: "And as for our boys, as many as shall be born to us, let us educate them here. For we ourselves shall be better, if we aim to set before the boys as good examples as we can in ourselves; and the boys could not easily turn out bad, even if they should wish to, if they neither see nor hear anything vicious but spend their days in good and noble pursuits" (7.5.86). In other words, Cyrus' sons are going to grow up in a traditional environment and to receive an education similar to the Persian *paideia* of their father, as described in book 1. So Plato does reject Xenophon's account on historical grounds, denying that Cyrus had received the education with which Xenophon credits him and that had seen to the proper education of his sons, as Xenophon's account implies. Plato seems to regard the *Cyropaedia* as an attempt at history and feels constrained to point out where Xenophon has gone astray.

August Boeckh, "De simultate quae inter Platonem et Xenophontem intercessisse fertur," in *August Boeckh's gesammelte kleine Schriften* vol. 4 (Leipzig, 1874), 25–26, claims that Plato would not have failed to realize that the *Cyropaedia*, like his own Socratic dialogues, was not intended as history, but that Plato's criticism must therefore be directed, not at Xenophon, but at readers who missed the point and mistakenly took the *Cyropaedia* as historical. Boeckh is taking a great deal for granted, simply assuming that the *Cyropaedia* laid no claims to historicity and forgetting that Plato's own dialogues were a curious mixture of history and fiction with a philosophic purpose. And even he is willing to concede that some fourth-century readers may have regarded the *Cyropaedia* as historical in intent.

117. Along similar lines, but hardly sufficient to account for Plato's conception, is the constitutional debate among the seven Persian conspirators in Herodotus (3.80–82). Herodotus adamantly insists that these Persian nobles had considered creating a democracy in place of the monarchy (6.43).

Chapter 5

1. Thomas Stanley, *Aeschyli Tragoediae*, vol. 2 (London, 1745), 790.
2. Meyer, *Geschichte des Altertums*, IV.1, 39 and n. 3.
3. Among Orientalists, Hans H. Schaeder, *Das Auge des Königs, Abhandlungen der königliche Gesellschaft der Wissenschaften*, Göttingen, Phil.-hist. Kl., ser. 3, no. 10 (Göttingen, 1934), 4; A. Pagliaro, "Riflessi di etimologie iraniche nella tradizione storiografica greca," *Rendiconti dell' Accademia Nazionale dei Lincei*, 8th ser. 9 (1954): 133; H. Lommel, "Die Späher des Varuna und Mitra und das Auge des Königs," *Oriens* 6 (1953): 324. Among classicists, Breitenbach, *Xenophon*, col. 1739; Lewis, *Sparta and Persia*, 20 n. 98.
4. Schaeder, *Auge*, 4; Lommel, "Späher," 324.
5. Aeschylus *Persae* lines 978–84; Herodotus 1.114; Aristophanes *Acharnians* lines 91–125; Plutarch *Artaxerxes* 12.1–3; Xenophon *Cyropaedia* 8.6.16. The Greek texts are reproduced in appendix A at the end of this chapter. Herodotus 1.100 is discussed below in n. 14 and Aristotle *Politics* 1287b29–31 in n. 19.
6. See Henry D. Broadhead, *The Persae of Aeschylus* (Cambridge, 1960), 233–34.
7. Translation of Arthur Sidgwick, *Aeschylus Persae* (Oxford, 1903), commentary ad loc.
8. Scholiast M explains the meaning as: σημείωσαι ὅτι βασιλέως ὀφθαλμὸς ἀριθμεῖ τὰς στρατίας—"Note that (the) King's Eye counts the armies." For the scholia, see G. Dindorf, *Aeschyli: Tragoediae Superstites et Deperditarum Fragmenta*, vol. 3 (Oxford, 1851), 90–91.
9. ἔξεισι τερατώδης τις, γελοίως ἐσκευασμένος, καὶ ὀφθαλμὸν ἔχων ἕνα ἐπὶ παντὸς τοῦ προσώπου—"Some monstrous figure comes out, ridiculously outfitted, and having one eye on (his) entire mask." The scholia can be found in G. Dindorf, *Aristophanis Comoediae*, vol. IV.2 (Oxford, 1838), 340–41.
10. On the reliability of Ctesias see Drews, *Greek Accounts*, 103–16. The remnants of Ctesias' *Persica* are available in John Gilmore, ed., *The Fragments of the Persika of Ktesias* (London and New York, 1888); König, *Persika*; Jacoby, *Fragmente*, III.C.1, 688. Gilmore's edition includes a running commentary. König provides a translation into German and notes on some topics.
11. See Ferdinand Justi, *Iranisches Namenbuch* (1895; reprint, Hildesheim, 1963) s.v. Ἀρτασύρας (3). Albert T. Olmstead, *History of the Persian Empire* (Chicago, 1948), index s.v. "Artasyras," also seems to identify him with a general of Darius II.
12. Aeschylus' tragedy and Aristophanes' comedy are manifestly fictional. For the character of Herodotus' testimony, see p. 108.
13. See Paul Krumbholz, *De Ctesia aliisque auctoribus in Plutarchi Artaxerxis vita adhibitis* (Eisenach, 1889). On the poor reliability of Dinon and Heraclides, see Drews, *Greek Accounts*, 116–21. Cousin, *Kyros le jeune*, xi, claims that Dinon treated the revolt of Cyrus in great detail and that Plutarch used Dinon as a source for his account of Cunaxa.

14. Herodotus, while discussing the Median kingdom of Deioces (1.100), claims that the Median king had *kataskopoi* and *katēkooi* everywhere in his domain. Some commentators see in those terms an anticipation of the Eyes and Ears of the later Persian Empire. But these terms mean something like "spies" and "eavesdroppers," which is not quite the same as the striking metaphor embodied in "the King's Eye." There may be a connection. But this cannot be taken as unequivocal evidence that Herodotus thought there was more than one Eye.

15. For example, Meyer, *Geschichte des Altertums*, 39; Mortéza Ehtécham, *L'Iran sous les Achéménides* (Fribourg, 1946), 57; Dandamayev, "Politische und wirtschaftliche Geschichte," 24.

16. Members of the royal family were occasionally dispatched on missions of importance. Note the testimony of Thucydides concerning the presence of members of the Persian royal household in western Asia Minor in the last phase of the Peloponnesian War. See Lewis, *Sparta and Persia*, 93–107.

17. In *Oeconomicus* 4.6 and 4.8 Xenophon speaks of *pistoi* who are sent out by the king to inspect military preparations and civil administration in the provinces. They are presumably to be equated with the *ephodoi* of this passage of the *Cyropaedia*.

The Hellenistic writer Megasthenes, who was a Seleucid envoy to the court of the Maurya ruler of northern India, Chandragupta, and who wrote a detailed work on India (the work has not survived, but is frequently cited by Strabo and Arrian), claimed that the sixth of the seven Indian castes was that of the Inspectors or Overseers (*ephoroi* in Strabo 15.1.48, *episkopoi* in Arrian *Indica* 12.5), who looked into what was being done in the kingdom and reported back to the king. Strabo mentions that the best and most trustworthy men (*aristoi kai pistotatoi*) are appointed to this office.

18. Unfortunately, none of the editions of Ctesias (see n. 10) has an index verborum.

19. The only other Greek writer of the Achaemenid period who may mention the King's Eye is Aristotle (*Politics* 1287b29–31). He is making the point that a king cannot oversee everything himself. He must appoint officials to help him, since many people will do a better job than one man: ἐπεὶ καὶ νῦν ὀφθαλμοὺς πολλοὺς οἱ μόναρχοι ποιοῦσιν αὐτῶν καὶ ὦτα καὶ χεῖρας καὶ πόδας· τοὺς γὰρ τῇ ἀρχῇ καὶ αὐτοῖς φίλους ποιοῦνται συνάρχους—"since even as it is monarchs make many eyes and ears and hands and feet their own, for they adopt persons that are friendly to their rule and to themselves as their fellow-rulers" (translation of H. Rackham, *Aristotle: Politics* [Cambridge, Mass., 1932]).

Some scholars regard this as a reference to the Persian offices of the King's Eye and King's Ears. (Schaeder, *Auge*, 4 n. 3, suspects that Aristotle is here parodying Xenophon *Cyropaedia* 8.2.10–12.) But this is far from certain. In the first place, Aristotle is speaking of kings in general, not of the Persian king in particular (although the Persian example might come first to mind for a Greek of the fourth century). And it seems probable that Aristotle is simply speaking metaphorically of the king's need to extend his capabilities. There need not be any intended allusion to an office of the King's Eye. Even if this were a literary allusion by one who has read his Aeschylus and Herodotus, it still cannot be asserted, on the basis of this passage, that Aristotle attests the existence of the King's Eye. At the risk of sounding ridiculous, it must be pointed out that there is no evidence for an official called "the King's Foot" or "the King's Hand." The point is that a ruler has many partisans who assist him in his task. They allow him to extend his surveillance and his capacity to act, serving as so many eyes, ears, hands, and feet. This is similar to the point made by Xenophon in *Cyropaedia* 8.2.10–12, where the Persian king, by his generosity in rewarding informers, gains the cooperation and services of many and thus is better able to keep watch over his vast empire.

20. This methodological distinction has not been employed by earlier writers on this topic, who tend to draw uncritically on references from all periods.

21. See Lewis, *Sparta and Persia*, 15, for an indictment of this all too common practice.

22. The following post-Achaemenid references have some bearing on the issue of the King's Eye: Dio Chrysostom 3.118; Hesychius s.v. βασιλέως ὀφθαλμός; Philostratus *Life of Apollonius of Tyana* 1.21; Themistius *Orations* 21.?255D; Pollux 2.84; Scholiast to Aristophanes *Acharnians* 91–94 = Suda s.v. ὀφθαλμὸς βασιλέως; Lucian *De mercede conductis* 29 and *Adversus indoctum* 23; Heliodorus *Aethiopica* 8.17; Aelius Aristides *Orations* 16, pp. 424–25 Dindorf. The Greek texts are reproduced in appendix A at the end of this chapter.

23. Meyer, *Geschichte des Altertums*, 39 n. 3, thinks Aristides derived his information from Xenophon.

24. It is generally agreed that there is a large element of fantasy in Philostratus' *Life of Apollonius of Tyana*. See the remarks of G. W. Bowersock, *Philostratus: Life of Apollonius* (Harmondsworth, 1970), 15–19.

25. Or "everyone." The Suda has *pantas* where the scholiast has *panta*.

26. Of course the title "King's Eye" would have arisen by such a metaphorical process. But the objective here is to establish whether a Persian official with this title actually existed, and this requires discriminating between Greek texts which make this claim and those which do not.

27. Translation of A. M. Harmon, *Lucian*, vol. 3 (London and New York, 1921), 463.

28. A more precise dramatic date probably cannot be determined. According to Otto Weinreich, *Der griechische Liebesroman* (Zurich, 1962), 41, Heliodorus does not attempt to represent real historical figures; he chooses Persian, Egyptian, and Ethiopian names merely to give an Oriental flavor to the narrative.

29. An example of the pitfalls afforded by this problem is Thomas Stanley's long discourse on the King's Eye in his eighteenth-century commentary on the plays of Aeschylus (*Aeschyli Tragoediae*, II, 790–91), still cited in modern scholarly works. Citing the testimony of Lucian, Heliodorus, the Aristophanes scholiast, and Philostratus, he claimed that eunuchs and satraps were numbered among the King's Eyes. But Philostratus

and Lucian are referring to the post-Achaemenid period, and Heliodorus uses the term metaphorically. As for the scholiast, his claim that satraps were King's Eyes finds no support in any author of the classical period. Thus Stanley's assertion is highly questionable. Stanley's additional claim that there were many Eyes and Ears is based on Xenophon, Lucian, and Aristotle. But the discussion earlier in this chapter demonstrates that this reading of Xenophon is incorrect. Lucian refers to his own day and is speaking metaphorically. Stanley also wants to have it both ways with Aeschylus, citing his testimony as proof for the high standing of the King's Eye (*contra* Dio) but rejecting his implication that there was but a single Eye.

30. In addition to the passages already surveyed in Pollux, Lucian, Scholiast/Suda, and Heliodorus, see Dio Chrysostom 57.12, Philostratus *Life of Apollonius of Tyana* 1.27. Cf. ps.-Aristotle *De mundo* 6.

31. Elephantine Papyrus 27.9 in Arthur E. Cowley, ed., *Aramaic Papyri of the Fifth Century B.C.* (Oxford, 1923). The *gaušaka* has been discussed by Schaeder, *Auge*, 5; Wilhelm Eilers, *Iranische Beamtennamen in der keilschriftlichen Überlieferung* (Leipzig, 1940), 22ff.; János Harmatta, *Studies in the Language of the Iranian Tribes in South Russia* (Budapest, 1951), 41; Emil G. Kraeling, *The Brooklyn Museum Aramaic Papyri* (New Haven, 1953), 37; Pagliaro, "Riflessi," 139; Ehtécham, *L'Iran*, 57; Richard N. Frye, *The Heritage of Persia* (New York and Toronto, 1963), 127; Lommel, "Späher," 324.

32. Schaeder, *Auge*, 5, points to a derivative in Armenian: *gušak*, "informer." In modern Persian *guš* means "ear."

33. Schaeder, *Auge*, 5, and Ehtécham, *L'Iran*, 57, see the King's Ears as some sort of secret police involved in espionage activities. Frye, *Heritage*, 127, believes they are either emissaries of the king or royal legal officers, perhaps a kind of state's attorney. Lommel, "Späher," 324, is probably right in his deduction that such officers, with their Persian titles, must have existed all over the empire, since they are found in far-off Upper Egypt.

Meyer, *Geschichte des Altertums*, 39 n. 3, observes that the phrases "Eye of the King" and "Ear of the King" appear frequently in pharaonic Egypt, but as honorary titles for important supporters of the pharaoh, not as offices. See also Adolf Erman, *Wörterbuch der aegyptischen Sprache*, vol. 1 (Berlin, 1955), 107, 205.

34. The Iranian root *spas/spa* is cognate with Greek *skopeō*, Latin *spicio*, German *spähen*.

35. Of course, "watcher/overseer" is not the same thing as "eye," but for the purposes of this discussion there is no need to go into the highly contrived and ultimately quite unconvincing explanation which Schaeder proposes to bridge the semantic gap.

36. Pagliaro, "Riflessi." Pagliaro demonstrates some of the shortcomings in Schaeder's monograph and claims in a footnote that in private correspondence to him Schaeder renounced the argument of *Das Auge des Königs* and accepted Pagliaro's identification of the Persian equivalent of the King's Eye.

37. It has formal and semantic parallels with Old Indian *adhyaksa*, "supervisor/superintendent."

38. However, Gherardo Gnoli, "Antico-Persiano *anušya*– e gli Immortali di Erodoto," *Acta Iranica* 21 (1981): 266–80, has mounted a series of strong arguments against Pagliaro's contention that "Immortals" is a mistaken translation of an Old Persian word meaning "Followers."

39. For the same reason, one can place little faith in the thesis of Eilers, *Beamtennamen*, 22–23. On the basis of Ossetic *käsag* = "good see-er," he postulates an earlier Old Persian **kasaka* as "the King's Eye." Needless to say, the **kasaka* appears nowhere in the Achaemenid documents and must therefore be regarded as no more than a guess.

40. Walther Hinz, *Altiranische Funde und Forschungen* (Berlin, 1969), 153. He transliterates the Middle Persian term as *bidyaxš*.

41. Walther Hinz, *Neue Wege im Altpersischen* (Wiesbaden, 1973), 98–101.

42. Kent, *Old Persian* s.v. *di–*, *didā*.

43. Heidemarie Koch, "Zu den Lohnverhältnissen der Dareioszeit in Persien," in *Kunst, Kultur, und Geschichte der Achämenidenzeit und ihr Fortleben*, ed. Heidemarie Koch and D. N. MacKenzie (Berlin, 1983), 30–31.

44. See now Perikles Georges, "The Persians in the Greek Imagination, 550–480 B.C." (Ph.D. diss., University of California at Berkeley, 1981). There is an analogy of sorts in the fabulous stories about the monarch circulating in the Roman Empire, for which see Keith Hopkins, *Conquerors and Slaves* (Cambridge, 1978), 231–32.

45. Yasht 10 preamble, 10.7 and 10.82. All translations of Yasht 10 are from James Darmesteter, *The Zend-Avesta* (New York, 1898). The italics in these quotations are mine. For "thousands of eyes and ears" see 10.91, 141, 144, 145. For "a thousand senses" see 10.107.

46. 10.24, 45, 46. For "ten thousand spies" see 10.27, 60, 63, 69, 82, 141. The word for "spy" in the language of the Avesta (an eastern Iranian dialect) is *spas*. See n. 34 above for cognates in other Indo-European languages.

47. But in this early stage he is not yet identical with the sun. One must be careful not to confuse Mithra in his early Iranian and Zoroastrian form with the considerably different deity of the later Mithraic religion so popular with the Roman army. For Mithra in Zoroastrian religion see Zaehner, *Dawn and Twilight*, chap. 4, and Gershevitch, Introduction to *Avestan Hymn*.

48. For example, *Iliad* 3.277: (the Sun) ὃς πάντ' ἐφορᾷς καὶ πάντ' ἐπακούεις—"who observes all things and hears all things."

49. 10.95, 103. Cf. 10.13, 44, 50.

50. Kent, *Old Persian*, DNa lines 31–36 (pp. 137–38).

51. Yasht 10.7, 17–18, 83–84.

52. Kent, *Old Persian*, DBI lines 20–24 (pp. 117, 119).

53. Ibid., DNb lines 5–11 (pp. 138, 140).

54. Zaehner, *Dawn and Twilight*, 109. Some scholars have posited an even closer connection between Mithra and the king. But John R. Hinnells, *Persian Mythology* (London and New York, 1973), 106, disputes the claim that the Persian "king was thought of as the incarnation of Mithra and that

on his accession to the throne he dramatically re-enacted the birth of Mithra in a cave," noting that the evidence for this is slight. It is true that the later Sassanian kings were definitely regarded as divine, and some commentators explain this as the continuation of a conception developed under the Achaemenid monarchs. Alternatively, the Sassanian concept of kingship might have been influenced, via their Parthian predecessors, by the developing notion of the divinity of the king in the Hellenistic Greek kingdoms.

55. Zaehner, *Dawn and Twilight*, 109, and Heinrich Lüders, *Varuna*, vol. 1 (Göttingen, 1951), 35, take the former position; Lommel, "Späher," 323–33, argues vigorously for the latter.

56. According to Yasht 10.109, Mithra confers sovereignty: "To whom shall I give in return, without his thinking of it, the awful sovereignty, beautifully arranged, with many armies, and most perfect; the sovereignty of an all-powerful tyrant. . . ?"

57. One is reminded of the *episkopoi* in the Athenian Empire. Not much is known about these officials (see Russell Meiggs, *The Athenian Empire* [Oxford, 1972], 212–13), but they seem to have been traveling commissioners sent out to inspect subject states and to assist or supervise the process of local government at times of crisis or transition. Thus they would seem to have combined the functions of supervision and gathering of information.

Jack M. Balcer, "The Athenian Episkopos and the Achaemenid 'King's Eye,'" *American Journal of Philology* 98 (1977): 252–63, tries to demonstrate that the Athenians copied the title and functions of the Achaemenid King's Eye for their imperial overseer, the *episkopos*. He argues that the Persian "Eyes" and the Athenian *episkopoi* were similarly involved in supervision of imperial territories, prevention of rebellion, and oversight of local governments. However, we know little enough about the Athenian *episkopoi*, and, as is argued here, in light of the tremendously contradictory Greek evidence, there is little or no secure information about the number and function of the King's Eye(s). Thus Balcer's thesis, which rests on an amalgam of Greek testimonies and the speculations of Orientalists, falls prey to the methodological pitfalls discussed in this chapter.

58. See Kent, *Old Persian*, 85.

59. Hesiod *Works and Days* 252–55: τρὶς γὰρ μύριοι εἰσὶν ἐπὶ χθονὶ πουλυβοτείρῃ / ἀθάνατοι Ζηνὸς φύλακες θνητῶν ἀνθρώπων / οἵ ῥα φυλάσσουσίν τε δίκας καὶ σχέτλια ἔργα, / ἠέρα ἑσσάμενοι, πάντῃ φοιτῶντες ἐπ' αἶαν.—"For upon the bounteous earth Zeus has thrice ten thousand spirits, watchers of mortal men, and these keep watch on judgements and deeds of wrong as they roam, clothed in mist, all over the earth" (translation of H. G. Evelyn-White, *Hesiod, the Homeric Hymns and Homerica* [Cambridge, Mass., 1943]). There are clear similarities to the eyes/spies of Iranian Mithra and Indian Varuna. Hesiod also speaks of "the eye of Zeus" (267–69): πάντα ἰδὼν Διὸς ὀφθαλμὸς καὶ πάντα νοήσας καὶ νυ τάδ' αἴ κ' ἐθέλῃσ' ἐπιδέρκεται, οὐδέ ἑ λήθει οἵην δὴ καὶ τήνδε δίκην πόλις ἐντὸς ἐέργει.—"The eye of Zeus, seeing all and understanding all, beholds these things too, if he so will, and fails not to mark what sort of justice is this that the city keeps within it" (Evelyn-White, *Hesiod*).

Other references to the eye of Zeus in the Greek tradition can be found in Martin L. West, *Hesiod: Works and Days* (Oxford, 1978), 224. West cites Raffaele Pettazzoni, *The All-Knowing God*, trans. H. J. Rose (London, 1956), for the universal occurrence of the motif of the god's spies or watchers, particularly in connection with sky or astral gods. But because of the similarities with the Indo-Iranian conception and the Indo-European background of Zeus, West thinks that both the Greek and Iranian notions of the eye of the god go back to a common Indo-European heritage. Is it not possible that the Greek conception was directly influenced by the Iranian mythological tradition?

This is not the only locus for the presence of Oriental mythological motifs in Hesiod. Richard Reitzenstein, *Studien zum antiken Synkretismus aus Iran und Griechenland*, Studien der Bibliothek Warburg 7 (Leipzig, 1926); Thomas A. Sinclair, *Hesiod: Works and Days* (London, 1932); and, most recently, West, *Hesiod*, 172–77, have all pointed to the similarity between Hesiod's myth of the Five Ages of the World (*Works and Days* 109–201) and certain Iranian and Near Eastern mythological conceptions. West argues that the mythological motif of metallic world ages originated in Mesopotamia and was disseminated to India, Iran, Israel, and Greece. There is, of course, considerable evidence in Greek art for contact between Greece and the Near East from the eighth century onward. It is therefore reasonable to assume that the Greeks were receptive to Near Eastern mythological motifs in the Archaic Period.

60. Briant, "Forces productives," 40–42, argues that the cult of Mithra became widely diffused throughout the provinces of the Persian Empire, the primary instruments of diffusion being the Persian garrisons.

In a stimulating article, "The Eyes of the Lord," *Journal of the American Oriental Society* 88 (1968): 173–80, A. L. Oppenheim cites a series of passages in the Old Testament which refer to "the eyes of the Lord" (*'yny yhwh*). The prophet Zechariah (Zechariah 4:10) sees a vision of a seven-branched candlestick, which is said by an angel to be "the eyes of Yahweh, which run to and fro through the whole earth." In 2 Chronicles 16:9 the seer Hanani tells King Asa of Judah that the "eyes" have reported the king's wrongdoing to God, who will punish him: "For the eyes of Yahweh run to and fro throughout the whole earth, to show himself strong in the behalf of them whose heart is perfect towards him." Oppenheim thinks that the variety and intensity of the passages in Zechariah (see additionally 1:8–11 and 6:5–7) are the product of a specific personal clash between Zechariah and the Persian secret service—that is, the King's Eyes—in the time of Darius I. Zechariah has transferred a political institution to the theological level. The royal officials who threaten him have been "demonized," changed into malevolent supernatural beings. Oppenheim goes on to cite several examples of such "demonization" of royal officials in ancient Mesopotamia.

This is all very interesting. But the image of "the eyes of the Lord" in the Old Testament passages does not strike me as negative or malignant. And the real affinities of these passages are with the Iranian mythological conception of the eyes/spies of Mithra. It looks very much as if the Hebrews, living under Persian domination, were influenced by Iranian mythological and religious traditions. Both Zechariah and 2 Chronicles were written sufficiently late to reflect this influence. For a discussion of the influence of Zoroastrianism on Judaism and further bibliography on the topic, see J. Duchesne-Guillemin, *The Western Response to Zoroaster* (Oxford, 1958), 86–102. Oppenheim also alludes to late references from India (second century A.D.) and China (seventh century A.D.) to officials called the "five senses of government" and "the ear-and-eye official," respectively. Of course these titles have no necessary bearing on Persian practice in the mid-first millennium B.C., since they could be independently derived or influenced by the myth of Mithra (for which there is an attested Indian counterpart).

In sum, Oppenheim has done nothing to strengthen the case for the existence of a Persian King's Eye. He even admits that "the documentary sources at our disposal hardly mention the day-to-day doings" of the informers, accusers, and spies who he thinks controlled and coerced ancient Near Eastern societies. However, by providing new insight into the spread of the mythological motif of the god's eyes or spies, his work may strengthen the likelihood that the Iranian myth reached the Greeks.

61. Yasht 10.7, 23.

62. I am indebted to Broadhead, *Persae*, xxx–xxxii and 318–21, for much of the following analysis, though I deviate from his conclusions in certain respects.

63. Some scholars, including Gershevitch, *Avestan Hymn*, think that the Mithra yasht, in which the eyes of the god play so prominent a role, was written or redacted in its present form in the mid-fifth century, that is, in the lifetime of Aeschylus.

64. None of the Persian emissaries to the Greek states mentioned in historical sources is ever referred to as "the King's Eye." Wilhelm Brandenstein, "Der persische Satz bei Aristophanes, Ἀχαρνῆς, Vers 100," *Wiener Zeitschrift für die Kunde Sud- und Ostasiens* 8 (1964): 43–58, makes a valiant attempt to recover an authentic Old Persian phrase from the seemingly nonsensical syllables spoken by Aristophanes' "Eye" in *Acharnians* 100. However, not only are the linguistic arguments strained and ultimately unconvincing, but, to accept this reconstruction, one must also accept the unlikely proposition that Aristophanes and his Athenian audience knew more than a little Persian. The most recent discussion (with bibliography of earlier studies) of the dramatic motives of this passage of the *Acharnians* is that of Charles C. Chiasson, "Pseudartabas and His Eunuchs: *Acharnians* 91–122," *Classical Philology* 79 (1984): 131–36.

65. For a detailed analysis of these events, see Lewis, *Sparta and Persia*, 85–136. Lewis stresses the importance of the Spartan embassy of 407 (*Hellenica* 1.4.2–3), maintaining that it led to a new treaty and to a significant transformation of Spartan-Persian relations.

66. Xenophon *Hellenica* 3.1.1–3.4.25 and Diodorus Siculus 14.35–81 for the overall sequence of events. Evidence that it was Pharnabazus who denounced Tissaphernes before the king is to be found in Justin *Epitome of Trogus* 6.1 and Nepos *Conon* 3–4.

67. Weiskopf, "Achaemenid Systems," 58–62, chaps. 4 and 6 passim.

68. Starr, "Greeks and Persians," 71.
69. See appendix B to this chapter for an evaluation of the evidence on intelligence networks in the ancient world.
70. See Georges, "The Persians in the Greek Imagination." The King's Eye is not the only case in which the Greeks exercised their imaginations regarding circumstances in the Persian Empire. Beginning in the classical period and accelerating in the Hellenistic era, they developed some very strange notions about Zoroaster, founder of the Zoroastrian religion which predominated in ancient Iran, and about the Iranian priestly caste of the Magi. See the discussions by Giuseppe Messina, *Der Ursprung der Magier und die zarathustrische Religion* (Rome, 1930), 39–55, and Arnaldo Momigliano, *Alien Wisdom: The Limits of Hellenization* (Cambridge and New York, 1975), 141–48.
71. For the Greek fascination with Cyrus the Great, see pp. 71–72.
72. O. Kimball Armayor, "Herodotus' Catalogues of the Persian Empire in the Light of the Monuments and the Greek Literary Tradition," *Transactions of the American Philological Association* 108 (1978): 1–9.
73. The demonstration of this Greek pattern of mind is one of the main concerns of Momigliano in *Alien Wisdom*. One of the best examples (though not one to which he pays much attention) involves Greek ideas about India. An Indian "myth" developed early, presumably based on tales picked up by Greeks traveling in the Persian Empire, and can be seen in the wondrous accounts of India given by Herodotus and Ctesias. The creation of such a fanciful tradition is understandable, given the vast distances involved and the almost complete lack of direct contact between India and Greece in the classical period. What is surprising, however, is that the Greeks continued to cling to the traditional conceptions even after Alexander had opened up India to the Greek world. Some of Alexander's companions and Megasthenes, the Seleucid envoy to the court of the Indian king Chandragupta in the third century, perpetuated these fantastic stories and stereotypical notions, even though they were in a position to discover the truth.
74. He tries to show that Herodotus' information about the Persians and their empire has few points of contact with the realities of that empire as revealed by Persian monuments and inscriptions. However, David Lewis, in a lecture titled "Persians In Herodotus," delivered at Stanford University in March 1983, has made a strong demonstration that much of the information about Persia in Herodotus' account can be confirmed from Oriental sources.
75. William G. Sinnigen, "The Roman Secret Service," *Classical Journal* 57 (1961): 65–72.
76. A. H. M. Jones, *The Later Roman Empire*, vol. 1 (Norman, Okla., 1964), 578–82.
77. In addition to Darius' conquest of the Punjab and the short-lived incorporation of this territory as a Persian satrapy, there is the likelihood of trade and diplomatic contacts between Persia and the kingdoms of northern India.

78. Thomas R. Trautmann, *Kautilya and the Arthashastra: A Statistical Investigation of the Authorship and Evolution of the Text* (Leiden, 1971).
79. See the cautions to this effect in R. S. Sharma, *Aspects of Political Ideas and Institutions in Ancient India*, 2d ed. (Delhi, 1968), 29–30; A. L. Basham, Foreword to John W. Spellman, *Political Theory of Ancient India: A Study of Kingship from the Earliest Times to circa A.D. 300* (Oxford, 1964), viii; Spellman, ibid., xxi–xxii.
80. D. D. Kosambi, *Ancient India: A History of Its Culture and Civilization* (New York, 1965), 142; A. L. Basham, *The Wonder That Was India*, rev. ed. (New York, 1963), 81; Charles Drekmeier, *Kingship and Community in Early India* (Stanford, 1962), 167.
81. Sharma, *Aspects*, 19.
82. A. S. Altekar, *State and Government in Ancient India*, 3d ed. (Delhi, 1958), 13–14.
83. T. S. Brown, "The Reliability of Megasthenes," *American Journal of Philology* 76 (1955): 18–33.
84. The syndrome of spy-paranoia is sufficiently well attested in modern times. The Ottoman Sultan Abdul Hamid II, who reigned in the late nineteenth and early twentieth centuries, was reputed to have so large a spy organization that "one-half of the population of Istanbul was employed spying on the other half" (Lord Kinross, *The Ottoman Centuries: The Rise and Fall of the Turkish Empire* [New York, 1977], 534). I am indebted for this reference to Dr. Leila Fawaz.
85. Sharma, *Aspects*, 192–200.

Chapter 6

1. Konstantinos I. Vourveris, Πλάτων καὶ βάρβαροι, 2d ed. (Athens, 1966), contains the texts of Plato's references to various barbarian peoples, a commentary on these texts in modern Greek, and a summary of results in German.
2. The following passages from the Platonic literary corpus can be construed as reflecting an attitude toward the Persians: *Alcibiades* 1.105B–C and 120–23; *Epistles* 4.320D and 7.332A–B; *Menexenus* 239B–246A; *Phaedrus* 258B; *Epinomis* 987E–988A; *Lysis* 209D–210B; *Gorgias* 470E and 524A–525E; *Republic* 5.470B–C and 8.553A–C; *Laws* 1.637D–E, 3.685C, and 3.692C–701E. This survey does not attempt to deal with the question whether all these passages are really Plato's.
The following passages mention the Persians but seem to reflect no particular attitude toward them: *Laches* 191C; *Minos* 316A; *Hippias Minor* 368C; *Epistles* 2.311B and 13.363C; *Lysis* 211E; *Gorgias* 483D–E; *Republic* 1.336A; *Sophist* 230D; *Meno* 78D; *Apology* 40D; *Charmides* 158A; *Euthydemus* 274A; *Statesman* 264C; *Phaedrus* 266C; *Axiochus* 371A; *Eryxias* 393D; *Laws* 1.642E and 4.707B–C.
The following passages are indicative of attitudes toward barbarians in general: *Statesman* 262D; *Theaetetus* 174E–175E; *Epinomis* 973D; *Republic* 5.452C and 5.469B–C; *Cratylus* 383B, 390A, 397C–D, and 409D–E; *Symposium* 182B–C and 209E; *Laws* 10.886A; *Phaedo* 78A.

3. See the remarks of H. C. Baldry in *Grecs et barbares*, Entretiens Hardt 8 (Geneva, 1961), 118: "The inconsistency between these passages [*Statesman* 262 C–E, *Republic* 469B–476C] is remarkable. It arises, I think, not from a change of mind on Plato's part, but from a difference of approach. The point I want to make is that when Plato approaches these questions incidentally, as it were, in the course of a philosophical argument, his thought is completely free from the prejudices which seem to underlie his statements in the *Republic*."

4. Aristotle is another matter. In a famous chapter of the *Politics* (1.2), he implies that barbarians are by nature slaves because they lack reason (*logos*). See E. Badian, "Alexander the Great and the Unity of Mankind," *Historia* 7 (1958): 440–41.

5. *Statesman* 262D.

6. *Theaetetus* 174–75.

7. *Cratylus* 390A, *Symposium* 209E.

8. *Phaedo* 78A.

9. *Gorgias* 524–25.

10. *Republic* 5.470B–C, *Menexenus* 239B–246A.

11. *Lysis* 211E, *Euthydemus* 274A, *Eryxias* 393D. Cf. *Apology* 40D, *Sophist* 230D, *Gorgias* 470E.

12. *Laws* 3.694A–D, *Phaedrus* 258B, *Epistles* 4.320D and 8.332A–B.

13. *Alcibiades* 1.120–23.

14. *Laws* 3.692C–701E.

15. *Laws* 3.697C–E.

16. Many scholars believe the *Menexenus* to be little more than a parody or satire of contemporary Athenian rhetoric. On the other hand, Kahn, "Plato's Funeral Oration," 220–34, believes it had the more serious purpose of influencing the policy of the Athenian state at the time of the King's Peace of 386.

17. Jüthner, *Hellenen und Barbaren*, 22–25, arrives at a more balanced judgment than Vourveris concerning Plato's attitude toward barbarians. He admits that Plato was affected by the Sophistic Enlightenment, though he maintains that Plato was still a proud Greek at heart and that his writings manifest this conflict between head and heart.

18. For Aeschylus' treatment of the Persians, see Gilbert Murray, "The *Persae*," in *Aeschylus. A Collection of Critical Essays*, ed. Marsh H. McCall, Jr. (Englewood Cliffs, N.J., 1972), 37–38; for Herodotus' attitude, Aubrey de Sélincourt, *The World of Herodotus* (Boston, 1962), 44–46. The new ideas of the Sophists are briefly discussed by Reverdin, "Crise spirituelle," 89–91.

19. Full references to the ancient sources can be found in A. B. Bosworth, "Alexander and the Iranians," *Journal of Hellenic Studies* 100 (1980): 1–21.

20. On the efforts of Isocrates and Aristotle to influence Alexander, see Philip Merlan, "Isocrates, Aristotle, and Alexander the Great," *Historia* 3 (1954–55): 60–81; Edmund Buchner, "Zwei Gutachten für die Behandlung der Barbaren durch Alexander den Grossen," *Hermes* 82 (1954); 378–84. For Aristotle's attitude toward barbarians, see Jüthner,

Hellenen und Barbaren, 25–28; Badian, "Alexander the Great," 440–44; S. M. Stern, *Aristotle on the World State* (London and Colchester, 1968), 30–32.

21. The most passionate exponent of this point of view was W. W. Tarn, *Alexander the Great*, vol. 2 (Cambridge, 1948), 399–449, who maintained that Alexander ultimately intended to bring about the universal brotherhood of mankind. More support can be found in the ancient sources for the thesis of Helmut Berve, "Die Verschmelzungspolitik Alexanders des Grossen," *Klio* 31 (1938): 135–68, according to which Alexander planned to fuse the Macedonian and Persian aristocracies into a new ruling class for the empire.

22. Notably Badian, "Alexander the Great," 425–44; Bosworth, "Alexander and the Iranians," 1–21.

23. In a speech in Arrian *Anabasis* 2.7 Alexander heartens his troops before the conflict at Issus by reminding them of the example of Xenophon and the Ten Thousand. To be sure, the fact that this claim occurs in a speech lays it open to some suspicion, since Arrian may have taken the ancient historian's customary liberties with speeches. The reliability of speeches in Arrian has been discussed most recently by Peter A. Brunt, *Arrian*, vol. 2 (Cambridge, Mass., 1983), 528–33. Arrian was keenly aware of the parallels between the march of Xenophon and the Ten Thousand and the expedition of Alexander, going so far as to give his history of Alexander the same name as Xenophon's memoir. It is hard to believe that Alexander was not also aware of that most famous of Greek expeditions to Asia since the Trojan War.

24. Buchner, "Zwei Gutachten," 383–84, suggests that Alexander was influenced by the teachings of the fifth-century Sophists and the cosmopolitan Cynics of his own time.

Bibliography

Adcock, Frank E. *The Greek and Macedonian Art of War*. Berkeley, 1957.
Altekar, A. S. *State and Government in Ancient India*. 3d ed. Delhi, 1958.
Anderson, John K. *Ancient Greek Horsemanship*. Berkeley, 1961.
———. *Military Theory and Practice in the Age of Xenophon*. Berkeley, 1970.
———. "Notes on Some Points in Xenophon's Περὶ Ἱππικῆς." *Journal of Hellenic Studies* 80 (1960): 1–9.
———. *Xenophon*. New York, 1974.
Armayor, O. Kimball. "Herodotus' Catalogues of the Persian Empire in the Light of the Monuments and the Greek Literary Tradition." *Transactions of the American Philological Association* 108 (1978): 1–9.
Badian, Ernst. "Alexander the Great and the Unity of Mankind." *Historia* 7 (1958): 425–44.
Balcer, Jack M. "The Athenian Episkopos and the Achaemenid 'King's Eye.'" *American Journal of Philology* 98 (1977): 252–63.
Basham, A. L. *The Wonder That Was India*. Revised ed. New York, 1963.
Beloch, Karl J. *Griechische Geschichte*. Vols. III.1 and III.2. 2d ed. Berlin and Leipzig, 1922–23.
Benveniste, Emile. "Relations lexicales entre la Perse et la Grèce ancienne." In *La Persia e il mondo greco-romano*, pp. 479–88. Rome, 1966.
Berve, Helmut. "Die Verschmelzungspolitik Alexanders des Grossen." *Klio* 31 (1938): 135–68.
Bigwood, Joan M. "Ctesias of Cnidus." Ph.D. diss., Harvard University, 1964.
Birt, Th. "Zu Antisthenes und Xenophon." *Rheinisches Museum* 51 (1896): 153–57.
Bizos, Marcel. *Cyropédie*. Paris, 1971.
Boeckh, August. "De simultate quae inter Platonem et Xenophontem intercessisse fertur." In *August Boeckh's gesammelte kleine Schriften*. Vol. 4, pp. 1–34. Leipzig, 1874.
Bos, Isaäc. *Plutarchus' Leven van Agesilaus*. Groningen, 1947.

Bosworth, A. B. "Alexander and the Iranians." *Journal of Hellenic Studies* 100 (1980): 1–21.
Bowersock, G. W. *Philostratus: Life of Apollonius.* Harmondsworth, 1970.
Boyce, Mary. *A History of Zoroastrianism.* Vol. 1: *The Early Period.* Leiden, 1975.
———. *A History of Zoroastrianism.* Vol. 2: *Under the Achaemenians.* Leiden, 1982.
———. *Zoroastrians, Their Religious Beliefs and Practices.* London and Boston, 1979.
Brandenstein, Wilhelm. "Der persische Satz bei Aristophanes, Ἀχαρνῆς, Vers 100." *Wiener Zeitschrift für die Kunde Sud- und Ostasiens* 8 (1964): 43–58.
Breebaart, A. B. "From Victory to Peace: Some Aspects of Cyrus' State in Xenophon's *Cyrupaedia.*" *Mnemosyne* 36 (1983): 117–34.
Breitenbach, Hans R. *Historiographische Anschauungsformen Xenophons.* Diss. Basel, 1950.
———. *Xenophon von Athen.* Stuttgart, 1966. Reprinted from Pauly's *Realencyclopädie der classischen Altertumswissenschaft,* vol. IX.A2.
Briant, Pierre. "Appareils d'état et développement des forces productives au Moyen-Orient ancien: le cas de l'empire achéménide." *La Pensée* 217–218 (1981): 9–23.
———. "'Brigandage,' dissidence, et conquête en Asie achéménide et hellénistique." *Centre de Recherches d'Histoire Ancienne* 21 = *Annales littéraires de l'Université de Besançon,* no. 188 (1976): 163–279.
———. "Forces productives, dépendance rurale, et idéologie religieuse dans l'empire achéménide." *Centre de Recherches d'Histoire Ancienne* 32 = *Annales littéraires de l'Université de Besançon,* no. 237 (1980): 15–68.
Bringmann, Klaus. "Xenophons Hellenika und Agesilaos." *Gymnasium* 78 (1971): 224–41.
Broadhead, Henry D. *The Persae of Aeschylus.* Cambridge, 1960.
Brown, Norman O. *Hermes the Thief.* New York, 1947.
Brown, T. S. "The Reliability of Megasthenes." *American Journal of Philology* 76 (1955): 18–33.
Brownson, Carleton L., trans. *Xenophon: Anabasis.* London and New York, 1921.
Bruns, Ivo. *Das literarische Porträt der Griechen.* 1896. Reprint. Hildesheim, 1961.
Brunt, Peter A. *Arrian.* Vol. 2. Cambridge, Mass., 1983.
Buchner, Edmund. "Zwei Gutachten für die Behandlung der Barbaren durch Alexander den Grossen." *Hermes* 82 (1954): 378–84.
Burckhardt, Jacob. *Griechische Kulturgeschichte.* Vol. 3. Berlin and Leipzig, 1931.
Burges, George, trans. *The Works of Plato.* Vol. 5. London, 1852.

Burn, Andrew R. *Persia and the Greeks*. London and New York, 1962.
Bury, R. G., trans. *Plato: Laws*. London and New York, 1926.
Caizzi, Fernanda. *Antisthenis Fragmenta*. Milan, 1966.
Carlier, Pierre. "L'idée de monarchie impériale dans la *Cyropédie* de Xénophon." *Ktema* 3 (1978): 133–63.
Cawkwell, George L. "Agesilaus and Sparta." *Classical Quarterly*, n.s. 26 (1976): 62–84.
———. Introduction to *Xenophon: A History of My Times*, trans. Rex Warner. Harmondsworth, 1978.
———. Introduction to *Xenophon: The Persian Expedition*, trans. Rex Warner. Harmondsworth, 1972.
Chiasson, Charles C. "Pseudartabas and His Eunuchs: *Acharnians* 91–122." *Classical Philology* 79 (1984): 131–36.
Chrimes, Kathleen M. T. *The Res Publica Lacedaemoniorum Ascribed to Xenophon*. Manchester, 1948.
Christensen, Arthur E. *Les gestes des rois dans les traditions de l'Iran antique*. Paris, 1936.
Connor, W. Robert. "A Post-Modernist Thucydides." *Classical Journal* 72 (1977): 289–98.
———. *Thucydides*. Princeton, 1984.
Cook, J. M. *The Persian Empire*. New York, 1983.
Costa, E. A. "Evagoras I and the Persians, ca. 411 to 391 B.C." *Historia* 23 (1974): 40–56.
Cousin, Georges. *Kyros le jeune en Asie Mineure*. Nancy, 1904.
Cowley, Arthur E., ed. *Aramaic Papyri of the Fifth Century B.C.* Oxford, 1923.
Dahmen, Johannes. *Quaestiones Xenophonteae et Antistheneae*. Diss. Marburg, 1897.
Dandamayev, M. "Politische und wirtschaftliche Geschichte." In *Beiträge zur Achämenidengeschichte*, edited by Gerold Walser, pp. 15–58. Historia Einzelschrift 18. Wiesbaden, 1972.
Darmesteter, James, trans. *The Zend-Avesta*. New York, 1898.
Delebecque, Edouard. *Essai sur la vie de Xénophon*. Paris, 1957.
De Sanctis, Gaetano. "La genesi delle Elleniche di Senofonte." *Annali della Scuola Normale Superiore di Pisa, Lettere, Storia e Filosofia*, 2d ser. 1 (1932): 15–35.
de Sélincourt, Aubrey. *The World of Herodotus*. Boston, 1962.
Dihle, Albrecht. *Studien zur griechischen Biographie*. Göttingen, 1956.
Dindorf, G., ed. *Aeschyli: Tragoediae Superstites et Deperditarum Fragmenta*. Vol. 3. Oxford, 1851.
———. *Aristophanis Comoediae*. Vol. IV.2. Oxford, 1838.
Dittmar, Heinrich. *Aischines von Sphettos. Studien zur Literaturgeschichte der Sokratiker*. Berlin, 1912.
Dougherty, Raymond P. *Nabonidus and Belshazzar*. New Haven, 1929.

Dover, Kenneth J. *Greek Popular Morality in the Time of Plato and Aristotle.* Berkeley, 1974.
———, ed. *Aristophanes' Clouds.* Oxford, 1968.
Drekmeier, Charles. *Kingship and Community in Early India.* Stanford, 1962.
Drews, Robert. *The Greek Accounts of Eastern History.* Cambridge, Mass., 1973.
———. "Sargon, Cyrus, and Mesopotamian Folk History." *Journal of Near Eastern Studies* 33 (1974): 387–93.
Duchesne-Guillemin, J. *The Western Response to Zoroaster.* Oxford, 1958.
Eddy, Samuel K. *The King Is Dead: Studies in the Near Eastern Resistance to Hellenism, 334–31 B.C.* Lincoln, Neb., 1961.
Ehtécham, Mortéza. *L'Iran sous les Achéménides.* Fribourg, 1946.
Eichler, Gustav. *De Cyrupaediae capite extremo.* Diss. Leipzig, 1880.
Eilers, Wilhelm. *Iranische Beamtennamen in der keilschriftlichen Überlieferung.* Leipzig, 1940.
Engels, Donald W. *Alexander the Great and the Logistics of the Macedonian Army.* Berkeley, 1978.
Erbse, Hartmut. "Xenophons Anabasis." *Gymnasium* 73 (1966): 485–505.
Erman, Adolf. *Wörterbuch der aegyptischen Sprache.* Vol. 1. Berlin, 1955.
Evelyn-White, H. G., trans. *Hesiod, the Homeric Hymns and Homerica.* Cambridge, Mass., and London, 1943.
Farber, J. Joel. "The *Cyropaedia* and Hellenistic Kingship." *American Journal of Philology* 100 (1979): 497–514.
———. "Xenophon's Theory of Kingship." Ph.D. diss., Yale University, 1959.
Fauth, Wolfgang. "Der königliche Gärtner und Jäger im Paradeisos. Beobachtungen zur Rolle des Herrschers in der vorderasiatischen Hortikultur." *Persica* 8 (1979): 1–53.
Finley, Moses I. "The Ancestral Constitution." In *The Use and Abuse of History,* 34–59. New York, 1975.
Fornara, Charles W. *Herodotus: An Interpretative Essay.* Oxford, 1971.
Fox, Robin Lane. *Alexander the Great.* London and New York, 1973.
Friedrich, Gustav. "Zu Xenophons Hellenika und Agesilaos." *Jahrbuch für klassische Philologie* 153 (1896): 289–99.
Frye, Richard N. *The Heritage of Persia.* New York and Toronto, 1963.
———. "The Institutions." In *Beiträge zur Achämenidengeschichte,* edited by Gerold Walser, pp. 83–93. Historia Einzelschrift 18. Wiesbaden, 1972.
Fuks, Alexander. *The Ancestral Constitution.* London, 1953.
Gabba, Emilio. "True History and False History in Classical Antiquity." *Journal of Roman Studies* 71 (1981): 50–62.
Gautier, Leopold. *La langue de Xénophon.* Geneva, 1911.

Gemoll, Wilhelm. Review of *Studi Senofontei*, by Luigi Castiglioni. *Philologische Wochenschrift* 43 (1923): 481–83.
Georges, Perikles. "The Persians in the Greek Imagination, 550–480 B.C." Ph.D. diss., University of California at Berkeley, 1981.
Gershevitch, Ilya. *The Avestan Hymn to Mithra*. Cambridge, 1959.
Gigon, Olof. *Sokrates. Sein Bild in Dichtung und Geschichte*. Bern, 1947.
Gilmore, John, ed. *The Fragments of the Persika of Ktesias*. London and New York, 1888.
Gnoli, Gherardo. "Antico-Persiano *anušya*– e gli Immortali di Erodoto." *Acta Iranica* 21 (1981): 266–80.
Godley, A. D., trans. *Herodotus*. Vol. 1. Cambridge, Mass., 1920.
Gomme, Arnold W. *A Historical Commentary on Thucydides*. Vol. 1. Oxford, 1945.
Grayson, A. K. *Assyrian and Babylonian Chronicles*. Locust Valley, N.Y., 1975.
Grimal, Pierre. *Les jardins romains, à la fin de la république et aux deux premiers siècles de l'empire: Essai sur le naturalisme romain*. Paris, 1943.
Guthrie, William K. C. *A History of Greek Philosophy*. Vol. 3. Cambridge, 1969.
Hamilton, Charles D. "Agesilaus and the Failure of Spartan Hegemony." *The Ancient World* 5 (1982): 67–78.
Harmatta, János. *Studies in the Language of the Iranian Tribes in South Russia*. Budapest, 1951.
Harmon, A. M., trans. *Lucian*. Vol. 3. London and New York, 1921.
Hatzfeld, J. "Agésilas et Artaxerxès II." *Bulletin de correspondance hellénique* 70 (1946): 238–46.
Helm, Peyton R. "'Greeks' in the Neo-Assyrian Levant and 'Assyria' in Early Greek Writers." Ph.D. diss., University of Pennsylvania, 1980.
Henry, William P. *Greek Historical Writing: A Historiographical Essay Based on Xenophon's Hellenica*. Chicago, 1967.
Hicks, R. D., trans. *Diogenes Laertius*. Cambridge, Mass., 1959.
Higgins, William E. *Xenophon the Athenian*. Albany, N.Y., 1977.
Hinnells, John R. *Persian Mythology*. London and New York, 1973.
Hinz, Walther. *Altiranische Funde und Forschungen*. Berlin, 1969.
———. *Neue Wege im Altpersischen*. Wiesbaden, 1973.
Höistad, Ragnar. *Cynic Hero and Cynic King: Studies in the Cynic Conception of Man*. Uppsala, 1948.
Holden, Hubert A. *The Cyropaedia of Xenophon*. Vol. 4. Cambridge, 1890.
Hopkins, Keith. *Conquerors and Slaves*. Cambridge, 1978.
Jackson, Abraham V. W. *Zoroastrian Studies*. New York, 1928.
Jacoby, Felix, ed. *Die Fragmente der griechischen Historiker*. Vols. II.1 and II.2. Berlin, 1923–26. Vol. III.C.1. Leiden, 1958.
Jaeger, Werner. *Paideia: The Ideals of Greek Culture*. Vol. 3. Oxford, 1943.

Jones, A. H. M. *The Later Roman Empire.* Vol. 1. Norman, Okla., 1964.
Jüthner, Julius. *Hellenen und Barbaren.* Leipzig, 1923.
Kahn, Charles H. "Plato's Funeral Oration: The Motive of the *Menexenus.*" *Classical Philology* 58 (1963): 220–34.
Keller, William J. "Xenophon's Acquaintance with the *History* of Herodotus." *Classical Journal* 6 (1911): 252–59.
Kent, Roland G. "The Oldest Old Persian Inscriptions." *Journal of the American Oriental Society* 66 (1946): 206–12.
———. *Old Persian: Grammar, Texts, Lexicon.* 2d ed. New Haven, 1953.
Kinross, Lord. *The Ottoman Centuries: The Rise and Fall of the Turkish Empire.* New York, 1977.
Knauth, Wolfgang. *Das altiranische Fürstenideal von Xenophon bis Ferdousi.* Wiesbaden, 1975.
Koch, Heidemarie. *Die religiösen Verhältnisse der Dareioszeit.* Wiesbaden, 1977.
———. "Zu den Lohnverhältnissen der Dareioszeit in Persien." In *Kunst, Kultur und Geschichte der Achämenidenzeit und ihr Fortleben,* edited by Heidemarie Koch and D. N. MacKenzie, pp. 19–50. Berlin, 1983.
König, Friedrich W. *Älteste Geschichte der Meder und Perser.* Leipzig, 1934.
———. *Die Persika des Ktesias von Knidos.* Archiv für Orientforschung 18. Graz, 1972.
Kosambi, D. D. *Ancient India: A History of Its Culture and Civilization.* New York, 1965.
Kraeling, Emil G. *The Brooklyn Museum Aramaic Papyri.* New Haven, 1953.
Krömer, Dietfried. *Xenophons Agesilaos: Untersuchungen zur Komposition.* Augsburg, 1971.
Krumbholz, Paul. *De Ctesia aliisque auctoribus in Plutarchi Artaxerxis vita adhibitis.* Eisenach, 1889.
Lefevre, E. "Die Frage nach dem βίος εὐδαίμων: Die Begegnung zwischen Kyros und Kroisos bei Xenophon." *Hermes* 99 (1971): 283–96.
Lehmann-Haupt, C. F. "Der Sturz des Kroisos und das historische Element in Xenophons Kyropädie." *Wiener Studien* 50 (1932): 123–59.
Leo, Friedrich. *Die griechisch-römische Biographie nach ihrer literarischen Form.* Leipzig, 1901.
Lesky, Albin. *A History of Greek Literature.* Translated by James Willis and Cornelis de Heer. New York, 1966.
Levy, Reuben, trans. *The Epic of the Kings: Shahnama.* Chicago, 1967.
Lewis, David M. *Sparta and Persia.* Leiden, 1977.
Lommel, H. "Die Späher des Varuna und Mitra und das Auge des Königs." *Oriens* 6 (1953): 323–33.
Lonis, Raoul. *Les usages de la guerre entre grecs et barbares: Des guerres médiques au milieu du IVe siècle avant J.-C.* Paris, 1969.

Luccioni, Jean. *Les idées politiques et sociales de Xénophon.* N.p., 1947.
Lüders, Heinrich. *Varuna.* Vol. 1. Göttingen, 1951.
Mallowan, Max. "Cyrus the Great (558–529 B.C.)." *Iran* 10 (1972): 1–17.
Marchant, Edgar C., trans. *Xenophon: Memorabilia and Oeconomicus.* Cambridge, Mass., 1918.
———. *Xenophon: Scripta Minora.* Cambridge, Mass., 1925.
Mathieu, Georges. *Les idées politiques d'Isocrate.* Paris, 1925.
Meiggs, Russell. *The Athenian Empire.* Oxford, 1972.
Merlan, Philip. "Isocrates, Aristotle, and Alexander the Great." *Historia* 3 (1954–55): 60–81.
Messina, Giuseppe. *Der Ursprung der Magier und die zarathustrische Religion.* Rome, 1930.
Meyer, Eduard. *Geschichte des Altertums.* Vol. IV.1. 3d ed. Stuttgart, 1939.
Miller, Walter, trans. *Xenophon: Cyropaedia.* London and Cambridge, Mass., 1914.
Momigliano, Arnaldo. *Alien Wisdom: The Limits of Hellenization.* Cambridge and New York, 1975.
———. *The Development of Greek Biography.* Cambridge, Mass., 1971.
———. "Per l'unita logica della *Lacedaemonion Politeia.*" In *Terzo contributo alla storia degli studi classici e del mondo antico,* pp. 341–45. Rome, 1966.
Morr, Josef. "Xenophon und der Gedanke eines all-griechischen Eroberungszuges gegen Persien." *Wiener Studien* 45 (1926/27): 186–201.
Morrow, Glenn R. *Plato's Cretan City: A Historical Interpretation of the Laws.* Princeton, 1960.
Mosley, D. J. "Greeks, Barbarians, Language, and Contact." *Ancient Society* 2 (1971): 1–6.
Moulton, James H. *Early Zoroastrianism.* London, 1913.
Moynihan, Elizabeth B. *Paradise as a Garden: In Persia and Mughal India.* New York, 1979.
Münscher, Karl. *Xenophon in der griechisch-römischen Literatur.* Philologus Supplementband 13. Leipzig, 1920.
Murray, Gilbert. "The *Persae.*" In *Aeschylus: A Collection of Critical Essays,* edited by Marsh H. McCall, Jr., pp. 29–39. Englewood Cliffs, N.J., 1972.
Murray, Oswyn. "Ὁ Ἀρχαῖος Δασμός." *Historia* 15 (1966): 142–56.
Muscarella, Oscar White. "Excavated and Unexcavated Achaemenian Art." In *Ancient Persia: The Art of an Empire,* edited by Denise Schmandt-Besserat, pp. 23–42. Malibu, Calif., 1980.
Nicolai, [?]. *Die Politik des Tissaphernes.* Bernburg, 1863.
Nickel, Rainer. *Xenophon.* Darmstadt, 1979.
Norlin, George, trans. *Isocrates.* Vol. 1. Cambridge, Mass., 1928.

Nussbaum, G. B. *The Ten Thousand: A Study in Social Organization and Action in Xenophon's Anabasis.* Leiden, 1967.

Ollier, François. *Le mirage spartiate.* Vol. 1: *Étude sur l'idéalisation de Sparte dans l'antiquité grecque de l'origine jusqu'aux cyniques.* Paris, 1933.

———. "La renomée posthume de Gryllos, fils de Xénophon." *Bulletin Association Guillaume Budé* (1959): 425–37.

Olmstead, Albert T. *History of the Persian Empire.* Chicago and London, 1948.

Opitz, Alfons. *Quaestiones Xenophonteae: De Hellenicorum atque Agesilai necessitudine.* Breslau Philologische Abhandlung 46. Breslau, 1913.

Oppenheim, A. L. "The Eyes of the Lord." *Journal of the American Oriental Society* 88 (1968): 173–80.

Pagliaro, A. "Riflessi di etimologie iraniche nella tradizione storiografica greca." *Rendiconti dell' Accademia Nazionale dei Lincei,* 8th ser. 9 (1954): 133–53.

Pearson, Lionel I. C. *Popular Ethics in Ancient Greece.* Stanford, 1962.

———. "Prophasis: A Clarification." *Transactions of the American Philological Association* 103 (1972): 381–94.

———. "Prophasis and Aitia." *Transactions of the American Philological Association* 83 (1952): 205–23.

Pease, Samuel J. "Xenophon's *Cyropaedia,* 'The Compleat General.'" *Classical Journal* 29 (1934): 436–40.

Pelletier, A. "Les deux Cyrus dans l'Économique de Xénophon." *Revue de philologie,* 3d ser. 18 (1944): 84–93.

Petit, Thomas. *Tissapherne: Les mésaventures d'une ambition.* Mémoires de l'Université de Liège. Liège, 1978–79.

Prinz, Wilhelm. *De Xenophontis Cyri institutione.* Göttingen, 1911.

Pritchard, James B., ed. *Ancient Near Eastern Texts Relating to the Old Testament.* 2d ed. Princeton, 1955.

Rackham, H., trans. *Aristotle: Politics.* London and Cambridge, Mass., 1932.

Raditsa, Leo. "Iranians in Asia Minor." In *The Cambridge History of Iran.* Vol. III.1: *The Seleucid, Parthian and Sassanian Periods,* edited by Ehsan Yarshater, pp. 100–115. Cambridge, 1983.

Rahe, Paul A. "The Military Situation in Western Asia on the Eve of Cunaxa." *American Journal of Philology* 101 (1980): 79–96.

Rahn, Peter J. "The Date of Xenophon's Exile." In *Classical Contributions: Studies in Honor of Malcolm Francis McGregor,* edited by Gordon S. Shrimpton and David J. McCargar, pp. 103–19. Locust Valley, N.Y., 1981.

Rawlings, Hunter R. III. *A Semantic Study of Prophasis to 400 B.C.* Hermes Einzelschrift 33. Wiesbaden, 1975.

Reitzenstein, Richard. *Studien zum antiken Synkretismus aus Iran und Griechenland*. Studien der Bibliothek Warburg 7. Leipzig, 1926.
Reverdin, Olivier. "Crise spirituelle et évasion." In *Grecs et barbares*, pp. 85–107. Entretiens Hardt 8. Geneva, 1961.
Rice, D. G. "Agesilaus, Agesipolis, and Spartan Politics, 386–379 B.C." *Historia* 23 (1974): 164–82.
Riemann, Karl-August. *Das herodoteische Geschichtswerk in der Antike*. Munich, 1967.
Robert, Fernand. "Les intentions de Xénophon dans l'Anabase." *Information littéraire* 2 (1950): 55–59.
Rosenstiel, Friedrich. *De Xenophontis Historiae Graecae parte bis edita*. Berlin, 1882.
Sakellariou, M. B. "Panhellenism: From Concept to Policy." In *Philip of Macedon*, edited by Miltiades B. Hatzopoulos and Louisa D. Loukopoulos, pp. 128–45. Athens, 1980.
Schaeder, Hans H. *Das Auge des Königs*. Abhandlung der königliche Gesellschaft der Wissenschaften, Göttingen, Phil.-hist. Kl., ser. 3, no. 10. Göttingen, 1934.
Scharr, Erwin. *Xenophons Staats- und Gesellschaftsideal und seine Zeit*. Halle, 1919.
Schmitt, Rüdiger. "Der Titel 'Satrap.'" In *Studies in Greek, Italic, and Indo-European Linguistics*, edited by Anna M. Davies and Wolfgang Meid, pp. 373–90. Innsbruck, 1976.
Schneider, Carl. *Kulturgeschichte des Hellenismus*. Vol. 1. Munich, 1967.
Schwartz, Eduard. *Fünf Vorträge über den griechischen Roman*. 2d ed. Berlin, 1943.
Seager, Robin. "The King's Peace and the Balance of Power in Greece, 386–362 B.C." *Athenaeum* 52 (1974): 36–63.
Shahbazi, A. "The Achaemenid Tomb in Buzpar (Gur-i Dukhtar)." *Bastan Chenassi va Honar-e Iran* 9/10 (1972).
Sharma, R. S. *Aspects of Political Ideas and Institutions in Ancient India*. 2d ed. Delhi, 1968.
Sherman, C. L., trans. *Diodorus Siculus: Library of History*. Vol. 7. Cambridge, Mass., 1952.
Sidgwick, Arthur, ed. *Aeschylus Persae*. Cambridge, 1903.
Sinclair, Thomas A. *Hesiod: Works and Days*. London, 1932.
Sinnigen, William G. "The Roman Secret Service." *Classical Journal* 57 (1961): 65–72.
Smith, R. E. "The Opposition to Agesilaus' Foreign Policy, 394–371 B.C." *Historia* 2 (1954): 274–88.
Spellman, John W. *Political Theory of Ancient India: A Study of Kingship from the Earliest Times to circa A.D. 300*. Oxford, 1964.
Stanley, Thomas. *Aeschyli Tragoediae*. Vol. 2. London, 1745.

Starr, Chester G. "Greeks and Persians in the Fourth Century B.C.: A Study in Cultural Contacts before Alexander." *Iranica Antiqua* 11 (1975): 39–99 and 12 (1977): 49–115.
Stern, S. M. *Aristotle on the World State.* London and Colchester, 1968.
Strauss, Leo. *Xenophon's Socratic Discourse.* Ithaca, N.Y., 1970.
Stronach, David. *Pasargadae: A Report on the Excavations Conducted by the British Institute of Persian Studies from 1961 to 1963.* Oxford, 1978.
Susemihl, F. "Der Idealstaat des Antisthenes und der Dialog Archelaos, Kyros und Herakles." *Jahrbuch für klassische Philologie* (1887): 207–14.
Sykutris, Johannes. "Isokrates' *Evagoras.*" *Hermes* 62 (1927): 24–53. Reprinted in *Wege der Forschung: Isokrates,* edited by Friedrich Seck, pp. 74–105. Darmstadt, 1976.
Taine, Hippolyte. "Xénophon: L'Anabase." In *Essais de critique et d'histoire.* 10th ed. Paris, 1904.
Tarn, W. W. *Alexander the Great.* Vol. 2. Cambridge, 1948.
Tigerstedt, E. N. *The Legend of Sparta in Classical Antiquity.* Lund, 1965.
Todd, Joan M. "Persian *Paideia* and Greek *Historia*: An Interpretation of the *Cyropaedia* of Xenophon, Book One." Ph.D. diss., University of Pittsburgh, 1968.
Trautmann, Thomas R. *Kautilya and the Arthashastra: A Statistical Investigation of the Authorship and Evolution of the Text.* Leiden, 1971.
Vidal-Naquet, Pierre. "The Black Hunter and the Origin of the Athenian *ephebeia.*" In *Myth, Religion, and Society,* edited by R. L. Gordon, pp. 147–62. Cambridge, 1981.
Vourveris, Konstantinos I. Πλάτων καὶ βάρβαροι. 2d ed. Athens, 1966.
Walcot, P. "Odysseus and the Art of Lying." *Ancient Society* 8 (1977): 1–19.
Walser, Gerold. "Griechen am Hofe des Grosskönigs." In *Festgabe Hans von Greyerz,* edited by Ernst Walder, pp. 189–202. Bern, 1967.
Weinreich, Otto. *Der griechische Liebesroman.* Zurich, 1962.
Weiskopf, Michael N. "Achaemenid Systems of Governing in Anatolia." Ph.D. diss., University of California at Berkeley, 1982.
Wencis, Leonard. "*Hypopsia* and the Structure of Xenophon's *Anabasis.*" *Classical Journal* 73 (1977): 44–49.
West, Martin L. *Hesiod: Works and Days.* Oxford, 1978.
Westlake, H. D. "Individuals in Xenophon, *Hellenica.*" *Bulletin of the John Rylands Library* 49 (1966–67): 246–69.
Wiseman, T. P. *Clio's Cosmetics: Three Studies in Greco-Roman Literature.* Leicester, 1979.
Wood, Henry. *The Histories of Herodotus.* The Hague, 1972.
Zaehner, Robert C. *The Dawn and Twilight of Zoroastrianism.* London, 1961.

———. *The Teachings of the Magi: A Compendium of Zoroastrian Beliefs.* London and New York, 1956.

Zierke, E. *Agesilaos. Beiträge zum Lebensbild und zur Politik des Spartanerkönigs.* Diss. Frankfurt, 1936.

Index

Abdul Hamid II (sultan), 193
Abrocomas, 23
Acharnians, The (Aristophanes), 105–6, 110, 113, 131–32
Adversus indoctum (Lucian), 111, 113, 134
Aelius Aristides, 109, 112, 113, 125, 134, 139
Aeschylus, 71, 72, 105, 112, 113, 126–27, 131, 146, 171, 178, 187
Aethiopica (Heliodorus), 111–12, 113, 134
Agesilaus (king), 2, 22, 39, 61, 166; Arcadian campaign, 48; at Aulis, 46; compared to Artaxerxes II, 43–45; in Corinthian War, 46–47; Coronea campaign, 46; Egyptian campaign, 45, 53; and the King's Peace, 47, 52, 55; Leuctra campaign, 48, 52; and peace conference in 371 B.C., 48; as "Persian-hater," 42–43; meets Pharnabazus, 12; *pistis* of, 40–41; Sardis campaign, 41–42, 45, 54; Sphodrias affair, 48; Theban campaigns, 47–48, 52
Agesilaus (Xenophon), 5, 9–10, 26, 39–60, 94, 141, 156, 162; accuracy of, 164; apologetic nature of, 166; Catalogue of Virtues, 42–46; omissions covered by *Hellenica*, 46–57 passim, 164; Survey of Deeds, 40–42, 45–49, 55; Xenophon's purpose in writing, 49–55
Agesipolis, 52
agogē, 87
Ahura Mazda, 120, 121, 156

Akkadian, 115
Alcibiades (attributed to Plato), 143, 179
Alexander the Great, 154, 172, 192, 194–95; legendary Persian parentage of, 177; respects and adopts Persian customs, 135, 146; restores tomb of Cyrus the Great, 178
Amorges, 129, 173
Anabasis (Arrian), 195
Anabasis (Xenophon), 2, 14–38, 40, 64, 68, 72, 85, 94, 140–41, 162; Armenian episode, 32; date of composition, 154; four-part division of, 15–16; Orontas episode, 20–21; as propaganda, 14–15; self-deception in, 16; Seuthes episode, 34–36; speeches after Cunaxa, 29–31
Anahita, 13, 153
Analysts, 4
anaoša, 118
Anaxibius, 33, 34
andarz, 178
animal sacrifice, 180
Anshan, 76
Antidosis (Isocrates), 166
Antisthenes, 68, 71, 72, 149, 170, 172
Antony, 154
anušiya, 118
apistia, 28, 30
Apollonius of Tyana, 110
apology, 166
Apology (Plato), 83, 163, 166, 182
Apology (Xenophon), 166, 182
Aramaic, 115, 174
aretai, 39

Argoste, 73, 77
Ariaeus, 29
Ariaramnes, 73
Ariobarzanes, 48, 166
Aristarchus, 33, 34
Aristobulus, 178
Aristophanes, 19, 105–6, 112, 113, 131–32, 191
Aristophanes scholiast, 110, 112, 113, 114, 133–34, 186–87
Aristotle, 64, 65, 146, 151, 168, 185–86, 194
Armayor, O. Kimball, 130
Arrian, 138, 195
Arsames, 73
Artaozus, 29
Artasyras, 106
Artaxerxes II, 12, 19, 22, 43–45, 50, 74, 128, 164
Artaxerxes III, 49
Artaynte, 161
Artemis, 13, 153
Arthashastra (attributed to Kautilya), 137–38
Assyria, 61, 175
Astyages, 81, 82, 88, 153, 173, 176
athanatoi, 117–18
Atharvaveda, 120
Athens, 48, 58, 59, 128, 161, 173
Atradates, 73, 76
Aulis, 46
Avesta, 120, 152
Avestan, 117. *See also* Old Persian

Babylon, 77, 78, 80
Babylonia, 175
baji, 149
barbarians, 1, 29, 143–45, 150, 163, 194; oral traditions of, 68; trustworthiness of, 31, 34, 37, 41
Barca, siege of, 161
Behistun inscription (Darius I), 7, 73, 88, 121, 158, 176
Belshazzar, 77
bidix, 117
bitaxš, 117, 118
Boyce, Mary, 89–90
Breitenbach, Hans R., 50, 80

Bringmann, Klaus, 56–57
Broadhead, Henry D., 126
Buzpar tomb, 173
Byzantium, 33. *See also* Istanbul

Callisthenes, 165
Cambyses (father of Cyrus the Great), 73, 74, 76, 77, 98, 177
Cambyses (son of Cyrus the Great), 79, 83, 84
čaša/čašman, 117
Catalogue of Virtues, 39, 40
cavalry, 41, 87, 151, 179
Celaenae, 153
Chandragupta, 138
Charon of Lampsacus, 170
Cheirisophus, 30
China, 191
Christensen, Arthur E., 84
Cicero, 169
Cilicia, 88
Cleanor, 30
Clearchus, 20, 21, 23, 24–25, 26–29, 160, 172
Clouds, The (Aristophanes), 19
Coeratadas, 33
Conon, 58, 167
Constitution of the Lacedaemonians (Xenophon), 87, 92, 95, 164
contract. *See* Mithra/*mithra*
Corinthian War, 46–47
covenant, 99. *See also* Mithra/*mithra*
Crassus, 154
Crete, 171
Critias, 164
Croesus, 21, 78, 83, 130, 169–70, 176
Ctesias, 138, 149, 169, 176; on the accession of Cyrus the Great, 82; on Clearchus, 60; on the death of Cyrus the Great, 83, 84; on Menon, 160, 162; on Mithra, 19; on the parentage of Cyrus the Great, 73, 76, 172–173; as source for Plutarch, 106; as source for Xenophon, 68
Cunaxa, battle of, 87, 106
cupbearer, 88, 179
Cyaxares, 81–82, 176

Cynegeticus (attributed to Xenophon), 181
Cynics, 195
Cynisca, 165
Cyprus, 88, 167. See also Salamis, Cypriot
Cyropaedia (Xenophon), 5, 44–45, 61–100 passim, 141–42, 150; compared to Arthashastra, 138; epilogue to, 10, 91–97, 164, 181–82; genre of, 66–67; Greek vs. Persian elements in, 70–71, 171; "King's Eye" in, 101–5, 107, 125, 133; purpose of, 66, 70; sources for, 67–69; structure of, 85
Cyrus (Antisthenes), 68, 149
Cyrus Cylinder, 74, 76
Cyrus the Great, 144, 153; accedes to throne of Media, 81–82; captures Babylon, 77, 78, 176; conquest of Egypt ascribed to, 79–81; death of, 83–85; defeats Croesus, 77–78, 176; intelligence network of, 101–5; justice of, 7; parentage of, 76–77; Plato's view of, 97–100; as propagandist, 177; reputation of, among non-Persians, 171–72; similarities to Cyrus the Younger, 64, 72–76 passim, 82, 85–86; tomb of, 84
Cyrus the Younger: appointed to dual command in Asia Minor, 11, 128, 158; deceptions by, 21, 22–24; justice of, 7; and Orontas, 20–21; *pistis* of, 158–59; rebellion of, 2, 65, 80; relationship with Xenophon, 174–75; similarities to Cyrus the Great, 64, 72–76 passim, 82, 85–86; solicitude for agriculture, 8, 153; tomb of, posited, 173–74. See also Cunaxa, battle of

daevas, 156
Daniel, 161
Dara (Darius III), 172
Darab, 172
Darius I, 7, 121, 144, 152, 158, 192
Darius III, 172

Dascylium, 12, 153
dasmos, 149
deceit, 18–38 passim, 157, 161
Delebecque, Edouard, 49–50, 71, 92–97 passim
Delphi, 169–70
De malignitate Herodoti (Plutarch), 165
De mercede conductis (Lucian), 111, 113, 134
Derbici, 83, 84, 173
Dercyllidas, 2, 49
diaballei, 22
Dicaearchus, 165
lu di-dak-ku, 118–19
Dihle, Albrecht, 49
Dinon, 106, 184
Dio Chrysostom, 17, 109, 112, 113, 133
Diodorus Siculus, 52, 138
Diogenes Laertius, 12–13, 97, 168
Dioscorides, 165
Dionysius of Halicarnassus, 17, 169
Dionysius of Miletus, 170
*ditaka/*didiyaka, 118–19
dorata, 87
Draco, 7
drauga, 19
Duris, 165

Ecbatana, 80; inscriptions at, 73–74
education, 19, 64, 85–86, 87
Egypt, 45, 53, 79–81, 187
Elamite, 115, 118
Elephantine papyrus, 115
elevator shoes, 89
empire vs. *polis*, 64–65
encomium, 45, 50–51, 58, 166, 168
Epaminondas, 48
Ephesus, 13, 153
ephodoi, 88, 107, 185
ephoroi, 138
epinikion, 167
epiorkia, 19. See also oath-breaking
episkopos, 115, 116, 138, 189
Epistulae ad Quintum fratrem (Cicero), 169
epitaph, 167

epitropos, 117
erga, 39
Eryxias (Plato), 163
eti kai nun, 69, 92, 93, 95, 104
Eunapius, 17
Euthydemus (Plato), 163
Evagoras (Isocrates), 45, 57–60, 167
Evagoras (king), 58–59, 65, 167
"Eyes of Mithra," 120
"Eyes of the Lord" (biblical), 190

Ferdowsi, 84, 177
Free Square, 180
frumentarii, 136

gaušaka, 115
Gigon, Olof, 68
Gobryas/Ugbaru, 77, 78, 175–76
Gorgias, 166
Gorgias (Plato), 163
Graves, Robert, 90
Gryllos, 168
gušak, 187
gwšky', 115

Hammurabi, 152
Hecataeus of Miletus, 130
Helen (Gorgias), 166
Heliodorus, 111–12, 113, 114, 134, 186–87
Hellanicus, 170
Hellenica (Xenophon): as continuation of Thucydides, 17; deception in, 157, 161; involvement of Persia in Greek affairs, 128; material omitted from *Agesilaus*, 46–57 passim, 164; meeting of Agesilaus and Pharnabazus, 12; Persian military science, 87; on Tissaphernes, 22, 26, 159, 162
Heraclea, 32–33
Heraclides (agent of Seuthes), 34, 36, 162
Heraclides (writer of *Persica*), 106, 184
Herodotus, 71, 72, 108, 130, 146, 155, 174; constitutional debate of Persian conspirators, 183; on Croesus and Solon, 21, 68, 172; on Cyrus the Great's parentage, 73, 77; on the King's Eye, 105, 112, 113, 131, 185; on Persian education, 19, 86; on Persian social customs, 89
Hesiod, 124, 189, 190
Hesychius, 109, 112, 113, 133
Hidrieus the Carian, 165
Hiero (Xenophon), 71
Hieronymus the Philosopher, 165
Higgins, William E., 16, 50, 87
Hinz, Walther, 118, 119
Hipparchicus (Xenophon), 151
Historia Augusta, 136
Histories (Herodotus), 21, 68, 131
Holden, H. A., 91
Homer, 130
Homeric hymn to Hermes, 19
hubris, 21, 44, 83
hunting, 93, 179
hyparchos, 149
hypopsia, 16, 28, 162

India (Maurya Empire), 137–39, 191, 192
Indica (Arrian), 138
Indica (Ctesias), 138
Indica (Megasthenes), 138
intelligence-gathering, 127–29; in India, 137–39; in Persia, 134–36; in Roman Empire, 136–37
irony, 160
Isocrates, 3–4, 45, 57–60, 65, 72, 146, 154, 166, 167, 168, 194
ispasay, 115–16, 118
Istanbul, 193. See also Byzantium

Jaeger, Werner, 17
Jason of Pherae, 65
Jones, A. H. M., 136
Julian the Apostate, 154

kalokagathia, 180
karanos, 149
kasaka, 188
Kautilya, 137
Kay Khusro, 178
Kent, R. G., 74
khshathrapavan, 149. See also satrapes

Index / 213

King's Ears, 103, 109, 110, 115, 187
King's Eye, 101–39 passim; as Egyptian title, 187
King's Peace, 14–15, 52, 55, 57
kopis, 87

Laws, The (Plato), 64, 96, 97–100, 143, 164, 169, 171, 182–83
Leuctra, 48, 52
Lewis, David, 12
Lie, the 18–19, 121
Life of Agesilaus (Plutarch), 51, 52–53, 165
Life of Apollonius of Tyana (Philostratus), 109–10, 133
Life of Artaxerxes (Plutarch), 73, 106, 113, 132–33, 164
Life of Xenophon (Diogenes Laertius), 12–13
Lommel, H., 115
loyalty, 162–63. See also *pistis*
Luccioni, Jean, 15, 49, 50
Lucian, 111, 112, 114, 134, 186–87
Lycurgus, 7
Lysander, 8, 46, 173
Lysis (Plato), 163

Magi, 90, 178, 192
Mani, 115–16
Manichaean church, 115
Mantinea, 48, 53, 168
Manushtchihr, 178
marketplace, 180
Maurya Empire, 137–39
Median Wall, 176
Megabates, 43, 54
Megabyzus, 13, 153
Megasthenes, 138–39, 185, 192
Memorabilia (Xenophon), 150, 156
Menexenus (Plato), 142, 143, 145, 150, 194
Menon, 27–28, 35–36, 160, 162, 172
Messenia, 53
Meyer, Eduard, 103
Milesian exiles, 23
misobarbaron, 163
misopersēs, 42, 163
mistrust, 28

Mithra/*mithra*, 18–19, 25–26, 122, 125, 127, 188–89, 190
Mithridates, 29
Mitra, 120
Momigliano, Arnaldo, 130
Moralia (Plutarch), 151
Mordechai, 11
Morr, Josef, 14
Mysians, 150

Nabonidus, 77
Nabonidus Chronicle, 76, 77
Naqsh-i Rustam: inscriptions at, 121; tombs at, 173
Nebuchadnezzar, 175, 176
Nehemiah, 88
New Hebrides, 177
Nicocles, 58
Nicolaus of Damascus, 169
Nippur, 118
non-Greeks. See barbarians
Nussbaum, G. B., 15, 16

oath-breaking, 19, 29, 41, 161
Odysseus, 19
Oeconomica (Aristotle), 151
Oeconomicus (Xenophon), 5, 6–12, 86, 151, 175
oikonomia, 11
Old Persia, 61, 71, 74
Old Persian, 115, 117
On Horsemanship (Xenophon), 87, 151
oral tradition, 68, 172–73
Orations (Aelius Aristides), 113, 125, 134
Orations (Themistius), 110, 113, 133
Oroetes, 129
Orontas, 20–21, 172, 177
Orontes, 106

Pagliaro, A., 115, 116–18
Pahlevi, Reza (shah of Iran), 178
palta, 87
panhellenism, 3, 39, 46, 49–51, 55, 61, 65
Paphlagonia, 88
paradayadā, 149

paradeisos, 149, 153
paradises, 8, 89, 153
Parthians, 108–9, 136
Parysatis, 160, 173
pati, 117, 118
patrios politeia, 173
*patyaxš, 117–18, 124
Peloponnesian War, The (Thucydides), 17, 22
Persae (Aeschylus), 105, 113, 126–27, 131, 171
Persae (Timotheus), 149
Persepolis tablets, 118, 156
Persia: administration of, 8–9, 64, 87–89; agriculture in, 8–9, 86, 152; extent of empire, 80; intelligence gathering in, 127–29, 134–36; justice in, 6–8, 158; military practices, 8, 9, 11, 87; rebellions against, 2, 65, 139
Persian king: as Greek literary figure, 8–9, 44–45, 119, 163, 180; as Mithra's representative, 188–89
Persians: educational philosophy of, 85–86; exercise and diet among, 92; Greek attitudes toward, 2–3, 55; and hunting, 93, 179; religion and ethics of, 11, 18–20, 28–29, 89–90, 152, 156, 158, 161, 180; social customs of, 89
Persica (Ctesias), 68, 73, 76, 82, 83, 84, 106, 108, 149, 169, 184
Persica (Dinon), 106
Persica (Heraclides), 106
Phaedo (Plato), 83
Pharnabazus, 12, 22, 33, 34, 43, 53, 128, 129, 159, 191
philhellēn, 42
Philip (prince consort of Great Britain), 177
Philip II of Macedon, 65, 172
philobarbaros, 51, 53
Philoctetes (Sophocles), 19–20
philopolis, 42
Philostratus, 109–10, 112, 113, 133, 186–87
philotimia, 7
Phlius, 47, 157

Phoebidas, 47, 52, 57
Phoenician revolt, 65
phoros, 149
Photius, 83, 169, 176
Pisidians, 23, 150, 159
Pissuthnes, 129
pistis, 20–38 passim, 141, 157, 158
pistoi, 88, 185
pitiaxēs/pityaxēs, 117
Plato, 130, 163, 166, 171, 194; on barbarians, 3, 142–45, 150; on Cyrus the Great, 72, 172; idealizes Sparta, 163–64; on the *polis*, 64; praises Darius I, 7; rebuttal to the *Cyropaedia*, 96, 97–100, 169, 183; rivalry with Xenophon, 182; on Socrates' stamina, 44; and the Syracuse tyrants, 65
pleonexia, 59
Plutarch: on Agesilaus, 52–53, 165; on Artaxerxes II, 73, 132–33, 164; on Herodotus, 165; on horse fattening, 151; on the King's Eye, 106, 112, 113, 132–33; sources for account of battle of Cunaxa, 106
polis vs. empire, 64–65
Politics (Aristotle), 64, 138, 185, 194
Pollux, 109, 110, 112, 113, 114, 133
Polybius, 154
Polyclitus, 178
Polycrates, 21
postal relay, 88
Prinz, Wilhelm, 61
Prometheus, 19
prophasis, 23, 25
Proxenus, 36, 159, 160, 175
pseudesthai, 19
Pteria, 78
Punjab, 192

rb trbṣ, 117
Republic, The (Plato), 3, 64, 71, 138, 164
Rigveda, 120
Roman Empire, 136–37

Sacas, 88
Salamis, Attic, 126

Salamis, Cypriot, 58–59, 65
Sardis, 54, 77, 153, 176
Sargon of Akkad, 172–73
Sassanians, 108–9, 116, 136
satrapes, 11, 135, 149. *See also*
    Abrocomas; Ariobarzanes; Orontes;
    Pharnabazus; Tiribazus;
    Tissaphernes
Schaeder, Hans H., 115–16
Scharr, Erwin, 62
Schwartz, Eduard, 61
Scillus, 16, 153
Seleucid kingdom, 135
Seuthes, 22, 33–35, 36–37, 162
Shahnama (Ferdowsi), 63, 84, 172, 177
Sinnigen, William G., 136
Sinope, 32–33
Socrates, 8, 44, 83, 152, 156, 182
Socratic dialogues, 70
Solon, 7, 21, 83
Sophist (Plato), 163
Sophists, 178, 195
Sophocles, 19–20, 159
sophrosyne, 7
Sparta, 12, 15, 157, 163
spaθaka, 116, 124
speeches, 26–27, 30–31, 83, 159
Sphodrias, 48, 57
Spithridates, 43
Stanley, Thomas, 103, 186–87
Starr, Chester, 129
Statesman, The (Plato), 3
Strabo, 86, 89, 138, 161, 178–79
strategos, 11
Stronach, David, 174
Suda, 110, 112, 113, 133–34
Summary of Virtues, 39
Survey of Deeds, 39, 40–45
Susa, 80
suspicion, 16, 26–27, 28. *See also*
    hypopsia
Sykutris, Johannes, 58–59
syllogos, 10
Symposium (Plato), 44
Symposium (Xenophon), 150
Syracuse, 65

Tanyoxarkes/Tanaoxares, 83

Teispis, 74, 76
Theaetetus (Plato), 3
Thebes, 47, 52, 166
Themistius, 109, 110, 112, 113, 114, 133
Themistocles, 19
Theophrastus, 165
Theopompus, 165
Thirty Tyrants, 161
Thorax, 33
Thucydides, 17, 22, 128, 185
Thymbrara, 77, 78, 180
Timasion, 33
Timotheus, 149, 167
Tiribazus, 32, 159, 162
Tissaphernes, 19, 21–29 passim, 158;
    death of, 54, 162, 191; deceitfulness
    of, 41, 50, 160; as informer, 128,
    129; political intervention in
    Greece, 128; rewarded by Artaxerxes II after Cyrus' rebellion, 41
Tithraustes, 54
ti-ti-kaš/ti-ti-ya-kaš-be, 118
tribute, 11. *See also dasmos, phoros*
truce breaking, 22, 25–26, 28, 32, 40, 122
trustworthiness. *See pistis*

Ugbaru. *See* Gobryas/Ugbaru
Unitarians, 4

Varuna, 120, 189
Vidal, Gore, 90
Vishtasp, 178
Vourveris, Konstantinos I., 142–45

Weiskopf, Michael N., 129
Wencis, Leonard, 16

Xanthus, 170
Xenophon: career synopsized, 2; defends own conduct to army, 35; experiences as sources for *Cyropaedia*, 68–69; and Megabyzus, 13; personal relationship with Cyrus the Younger, 174–75; qualifications for command, 159; rivalry with Plato, 182; and Seuthes, 36–37, 162;

speech after Cunaxa, 29, 30–31
Xerxes, 21, 156, 161

Zaehner, Robert C., 122
Zarathustra/Zoroaster, 186, 192
Zeus, 189–90
Zopyrus, 11
Zoroastrianism, 18, 28, 89–90, 99,
    120, 152, 156, 191, 192